# "MY ENDLESS WAR
## ...AND MY SHATTERED DREAMS"

To Chris

Never Forget

Sonia Kaplan

# MY ENDLESS WAR
## ...AND MY SHATTERED DREAMS

Library of Congress Control Number TXu1-165-321

ISBN: 1-59457-558-4

To order additional copies, please contact us.
BookSurge, LLC
www.booksurge.com
1-866-308-6235
orders@booksurge.com

SONIA
KAPLAN

# "MY ENDLESS WAR
## ...AND MY SHATTERED DREAMS"

My survival of the Holocaust and
the recollection of my unforgettable
memories of my life BEFORE
World War II, my life DURING
the war with the Nazi Regime, my
life AFTER the war and all of my
happenings.

2004

# "MY ENDLESS WAR
## ...AND MY SHATTERED DREAMS"

# The Lost Years of My Life

Written by
Sonia Kaplan

# THE LEGACY OF GENERATIONS

My Beloved and Dear Children
David, Gloria, Ellen
My Grandchildren
Michael, Marc, Shayna,
Matthew, Jeffrey, Leah
My Great-Grandchildren
Liana, Jenna, Zackary

# DEDICATION

*This book is dedicated in memory of
my dear loving parents,
Boruch Moshe and Gittel Hannah
and the rest of my family who perished in the
Holocaust among the six million Jews.*

# TABLE OF CONTENTS

# ACKNOWLEDGEMENTS

Since the war ended, I have to admit that I never wanted to bring back my wartime memories. Instead, I tried to pretend that this never happened. Finally, after sixty years of silence, thanks to my daughter, Ellen, who gave me the courage, strength and support to open my wounds and face the reality, little by little I started to reveal my past to her and bring it out in the open.

Without her total support, encouragement, devotion and help, this memoir would never have been achieved. Her inspiration and involvement made it possible. She devoted a great deal of her time and spent countless hours and many weekends typing and retyping this manuscript until it looked right. For all of her effort and dedication, I express my gratitude, and many thanks.

I also express my appreciation to Dr. Marcia Littell, Professor and Founding Director in Holocaust and Genocide Studies at the Richard Stockton College of NJ. She took the time to read my manuscript and I am very grateful to her for all of her effort. I express my sincere appreciation and thanks for her support.

I express my thanks to Rabbi Gordon Geller of Temple Emeth Shalom in Margate, NJ. Rabbi Geller read my manuscript and expressed his valuable opinion. He appreciated my way of describing the Jewish way of living in the older days in Europe, before the war. Thank you Rabbi Geller.

I want to express my thanks to my friend, Trish Marion. I am very grateful for all of her effort, and thoughtfulness, by helping with the editing of my manuscript. She dedicated a lot of her time and I do thank her for it.

I want to thank my son-in-law, David, and granddaughter, Shayna, for their suggestions, technical help and for taking the time and interest in helping with the formatting of my manuscript. They did this with caring and love.

I thank my daughter, Gloria, for helping with the final touches of the manuscript and for helping with the technical aspects. Gloria helped with the selection of the pictures that were used in my book. I express my sincere appreciation to her with many thanks.

# INTRODUCTION

This book was written in my original voice, and from my own experience. It is my personal recollection of all of the happenings to me, my family, and the rest of the Jews in our city, Wlodzimierz Volynski, during the time of the Nazi Regime. I am living proof of it and I, myself, witnessed these unbelievable, inhuman, and cruel actions. All of this brutality towards us will remain in my memory and in my thoughts forever.

**Sonia Kaplan**
**AUTHOR**

# THE STORY OF MY LIFE

Before I begin my autobiography, I have to admit that after so many years, which was almost a lifetime of suffering, it is still very painful for me to bring back my memories of my past. So many years of misery and horror that the war inflicted on me, left a deep scar in my memory. Looking back and analyzing everything that really happened to me, makes it very hard for me to face the reality and when I do, I get very emotional and tears fill my eyes.

When I start to bring back the thoughts and all of the cruel happenings of my past, at the time of the Nazi Regime, the whole terrible painful picture of my life by Adolf Hitler is flashing in front of my eyes, and I do feel that I am reliving the terrible happenings and their brutality all over again. I kept on hoping that time will heal my pain, but it was not so. It looked to me that time stood still. The memories of the Nazi brutality remain fresh in my mind forever. I always tried to erase the horrible wartime memories of my mind and not to think or look back, instead I tried just to pretend that nothing ever happened, but no matter how hard I was, and still am trying, and what kind of pretenses I was using, nothing helped. Unfortunately, I never could succeed.

Finally, I came to a conclusion that it is the highest time for me to stop pretending and face the reality of the awful, unbelievable happenings like the loss of my family by the Nazis, of taking our rights away from us, destroying our synagogues, properties and businesses, the constant humiliation by labeling and forcing us to wear the Yellow Star of David and being put into ghettos. My memories of the war by being hungry, sick, degraded, humiliated, lonely and confused left me with mixed emotions and without any hope that I would ever survive.

All of these were unbelievable and inhuman acts that Hitler's Nazis inflicted on me. Whenever anybody asked me about the war I always said in a nice and polite way that I would rather not talk about it. Even when my children asked me all kinds of questions, I did not say too much to them either. I guess I was not ready for it. I do not think that I will ever be completely ready and free to talk about my past and of my wartime memories without ever getting emotional, but unfortunately I never had another choice, only to go on living with them all of my life.

For many years, my children kept on asking me about my life before the war, my family, my upbringing and how I managed to survive the Nazis, but I just could not bring myself together to talk about it and open all of my wounds.

After sixty years of trying to hide my past I realized that it is time to reveal it to them because my children and my grandchildren have a right to know about their heritage and also about all of the happenings in my life. Finally, I broke my silence and little by little I started to bring it out in the open.

No matter how painful it has been for me, I know that I have to learn to deal with it. I realized that I must also tell the world what happened to me and to the six million Jews during the years of the Holocaust. I know that it is really the highest time to tell the story of my life and all of my suffering by the Nazis, and their brutality and inhuman doings towards other human beings. No matter how unbelievable it sounds to most of the people, the reality of it is that all of these things really did happen because I am a living proof of it. I do wish to tell my story, and I hope that people will be united and stick together from now on in order to prevent, in the future, a brutality like this of happening again. The Nazis actions should never be forgotten and their brutality towards us should be remembered forever. I am trying to tell the world of all of these happenings to me and to the rest of the Jews during the Nazi occupation.

This book is written in three parts. The first part is written of my childhood years before World War II. The second part is written of my life in World War II, first under Communism and then under the Nazis Regime. The third part is written about my life after the war until now. It is written about my life, my upbringing, my surroundings, my actions and my way of coping with my problems, first to understand them and then to try to solve them. I also have to mention my determination to survive, even at times when the whole situation looked and seemed to be hopeless.

In order to begin the story of my life I have to fill you in and familiarize you with my family that I was born into and how I was raised and brought up. From the minute I was born and I started to understand certain things, my parents started to teach me and to drill in my memory that I have to grow up and become a good Jew and a good person. To be a good Jew and a good human being, I was taught that I have to believe in kindness, truthfulness, honesty, unselfishness and most of all I had to believe in God and in the Ten Commandments.

I would also like to familiarize you with our religious traditions and customs of the Jewish life, which we always believed and observed before the tragedy of the war. I would like to describe the city in which I was born in and lived, until the Nazis came to us. I also would like to get you acquainted with our everyday living with each other and between each other in our Jewish community.

We mostly lived within ourselves and we had our ways of living. We had our culture, our traditions, our religion, which we observed and respected. I would like to fill you in how the Jewish holidays were celebrated and most of all how my family and I lived a peaceful, normal and respectable life in every way until the awful tragedy started when the Nazis came to our city, and immediately interrupted our lives. Besides taking over our way of living they took over our right of existing in this world. They became our judge, jury and persecutor, and their verdict was to erase all of the Jews completely off the face of the earth.

# PART ONE

# CHAPTER I
# THE HISTORY OF OUR CITY, WLODZIMIERZ VOLYNSKI
# (VLADIMIR, LUDMIR)

I would like to describe and familiarize you with the European life in the older days, especially the life of the Jews in my city, before World War II. Our city, Wlodzimierz Volynski, Poland, where I was born, was known for having a traditional Jewish population. Our city and the surrounding vicinity consisted of 36,000 Jews. It was a very agricultural and industrial city. We were surrounded by villages, farms, and forests.

We always saw in the city, Polish uniformed soldiers around, because a unit of the Polish army (A.K. Armia Krajowa) was stationed in the koshare (army base), which was located in the downtown area of our city. We had a big train station, (Stacja Kolejowa in Polish), a lot of churches, shuls (synagogues), shtibels (temples), two jails, one small town jail and one big jail (prison). We also had four beautiful parks, and a river named the Luga River, which went through our city. We had a lot of orchards with fruit trees. Some orchards belonged to the city and some belonged to private families.

The ones that belonged to the private families were passed on from generation to generation. This was their income. In the summer, when the fruit got ripe, they hired workers to pick the fruit and pack them in the crates. They had their steady customers who they sold wholesale to, and most of the time they were exporting the fruit to other countries. I remember my mother always said that it was a good business, but it had its advantages and sometimes disadvantages. A lot of times in winter, the fruit trees got affected from the freezing weather, and in summer the fruit could get attacked by the insects and it would damage the fruit and they were not getting a good production. Either way, the result would be that they would not even make enough to cover their expenses. It was a business just like any other business. Sometimes it was good and sometimes it was bad.

In our city we had a Polish public school, and a Jewish Hebrew school (Tarbut), a city hall (Magistrate in Polish), two police stations, two fire departments, banks, drug stores, hospitals, cemeteries, and marketplaces. We also had a couple of small factories, but the most that we could see in our city were different kinds of businesses. In general, most of the city was a business place with a lot of stores. We also had some wholesale magazins (stores) where the storekeepers were buying their merchandise. We could find homes next to the stores because our city actually did not have too many residential-only sections.

A lot of the buildings in the business section were built the way a business was on the street floor, and the living quarters were on top of the business. The owner of the business lived in these quarters. Most of the time the businesses and the homes were on the same street. We also had some business sections that sold a better quality of goods. The majority of the Jewish lifestyle was mostly primitive. The Jews were between a poor and middle class category. The Jews in our city knew each other and they also knew each other's needs. They got involved in each other's problems and they always tried to help one another in any way they could.

The Jews had their own culture and their unique style of living in their communities. No matter how they were - rich or poor, they still were content and they always took pride in their ways of living. We had a large Jewish population in our shtut (city) and in the vicinity. Most of the Jews lived in the cities and in small shtetls (towns), because it was easier for them to earn their parnuse (livelihood). Besides that, they felt that the cities offered more opportunities to develop their talents and mind and in a way they were right.

Most of the Jews came from a good background. They were well educated, religiously and intellectually. Jews who were professionals were financially well off most of the time. The Jews were well mannered all the time. They spoke softly and they were always polite. They did not have many bad habits, like drinking, smoking or bad language. Most of the Jews spoke only Yiddish (Jewish) to each other. They read Yiddish books, went to see Yiddish theatre and they attended all of the Jewish ceremonies.

The Jews, also, were in different professions, like some were Yiddish (Jewish) writers, a lot of Jews were artists and much more. We also had, in our city, Jewish doctors and lawyers, but most of the Jews were in different businesses, like merchants, traders and salesmen. The Jews also had different trades like blacksmithing, carpentry, bookbinding, pottery, carving, tailoring, hat making, shoemaking and many other trades.

Most of the Jews lived a very ordinary life. Many Jews were very poor. Some Jews were factory workers, some were shopkeepers, some had religious positions, some Jews were peddlers, and some Jews were drifters and they drifted from one job to another. No matter what kind of profession, business or job they had, it came down to one thing, that every Jew tried in an honest and respectable way to make a living for their families without doing any harm to anybody. The majority of non-Jews settled down in the outskirts of the city, which was in the villages and many became farmers. It seemed to me that they liked the village life better than the city life.

The village life had some advantages, like fresh air, more space, free of the city hustle and bustle, and freedom of doing what they wanted to do and not have to be dependent on others or be connected with others. In other words, they were their own bosses. The farmers were very independent and did what they wanted to do because it was their choice and their decision how to manage their farms and decide on what would be the best and most productive things for them to grow.

They grew all kinds of crops, like wheat, corn, and all kinds of vegetables. They also grew cotton in order to make their own materials. A peasant would grow as many things as he was able to in order to make his farm profitable. The peasants worked very hard to accomplish what they wanted to, and they always tried their best because the peasants knew that the more crops they would have to sell, the more profit they would make.

The peasants also raised livestock for meat, eggs, and milk. They raised chickens, geese, turkeys, cows, horses, goats, calves, and other animals. Everyone knew that the peasants played a big part in our daily life. We always had fresh fruit, vegetables, meat, chicken, eggs and all of the dairy products. The fact was that the farmers knew everything in the farming field, and on the other hand, the city people were mostly knowledgeable in the business industry. Besides that, some farmers had little shops on the highway and they sold all kinds of handcrafted items like tablecloths, doilies, pictures, and knickknacks that the women made themselves, in their spare time. They also made hand braided straw baskets and all kinds of woven things. Some of the farmers were also innkeepers. Before the war, everyone tried to manage their life the way that made them happy and content, and also the best way they could and would be able to make a living for their family.

Most of the population was happy with what they did and how they managed their life. Everyone had their own way of living, their own culture, their own style of dressing, their own tradition and their own language. It was okay, because everyone had the same right to live their lives the way they chose to, as long as they did not do any harm to others. I think that nobody was given the authority of mixing into somebody else's life and telling them what to do or what not to do. I think that it was really nobody's concern how other people were choosing to live their life, and I also think that it would have been much better for everyone around, if this kind of people would take care of their own lives, instead of trying to run the lives of others.

The Jews also were supposed to have the same right to live in the world according to God, and they could live the way they chose because everyone was supposed to be created equal. Also, the Jews were put on this earth for the same reason like the others, and like the others, the Jews had to be treated with equality and without any discrimination against them or their religious beliefs. God gave every human being in the world the same rights and privileges, including the Jews, and they were entitled to exercise their rights the way that it felt and looked good to them.

## CHAPTER II
## THE SHULS (SYNAGOGUES) and SHTIBELS
## (TEMPLES)
## IN OUR CITY OF WLODZIMIERZ VOLYNSKI

## OUR BIG SYNAGOGUE

In our city, most of our Jewish population was religious and some Jews were very strictly religious. These were the Orthodox Jews, but overall, all of the Jews belonged to one or the other Jewish congregation. We had in our city a lot of shuls (synagogues) and many shtibels (temples). Practically every Jewish neighborhood had their temple. Some Jews came to pray everyday, some even came twice a day in the morning and in the evening.

The shtibels (temples) usually were small buildings. It was mostly built for the Jews who lived in the neighborhood. We also had in our city, shuls (synagogues). A shul (synagogue) was a big building and it had small buildings attached to it. One building was for a Beth Midrash (House of Study); one building was for the Cheider (Jewish School), one building was for a Yeshiva (for higher studying of Judaism), and one building was for a Mikvah (Traditional Bath House for Ritual Ceremonies).

Some synagogues were small and some were big. The biggest synagogue was in the center of the city. It was a beautiful synagogue. The ceiling was high and around the ceiling were glass windows made out of little square pictures with different names of the people who donated them. The walls were filled with traditional pictures. The windows were made out of Venetian glass with Jewish writing and Stars of David. Before we opened the door of the synagogue, to your right of the doorpost was hanging a mezuzah. (a mezuzah is a hand written scroll with shema yisrael in it) and before the people came in, they touched the mezuzah with their fingers and then kissed their fingers. Straight ahead we came into the synagogue. I have to mention, that in my days, every Jewish house had a mezuzah on the right side of the door, especially the Orthodox Jews.

As we were coming into the synagogue, we saw the Bimah (area to pray) and on the Bimah was a podium (high table), called a lectern or shulhan, from where they were reading the Torah. Right on the Bimah was a section for the Torah scrolls called the Arum Kudish (Holy Ark). The Holy Ark was covered with a special curtain called an aporoiches. The aporoiches was embroidered in golden letters with a symbolic design. In the middle of the aporoiches was the Ten Commandments. On both sides of the Ten Commandments were two lions and on top of the aporoiches was a crown and a Star of David. On both sides of the Holy Ark, on the wall, hung two big, lit up menorahs (lamps or candelabras). All the things in the synagogue had a very deep symbolic and specific religious meaning. The Torah scrolls were written by a Jewish writer who was called a sofer (rabbinic scribe). He was a special Jew who was learned in the Torah.

It was written in script letters, on parchment, with a goose feather, with the point of the feather dipped in ink and every letter was written separate. After the Torah was written and finished, the scribe took it into the synagogue and the whole congregation of the members of the synagogue started to celebrate the new Torah. They walked around with the Torah and everyone was singing and dancing and rejoicing the new Torah.

In the Jewish religion, the Torah was and still is the most symbolic and holy possession of all. On every Jewish holiday, they took the Torahs out of the Arum Kudish (ark) and they kept on walking around with the Torahs and everyone was and still is, up to this day trying to touch and kiss the torah. All of the Jews considered this a mitzvah. This meant a good deed. In a way, by touching the Torah, it made every Jew happy to be connected to something holy.

I still remember that in our big synagogue, they had rows of wooden chairs covered with blue velvet. The floor was also wood without any covering. Every member of the synagogue had a chair assigned to him with a number on it. In the older days men and women were not allowed to sit together in the synagogue. When the women and the girls came to synagogue, they had to sit in the gallery. We could see everything and hear the davinnen (praying) by sitting in the gallery because the whole front was open and it looked like a balcony. When we looked down we could see the men with the boys and the whole synagogue with everything in it.

In our city, we had two groups of Chassidim (a sect of religious Jews). One group was called Triska Chassidim and the other group was called Bluedafska Chassidim. Most of the Jews were very much involved in the Jewish religious life. The synagogues were very symbolic places and it was the house of God for every Jew. Besides the religious ceremonies and prayer, the synagogue also served as a social and personal place for activities and events. The Jews felt very comfortable coming into the shul (synagogue) or shtibel (temple) anytime they felt and had a need to, and they were sure that there would always be somebody to talk to and there always was.

The women were not as much involved in the synagogue as the men. Some women were mostly busy running businesses, working and taking care of the household. In the older days, when a man had a religious position or they studied the Torah in order to get a religious position, they did not get involved in anything else, only in studying. So in these cases the wives had to carry all of the responsibilities of their families on their shoulders. They had to make a living and take care of the whole household all by themselves.

Some Jews, besides being religious, had other interests, too. A lot of Jews had different interests, like they belonged to political, social, cultural, and spiritual religious organizations. They had a strong sense of ethics and they always celebrated our traditional holidays in order to preserve the Jewish and religious identity.

The members were gathered together and they had discussions about different subjects. The Jewish people were always interested in economy, history, education and much more. They also performed Brit (circumcision), death, and all of the life events according to the traditions. In order to perform a religious and traditional ceremony in the synagogue meant that the Jewish man had to know the Torah and the Ten Commandments, which teaches us also, all the rules and regulations. It was, for every Jew, the same religion and the same belief in God because God created the world.

All of the other things like our traditions were made up by Jewish people for many thousands of years and they could be changed. The fact was that many countries and cities, found that the Jews had different traditions in certain places, but they were very similar to each other and they had the same meaning. The synagogue not only functioned for religious purposes, but some personal matters also were taken care of in the shul (synagogue) or shtibel (temple).

For instance, when somebody was in need and was too proud to ask just anybody for help, they came to the synagogue. When the members saw a stranger, they knew already that he needs help, so without embarrassing him, they found a way to help him. In the Jewish religion the Torah said to give zducke (giving charity) to someone and that to help someone in need was the most important thing in life and it was considered of being the biggest mitzvah in the world. It meant that you were doing a good deed for somebody, and God will repay you.

In our shtut (city) were some oishers (rich), Jewish people who did not want to socialize or help the poor. They were very selfish and nobody in the city wanted to bother with them. There was another class of Jews, Balbatisher (respectable) who tried their best to help with what they could. The third class of Jews was Kapzen (the poor). These Jews would have liked to help others, but they could not afford to, because they were too poor to help. Almost every Jewish person in our city who could, would help others anyway they were able to, like they would lend a helping hand, and they would offer friendship and dedication. They also helped in many other ways like donating their time, or giving money or by cheering somebody up or taking a part in their happiness, like simchas (parties), in other words, being a real friend to you and being there for you in every situation. A Jew with a will to help others in joy and in sorrow was known as a chuchem. He was known as a smart person and well educated in the Torah and in Talmud. They always had an expression that "it was better to give than to receive".

## BETH MIDRASH-The House of Study – The Torah

Beth Midrash was the house for study of the Torah. In the older days, a lot of Orthodox Jewish men did not work and all day long, they studied the Torah. In Poland, most of the religious men were sitting in Beth Midrash and studying the Torah while their wives were working.

Either the wives worked for someone or they had their own businesses. No matter what they were doing, they were busy all day and most of the evening. In the older days, no man would help his wife with any housework or any other kind of work. In these days, every and any kind of a job was the woman's job according to the man. The women were treated by their husbands like a slave, but they did not know any better or know a different way of treatment, so they went on living this way for generations and generations and they were pretty happy with it.

In the older days, the men thought of his wife and children, as they were his property. He owned them and he could do whatever he wanted to do because at that time the women knew one thing, to obey their husband's wishes, so while the wives were working, they had to be the providers and breadwinners in the family. They also had to take care of all of the other problems that would arise mostly every day of the week.

As it always was, the Jews, especially the Orthodox Jews, had specific traditional rules and regulations. One of them was that their sons had to follow their father's footsteps if they liked it or not. They had to study the Torah in order to get a religious position. I think and I know that it sounds a little strange now, but that was how it was in my day. When I was born and raised in Poland in my parents' home, this was our Jewish way of living, this was our culture, our religion, our traditions and it did not bother us at all because we never knew another way of living or another way of doing things.

In the Jewish religion, if a Jew wanted to davinnen (pray) he had to have a minyan. This means he had to have ten people to pray. Some Jewish men came to synagogue to pray three times a day. These were mostly the Orthodox Jews, like my father was, but when they were just studying the Torah, they could study by themselves. They also saw the rabbi sitting and studying there. In the synagogue, they had a steady man called a shammes (caretaker) who looked after everything. It was his job to take care of cleaning up and helping with what he was asked to, because he got paid a weekly salary for it from the Kehilah or Gmeana (Jewish organization).

## THE CHEIDER (Yiddish School for Beginners)

Every synagogue had a special room for a Cheider (Yiddish School).

The Cheider was a long room with a long table and on both sides of the table were wooden benches for the children to sit on. A Melammed (a Yiddish teacher) was coming in and teaching the children the everyday davinnen (praying) and he was teaching them Yiddishkeit, (Judaism). He was also teaching them all the bruchas (prayers) over bread, over water, over meat, over milk and more. The Melammed sometimes was also teaching the children a little Hebrew. Hebrew was a language, which they were speaking mostly in Palestine (Israel). In Poland, the Jews spoke only Yiddish to each other. The children attended the Cheider (Yiddish school) twice a week, on Monday and Wednesday after they came home from the elementary school. The rest of the week they went to elementary school only. On Saturday and Sunday they had off and did not go to school. If the children would not learn and they did not concentrate in Cheider, the Melammed (Yiddish teacher) had a kanchik (a strap with leather fringes) and he hit them hard enough with it so they knew better for the next time.

In the older days in public school a lerehr (teacher) was allowed to spank a child for doing something wrong, like for instance, not obeying the lerehr's (teacher's) orders. The same was in Cheider (Yiddish School), when the Melammed (Yiddish teacher) was trying to lerrennin (teach) the children and they were not paying attention, the children got punished.

The parents were also allowed to discipline their children the way they saw fit. Every child learned in their early age to have the greatest respect for their parents, to obey them and look up to them. They also were taught to show respect to elderly people. No matter how the children felt about all of these rules and regulations, they still would never dare to be disrespectful to their parents and go against their wishes. Instead, they would carry out their parents' orders. Some children did not attend the elementary school or the Cheider. They went to the Tarbut (Hebrew School) and they just learned Hebrew. They never learned Polish or Yiddish, so they did not know too much Polish or too much about Judaism. The only thing that they knew was that they were Jewish, but this was not enough. In order to become a good person and a good Jew, and know the difference between right doing and wrong doing, first we had to believe in God and in the Ten Commandments and we also had to know our heritage.

In the older days, the girls were not accepted in the Cheider. Those parents who wanted the girls to study the Jewish religion, had to hire a private Melammed (Yiddish teacher) to come to their house and tutor them. When the parents hired the Melammed they made an agreement with him how many times a week he had to come and also how much he would be paid each week. After everything was settled, he started to teach the children. He taught them whatever he thought was important for the children to learn, without any interference from anybody.

The Melammed taught all the children in the household for the same fee. He was like a private tutor, even better because the Melammed stayed as long as the children could concentrate. He always was very serious about his teaching the children Yiddishkeit (Judaism). He taught them all of the basic things about Judaism, like all of the Jewish traditions and the religion. When he saw that the children had enough knowledge in this respect, he told the parents that his job here was done.

We had quite a few Melammeds in our city and they were always very busy tutoring the children. Besides making a living by tutoring the children, the Melammed felt some accomplishment. They really got a lot of satisfaction out of it, because they taught the children Yiddishkeit (Judaism) and this was what made the Melammed feel very good.

## YESHIVA-High Studying of Judaism

In the older days, when a Jewish man wanted to continue with his Jewish education and he wanted to learn about higher Judaism, like Humesh, Gemmorah, Rashi and more, he had to attend the Yeshiva. The Yeshiva was like a college. They studied the Torah, and Talmud, and they learned everything about the Jewish traditions and religion. When a man finished the Yeshiva, he had learned most of Judaism, and what he wanted to know about the Jewish religion and the traditions.

Most of the Orthodox parents were sending their sons to the Yeshiva to get the higher education in Judaism, in order to become a strictly Orthodox Jew and follow the father's footsteps. Only boys could attend the Yeshiva. There were quite a few Yeshivas in Poland, and they were located mostly in the big cities. The boys who wanted to attend the Yeshiva and did not have any Yeshiva in their shtetl (town), had to leave their families, friends and everything else behind them and come to the cities in order to attend the Yeshiva.

The boys who came from other towns had to settle down within walking distance in order to be able to walk to the Yeshiva every day. They also had to be within walking distance of a synagogue, especially on Friday, after sundown until Saturday, after sundown, when Jews were not allowed to ride and everyone had to walk to synagogue.

The Jewish community of the city took care of the Yeshivanikas (Yeshiva students) by providing them with room and board in the homes of the synagogues members for no cost to them at all. They even got spending money from those they lived with. The studying in the Yeshiva took three or four years, like they were learning a profession. On the holidays, they were allowed to visit their families and celebrate the holidays with them. Also on weekends, they could do whatever they wanted to. Sometimes, they went home for the weekend and sometimes, the parents came to visit them, before the Sabbath.

After graduation, the Jewish men could become a Shoichath (ritual way of slaughtering animals), a rabbi, or a head of the rabbis. They had a choice of other high religious positions. The very religious Yeshivanikas had very strict customs, like they were always dressed in long black coats called kapotes. They wore black shoes and on top of their heads they wore a yarmulke (skull cap) or a hat.

There was also another group of religious Jews who were always studying the Torah. They were dressed in a kapote (long coat made out of silk). They wore a big black hat or a shtreimel (hat) made with mink tails around the shtreimel and they had a long beard with curly sideburns called payahs. They were studying the Talmud and higher studies. These Jews were the most religious Jews and they were called Chassidim. One was called Chussid. It was a spiritual orthodox movement and they felt a certain pride and obligation to their faith and beliefs. They observed the Ten Commandments and most of all they believed in God and preserved all the Jewish traditions. When the Chassidim got married it had to be to a girl from a very religious family in order for her to know all of the strictest traditions and to observe them. When they had children, they were raised in the same way. The children had to, and they did follow their father's footsteps. On Saturday, when they were going to synagogue, the husbands wore their mink or fur-lined hat, the shtreimel, and their wives had to wear a shathl or paruck (wig). The husband was not allowed to look at another woman, only his wife. This was our tradition in the older days.

# CHAPTER III
# TRADITIONAL AND RITUAL CEREMONIES

## MIKVAH

In the older days we did not have any baths in our homes. In order to be able to take a bath we could go to the public bathhouse for a small fee. The bathhouse was always full of people, especially Thursday. Thursday evening everyone wanted to be clean for Shabbos (Sabbath), which was from sundown Friday to sundown Saturday. In the wintertime there were more people coming to the bathhouse because wintertime nobody could go to the lake to wash themselves.

Each synagogue had a ritual ceremonial bathhouse for women, which was called a Mikvah. This was a bath for ritual purification and it was a part of the Jewish custom. It was written in the Torah that a woman after seven days being clean of menstruation, in order to have marital relations with her husband, had to go first, to the Mikvah. The Mikvah was built like a big swimming pool, with four walls and steps on one side of one wall, in order to go down into the water. The Mikvah was as deep, more or less, as a woman's height.

The water kept on circulating. A special woman called Tukerin was there all the time to supervise the women in the Mikvah. When the women came to the Mikvah, the Tukerin was in charge of telling them what to do, step by step. First, they undressed and then they went down the steps into the water and washed themselves with soap. Then, the Tukerin said a brucha (prayer) and she told them to dip down three times. After that she brought a pot of water and spilled it on their head. After the whole ceremony was over she told them that they could come out of the water, dress, and go home.

Everything that the Tukerin performed of the religious ceremony was very important to our tradition. In the older days, the night before the women got married, they had to go to the Mikvah, in order to go through all of the ritual ceremonial acts. They had to get an okay from the Tukerin that the bride already became pure. The Mikvah was supported by the Kehilah organization, which got donations from the Balebatim. It means that donations came from the Jewish members of the synagogue.

I have to mention that I still remember when my mother went to the Mikvah and every time she went she used to take me with her. I was happy that she wanted me to go with her because in our home we had a small vanne (washtub) like for a baby and it was not too comfortable to wash yourself in it. I remember that most of the time the water spilled all over the kitchen floor, but in the Mikvah there was a lot of room and plenty of water to wash yourself. I was too young to know about the ritual ceremonies. I only thought about taking a bath there.

They also had public baths in our city for men and women, and almost everyone went to take a bath there. When my father went to the bathhouse, he used to take my brothers with him almost every Friday. I still remember that summertime, on Friday, when my mother sometimes finished with her cooking for Shabbos, a little earlier than usual, she took us to the lake, which was about four blocks from us and we washed ourselves with soap and water. Then when we came home we dressed and we were ready for Shabbos. In wintertime, we children had to take a bath in the little vanne, but we tried to manage. Those were the good old days.

## BRIS (Circumcision)

In my days when somebody got married, divorced, Bar Mitzvah, or bris (circumcision), all of these ceremonies were observed according to the Jewish tradition, faith, and belief. When a baby boy was born, after the first seven days of the baby's life, they had a bris for the baby boy. A special religious Jewish man who went to a special religious school to learn to become a moil performed the bris (circumcision) for the baby boy. It was a very painful procedure. The baby kept on crying all the time while the moil was performing the circumcision. After the circumcision was over, the moil gave the baby a name. In the Jewish religion, when they were giving a baby a name, it had to be after a dead person. The reason for it was to keep our dead family members names alive. By hearing their name, it felt that they were remembered.

After the ceremony was over, the parents had a party for the baby with all kinds of food and drinks. Everyone drank L'Chaim (to life). It also was customary to have arbes (chick peas) at the bris. After the bris was over, the moil came sometime later in the day to check on the baby, and then everyday after to change the dressing. He was checking to see if everything was okay, like a doctor. After a couple weeks, it was all healed up and everyone was glad that the circumcision was over. These were our religious traditions in my days and we had to follow them.

# A CHASENEH (in Yiddish)-A Traditional Wedding

In the older days, they had professional matchmakers or the parents were the matchmakers. They negotiated with each other and both sets of parents had the authority to decide what was right for their children. The children were never asked if they liked each other or not. If the parents thought it was okay for their children to get married to each other, then they would have a wedding. A lot of times, the children never met before the wedding. They met after the wedding was over and only then they were introduced to each other for the first time.

Not long before the war, when people started to become more advanced and they started to live a more modern life, some people tried to accept the new ways and they started to change a little. Occasionally, a boy and a girl met and they fell in love. They really wanted to marry each other, but they still had to persuade both sides of parents that they loved each other. It was not so easy, but the children at least knew that they had a chance. They thought, maybe by trying hard enough to reassure their parents of their certainness that they really love each other, the parents would agree to it. The children kept on hoping and praying that it would work out.

After a certain time trying, over and over again, sometimes, finally, both sides of parents would agree to it and they seemed to be happy. In the older days, most of the Jews did not believe in divorces. Everyone got married for better or for worse, until death did them part, and that was how it worked when a couple got married. They never thought of their happiness, instead, they only thought of the spouse's happiness. In other words, nobody was selfish enough only to think about themselves. Everyone thought to make the other person happy, so the result was that they both wound up being happy.

I remember we had in our city, women who were doing their matchmaking. They were called shatchente (matchmaker). They did their matchmaking for a fee. In order to introduce the girl and the boy to each other, both sides of the parents discussed where to meet. Finally, they had arranged the meeting with the girl and the boy in the girls' parents' house, most of the time, anyway.

It was mostly up to the children to decide if they liked each other or not. After seeing each other a couple of times, they had to decide yes or no. If they liked each other, there was going to be a wedding. If the children did not like each other, the matchmaker said to them, "Don't worry, I have a better match for you", and everyone was happy. Looking back at the good old days and their old ways of doing certain things, like, for instance, when a boy and a girl wanted to get married, normally, they did not have any voice in this matter, instead, the parents decided what was proper for them. As the years went by the times changed for the better because finally, it was up to the children also, and not just up to the parents.

I remember one shatchente (matchmaker), in our city was a heavyset woman, and dressed in a thousand rags and all day she was walking around from place to place. She knew every Jew in the city and she knew how many children every family had and how old they were. She always seemed to be busy going from one house to another and trying to match the children up with each other.

She probably did not care if they were a good match or a bad match, the only thing that she wanted to do was to make some money. After all, this was her parnuse (earning a living). I still remember that she talked very loud and fast. Most of the time I could not even understand her. She used to come into our store to look for my mother. She always liked to talk to my mother and my mother liked to talk to her, also. My mother always told me that the matchmaker was a very smart woman and whenever she came in, and it was not too busy in the store, my mother was glad to talk to her and hear all the funny stories that she was telling her. Mostly, she talked about her matchmaking profession. The way she expressed herself and told about her incidences, we could not help laughing, because they really were hilariously funny.

I remember that she always looked everyone over. She looked at me, also, and I was only seven or eight years old at the time, and she probably thought that "Soon I'll have a match for her, too." In the older days, boys and girls got married very young. They were only about thirteen or fourteen years old. After this age they considered them as being old, especially girls.

Besides the fact that they had to be young in order to get married, the girls also had to have a naden (dowry). The girl's parents had to give the boy a certain amount of money that they agreed to for marrying their daughter. A lot of times in these days when a family was poor and they had a couple of daughters, they could not marry them off without a naden (dowry), no matter how pretty or smart they would be. Eventually they became old maids and they never got married. Occasionally, sometimes, it happened that a boy fell in love with a poor girl and they got married without having to give the boy a naden (dowry). I remember that all of the years the traditional wedding ceremony did not change too much from the older days until now. After so many years, most of the Jewish traditions remain the same.

When the boy and the girl were ready to get married, on the day of their wedding, they had to follow some rules and regulations and they had to go through certain procedures. The evening before the wedding, the kalleh (the bride), had to go to the Mikvah (ritual bathhouse). The Mikvah was the place for a ritual ceremony, in order to cleanse herself from all of her sins. The chussin (groom) was not allowed to see his bride on the day of the wedding. Also, the day of the wedding, the bride and groom had to fast until after the ceremony under the chuppah (the wedding canopy) was over. In the older days, a wedding celebration in our city lasted for seven days. People were coming from all over and whoever was coming to the wedding had a good time. A lot of times people were coming even without being invited and it was okay, too.

To get married, the couple had to stand under a chuppah, which looked like four poles holding up a white sheet in four corners. The rabbi said a brucha (a blessing) and the groom put the ring on the bride's finger and he said a brucha and then with his foot he broke a glass, which was lying on the floor. After that, everyone hollered, "Mazel tov," which means good luck. Finally, they were married. The music started to play happy tunes and everyone was singing and drinking and eating and dancing and having a very good time. These affairs were sometimes taking place in the park, or in a hall, or in the parents' house.

In my times, it was not allowed for religious Jewish men and women to dance together, so men were dancing with men and women were dancing with women. They were in the same room, but there was a divider in the middle of the room. They danced a hoira (a traditional Jewish dance). They made a big circle and they lifted up the groom with a chair on the men's side, and they lifted up the bride on the women's side. They were given a handkerchief and the bride and groom were holding an end of the handkerchief and this was their way of being connected with each other. The Klezmurim bands, and fiddlers, (violinists) a group of musicians, were playing beautiful Jewish, festive songs. After the chuppah, when the eating, dancing, and singing were over and it was almost daybreak, everyone was tired and went to their sleeping places, and so did the bride and groom.

In the older days, a husband and wife did not sleep in one bed. In the bedroom were always two beds. This was the traditional way. In the morning, the celebration started all over again. After everyone had their breakfast meal, which the bride's parents had supplied all the meals and shelter for everyone, they started to sing and dance in the streets with the bride and groom and their families. The celebration continued for seven days and, no matter how everyone was still having a good time, most of the guests were getting tired. When the seven days were over, everyone went home and the couple was finally alone. Now, according to the tradition they were married to live happily ever after.

# BAR MITZVAH

## A Jewish Tradition of a Boy Becoming a Man

In the Jewish religion, a Bar Mitzvah was a very important traditional ceremony for the Jewish boy. On this day, the boy goes through a transformation from being a thirteen-year-old boy of becoming a thirteen- year- old man. In order to become a man, the boy had to follow all the procedures that he was taught by the rabbi for a whole year.

When a boy gets to be thirteen years old, he had to have a Bar Mitzvah and it was conducted according to the Jewish tradition. The family and friends were invited to share the simcha (happiness) together. Everyone was gathering in the synagogue.

The Bar Mitzvah boy was called up to the bimah, and the rabbi was putting a tallas (religious prayer shawl) on him. The Bar Mitzvah boy was starting his praying from the seifer or siddur (prayer book). He was directing the formalities of the whole ceremony. The rabbi was staying right next to him. Then they were taking the Torah out of the Arum Kudish (Holy Ark) where the Torahs were kept, and the Bar Mitzvah boy started reading from the Torah. After the reading was over, the Bar Mitzvah boy was giving a speech, thanking his parents and grandparents for helping him become a man. Everyone was throwing candy at him, to symbolize a sweet life. When the ceremonies were over they had a Kiddish and they were drinking L'Chaim, which meant to drink "to life". In a short time everyone in the synagogue, where the parents were making the affair for the son, started to celebrate his Bar Mitzvah. Besides all of the members of the synagogue, whoever wanted to join in the simcha (happiness) were welcomed. It was a big crowd and all of the friends came and they celebrated the simcha together.

It was a big celebration with a lot of food and drinks. They were singing, dancing, and everyone enjoyed themselves. After so many years of studying Judaism and all of the preparations for the Bar Mitzvah and having a lot of excitement, now everyone could relax, and they were happy that the ceremony was over. For the Bar Mitzvah boy, from now on, it started a new beginning because his life changed from being a boy to becoming a man. Now he had to accept a lot of responsibilities and be ready to try to make some decisions on his own in the best way he could. He had to try to show his maturity and independence, and also to try to remember what he learned all year long in order to become a good Jew and a good man.

# CHAPTER IV
## MY MOTHER'S FAMILY

My mother, Gittel Hannah, was born in 1912, in the town of Hrubieszow (Polish), or Rabeshoiw (Yiddish), Poland. It was about 30 kilometers from Wlodzimierz Volynski, Poland. My mother's family consisted of her mother, her father, three brothers and herself. Because she was the only girl in her family she was pampered by her parents and her brothers. Besides her family, everyone liked her. From what my mother and my grandmother told me, I could figure this out, that everyone was spoiling her in many ways. She also always had everything that money could buy.

Her parents owned a big house near the lake and all summer most of the days, she was in the water. My mother always said that she enjoyed swimming and was a good swimmer. She also told me that she liked reading and used to read a lot. My mother once mentioned that the best thing that she really enjoyed doing was to come to her mother's store, talk to the customers, and try to sell some goods to them.

My grandmother, her mother, used to tell me stories about my mother, and one of the things was that she never wanted to help with any housework. They let her get away with it because my grandmother saw right away that she had a special dislike towards housework. My mother also hated cooking, so besides attending elementary school, coming home and finishing the lessons, she had the rest of the day free and she could do whatever she wanted to do. I think she grew up carefree without any responsibilities or any worries in the world. My grandmother once mentioned that when my mother turned fourteen years old, they started to look for a husband for her. A lot of times the matchmaker tried to match her up. My mother's parents would like the boy, but my mother said no, until my mother met my father, also through a matchmaker, and they got married.

My grandparents had a store in Hrubieszow and they also had a big house. When I was two years old, my father took sick and I lived with my grandparents for a while. My mother had her hands full with my father being sick and taking care of her two businesses, and being pregnant. Having all the responsibilities on her shoulders, it was a little too much for her to handle all by herself. After all, she herself was very young at the time. My parents decided that it would be better for everyone around for me to stay with my grandparents for a while.

When my parents came to take me home, I remember that I really did not want to leave. I loved my grandparents and they loved me. When I came home, my brother had already been born. He must have been about one year old. I remember that he was already walking and talking a little. In no time, I got used to being home again and having a brother and my parents near me, but I still missed my grandmother and my grandfather. When my mother got a letter from my grandparents, I remember that she used to read the letter out loud to me and they were saying that they love me and miss me a lot.

My mother was very dedicated to my father and she always worried about his health. One day my mother told me that when the shatchente (matchmaker) introduced her to my father, she liked him right away. I think that she really was in love with him. I guess that opposite attraction counts. Apparently, he liked her, also. My mother was a very smart woman and she knew when to talk and when not to. On the other hand, my father was not too much of a conversationalist.

My father was a very gentle person. He spoke softly and always to the point. He was also a very serious type of a person and carried himself very dignified, like a gentleman.

My mother was the opposite of my father. She was always smiling and she talked to everyone about everything and anything. In general, she was a "happy go lucky" person. Everyone liked to be around her and in a way she always cheered everyone up and made them laugh. My mother always had a smile on her face, even sometimes when she was upset for some reason or another. In spite of it, she still hid her feelings in front of everyone and kept on pretending that she does not have any worries in the world. In a lot of ways I am a lot like my mother was.

I remember that my mother was very beautiful. She had a nice figure and a very pretty face. She also had beautiful, long, pitch-black hair, but she had to cover her hair by wearing a scarf or shawl. On Shabbos (Saturday), she wore a paruck (wig) or shathl (wig) because in the older days the wives of the religious Orthodox husbands, like my father was, were not allowed to show their hair to anybody. They would consider it going against our religion and this would be a sin. That was why she was covering up her hair all week with the scarf. Just in the front she could show some of her hair. I remember that when the gypsies came to our city, and they looked at my mother's hair, they envied her, because the gypsies had black hair, but not as black as my mother's.

My mother's, mother and father, my grandparents, observed the Jewish religion and all of the traditions and they were also religious Jews, but not as religious as my father's family. My father's family were strictly Orthodox Jews. My mother and her family lived in Rabeshoiw (Yiddish) or Hrubieszow (Polish) for generations. It was a small town and they had a nice Jewish community. Everyone knew each other and they treated each other with the greatest respect. It was like one big happy family. My mother's family loved this town with all the Jewish people in it, because everyone was their real friend and the Jews were happy to know that they could depend on each other.

The most important part of the town of Hrubieszow was the Central Square. On Central Square they had the nicest stores with the most expensive merchandise, and besides that they had the nicest buildings there, also. From Central Square the streets were spread out in different directions of town. The back streets had some small shops. Some streets were made out of bricks, but not too many. Most of the streets did not have any bricks or cement and they were mostly covered with mud.

Next to Central Square, behind the stores, like in an alley, was a very narrow street with stores on both sides of the street. My grandparents and my uncle had their stores on this street. It was called Targowa Ulica (in Polish for Targowa Street). The street was long and narrow. At the beginning of the street from Central Square, they had a few steps to walk up to Targowa Ulica, and with the same steps we could walk down to Central Square. On Targowa Street, they had small stores with less expensive merchandise. Mostly, the peasants came to do their shopping there because they only needed work clothes.

Most of these businesses on Targowa Street belonged to Jewish people. My grandparents had a yard goods store and because most of the people in Poland bought yard goods to have their clothes made to order, my grandparents did very good business in their store. In the older days if we wanted to be dressed in nice clothes that looked good on us and fit good we had to have it made to order. The peasants bought their clothes ready made, but the city people dressed much nicer.

In our city we had a lot of bolmeluches (specialists in their trade). When for instance, a man or a boy wanted a suit, jacket, coat or a pair of pants to be made to order, they went to a shnaider (tailor). The tailor told them how many yards of material they needed. Then they went to a yard goods store and they bought the material that they liked and as much as they needed. They went back to the tailor to pick a style from a fashion book. They picked what they liked. Now the procedure began and the tailor started to prepare the garment for the first fitting.

In order for the garment to come out good and to be done right, they had to come for at least three fittings, three separate times. When the tailor thought that everything looked good and it was to his satisfaction, then he finished the garment. Now the man or boy was happy that he was getting a new piece of clothing. In the older days, practically most of the people had only one set of clothing for the yom-tov (holidays) and special occasions.

The majority of Jews wore the holiday clothes for as long as they could. When they decided that the holiday clothes did not look yomtovdik, which meant that it did not look nice for the holidays anymore, they took the holiday clothes to be used for everyday and for the holiday they definitely were getting new clothes.

I remember that in our city we had a lot of shnaiders (tailors), but one particular tailor had the best reputation, because he was doing the best job possible. That was why he was always very busy and everyone went to him. It took a long time for him to make the clothes, and when he was done, it came out perfect. He was more expensive than the other tailors, but everyone knew that he did a better job than the others.

His wife helped him with his sewing and she did everything that he told her to do. Most of the time she did the finishing touches on the garment. Now, when a woman or a girl wanted a dress, blouse, coat, or skirt, she went to a shnaiderin (dressmaker). Usually the dressmakers who had the best reputation, of doing the best job and making the clothes to fit right, had the most work. We had to go through the same procedure, like at the tailor.

When a woman, a man, and children wanted a pair of shoes

they went to a shister (shoemaker). The shoes were made by hand and everyone could pick a style and the color of the leather that they wanted. The shoemaker took the exact measurement of both feet and he made the shoes. Practically, most of the time the shoes did fit very good and they lasted forever. Even when children outgrew their shoes, they were passed on to the younger children in the family household.

We also had shops that made all kinds of hats. When a man got a new coat or suit, the tailor made sure to have a piece of material left over for a hat in order to match their new outfit and the same was true for the dressmaker. After they cut the lady's suit or coat, they always had a piece of material left over for a hat. Sometimes the children also had a hat made to match their outfit.

My grandparents were very busy with their business in their yard goods store, because there was such a demand for this item, that they hardly had time to come to see us. My mother visited them quite often. My mother did not have any sisters, she was closer to her mother, and they always shared all of their happenings together. My mother always tried her best to visit her parents, as often as she could. A lot of times, after closing the stores, my mother decided to take a ride and go to see her parents and her brothers. She always used to rent a horse and buggy and a driver. In the old days, this was one of the best ways to travel short distances.

I remember every time my mother went to see my grandparents she always asked me if I wanted to come along and of course, I said yes. I also remember that I used to go with my mother all the time and I was very happy to go and see everyone. A lot of times we used to go on a Saturday evening and we stayed there until Sunday evening, so we had a whole day to visit with my grandparents and with my uncles. I did not have to miss school, either.

My grandparents loved to see me and I loved to see them, too. I really missed them a lot. I still remember that every time, when I came to visit them, they always gave me a lot of material. I had enough for everything that I wanted to make out of it, like dresses, skirts, blouses and whatever I would decide to do with it, I could do.

When I came home I went to the shnaiderin (dressmaker) in order to have my clothes made. I picked out a style from a fashion book and the dressmaker made everything the way I told her. I still remember that I used to pick a style of a dress, but for some reason or another if I did not like, for instance, the collar or the sleeves of this model, I picked a collar and sleeves from another model and the dressmaker made it the way I wanted it.

This particular dressmaker was more expensive than the others, but my mother did not mind it at all because she knew that I was very particular and everything had to be done right. My mother also knew that if the dressmaker would not do a good job, my mother would not hear the end of it from me. Among all of the other things, was that if I did not like the way the clothes looked on me, I would never wear them.

I had to come three times for a fitting. As long as I can remember I always liked nice clothes. The dressmaker always had problems with me. She knew that everything had to be made perfect because I was a perfectionist and when I saw something not done right I was not too happy with it and I let her know. Even until this day, I will try my best to do and make things perfect. No matter how hard it will be for me or how long it takes me, I will still keep on trying until I get it right. I know that they had and still do have an expression, "if you don't succeed the first time, try again and again until you will succeed."

One of my uncles, my mother's brother, served in the Polish army in the Kawalerja battalion (infantry unit) for four years. He visited with his parents, my grandparents, and he also came to visit us on his leave, as often as he could. He was a very good-looking man, like a movie actor. I remember when he came to visit us I was very young, but I was also a very curious child. I wanted to know what the object was that he had on the side of his uniform. He had a heavy belt and what he had on, was a sword that was covered by a holder.

I could only see the shiny handle. I kept on looking at the handle and the more I looked at it the more curious I became and finally I asked my uncle if I could see it. He said, "Why?" then I replied because I really want to see it. I was very curious to know what it was, and I kept on insisting on seeing it. Finally, he pulled it out of the holder and swung it over his head. It looked like a big, long knife to me and I was fascinated by the shine of it. I wanted to touch it, but he did not let me because it was very sharp. He said to me that little children were not allowed to touch sharp things and, of course, I asked why. When he explained it to me, I could understand the reason why he did not let me touch it.

It was a sword weapon that the soldiers in the infantry were using in the war. After a while my uncle put it back into the holder, picked me up and kissed me. My uncle had a lot of patience with me, and he always got a kick out of hearing me asking so many questions and I never gave up until I got the answers. I was always a very persistent child and I guess this was my personality, to want to know everything. When I asked a question I never accepted "because". I always wanted a real answer with an explanation and I kept on nagging until I got my answer and only then I was happy.

After my uncle finished his term in the army and he was discharged he came home and he lived with his parents in Hrubieszow (Rabeshoiw). Nobody exactly knew what his plans were for the future and apparently, he did not tell anybody what he intended to do. For some reason or another, without telling or asking anybody's advice, he decided to join the Communist underground party. For a long time nobody of the family members really knew what he was doing and nobody even had the slightest idea or any thoughts in their mind that he chose to become a Communist.

When he came to our city he stayed with us for a couple weeks. I remember one evening he asked me if I wanted to take a walk with him. I was very happy and I said yes, of course with my mother's permission. He took me with him and we went to the main street of our city and I watched him hanging some paper signs on every place he could find where the people would see and read them. At the time I really did not pay too much attention or understand what he was doing, instead I was very happy that my uncle was taking me with him for a walk. My mother did not have any objection to it, either. She did not have any reason to suspect that something was going on because she really did not know anything.

I guess the reason he took me along was not to attract too much attention to himself. I went with him quite a few times. My mother never got suspicious because she really did not have a way of knowing what he was really up to. Eventually, he told my mother the truth and, of course, my mother became very worried. From then on she was in fear that sooner or later the police would catch up with him and he would be arrested.

The Communist party was illegal in Poland, and because of this, when the Polish police caught a Communist, they arrested them and put them in jail for a long time. My mother was scared that some of our neighbors would find out that he was hiding with us and she also knew that I was a very talkative kid, like most of the children were. Whatever they saw or heard, they would repeat to others. Of course, she knew that I would say wrong things without even knowing what I was saying, so just to make sure, my mother had a talk with me.

She told me that when I will play with the children I should not tell them that my uncle was staying with us and that he was hiding out with us. When I went out to play, I said to the children, "I won't tell you that my uncle is staying with us, and he is hiding out with us." At that time the police were looking for the Communists who were putting out all the posters with the propaganda about Communism. The police knew who was doing it, but they did not know where they were hiding. Little by little, the police were catching them and one by one, they were arrested.

The Communist party was working like an underground group, and their job was to turn everyone into a Communist. My uncle was working for them, also. I remember that when I came back into the house, I felt very good about myself. I told my mother what I said to the children, exactly what she told me to say to them. I expected that my mother would be pleased with it, but instead of giving me a pat on the back, it turned out the other way around. She got very upset and she started to scream at me. At the time I got very confused and I was very surprised by her actions. I thought that I did exactly what she told me to do and I really could not understand why she was so angry with me, since according to me I did not do anything else, but only what I was told to do. I really did not know what I did to make my mother so angry. I kept on thinking to myself and asking myself, "What did I do wrong?" but I could not think of anything.

My mother knew, right away, that there would be trouble. My uncle packed his things and he left in a hurry. I just could not understand what I did wrong, because according to me, I only said what my mother told me to. Right away, somebody reported my uncle to the Polish authorities because apparently, one of the children told their parents what I said and they probably did not like Communists, so very shortly after, the police came to look for my uncle.

They told my mother that they looked for him in Hrubieszow

and they tried to arrest him there and that was why he came to our city to hide out. Everything would have been okay, if I only would not say what I said. Me, without realizing what I was saying, got my uncle into trouble and I really did not know what I did wrong until after my mother explained to me. Then I started to understand what I did and I felt very guilty and miserable that because of me, my uncle had to leave. I guess from then on I understood that when somebody told me not to tell anybody what they said, I should just keep quiet and not say anything.

My uncle probably got in touch with his contact. We did not hear from him for a long time. One day a man came to us, who was working in the underground, also, and he told my mother that my uncle was in Russia and that he was okay. The man gave my mother a picture of my uncle. After that, nobody knew where my uncle was or what he was doing.

From time to time I asked my parents where my uncle was and they never told me. They never gave me an answer. I guess that they really did not know themselves where he was, and what happened to him. They were very uncertain if he was dead or alive. Every time I heard my parents talking to each other and mentioning his name, I looked at them and I saw in their faces that they were very worried and they wondered if they would ever know what happened to him. One day, I overheard my parents talking about my uncle and they stated a fact that the last time they heard about my uncle was that he left the Russian revolutionist party. This meant that now he was working against the Communist party. Apparently, he did not like Communism anymore. My uncle exiled from the Russian revolutionists party and he joined Trotsky's party.

I overheard my parents' conversation saying that the Russian authorities arrested him and sent him to Siberia and since that time nobody exactly knew what happened to him. Everyone in the family assumed that he was killed or died in Siberia because very few people who were sent to Siberia could survive. First of all, it was very cold there, only white bears lived there. Besides the cold climate, the slave labor camps were like death camps. The work was very hard there. Whoever was sent to Siberia to be punished knew that they would not come out of there alive because the Siberian labor camps were working the prisoners to death, especially the political ones.

My second uncle was a goldsmith. He had a workshop in

Hrubieszow. He made different things out of gold, like rings, necklaces, bracelets, pins and many other items. Everything was hand made and he did very well in his shop, but he was not too happy to live in Poland. He did not like most of the Polish and Ukrainian people and he knew very well that the feeling was mutual. In spite of them doing business together, there still was not any friendship between them. My uncle was a very warm and good-natured person and he liked to live among friends, not enemies. Most of the time the Poles and Ukrainians were not our friends. Even when every one of them tried to hide how they really felt towards us Jews, we always knew the truth. We knew that they do not like us and on the other hand we did not like them, either.

The anti-Semitism was always playing a big part in the Jewish life. It started to become very bad in Poland and my uncle really did not like living with the Polish and Ukrainian anti-Semites and narrow-minded people. He said that Palestine was our country and someday he will settle down in Palestine. Finally, the day came and he was on his way to Palestine. I do not remember exactly when he left, but I know it was not that much earlier than before my father died. It was around the year of 1935.

After he settled down in Palestine, he opened the same kind of business and worked as a goldsmith. He was very happy in Palestine. Very shortly after, he got married and had a baby. He kept on writing to all of us to pack up and come to Palestine, but nobody in the family thought of it too seriously. Even though the anti-Semitism got worse, nobody was ready to leave the old life behind and start a new life. Everyone was set in their ways and they had their homes, their businesses, their friends and everyone had their way of living and their daily routines.

Most of the reason was that when people were getting settled in one place and getting used to it, it was very hard to give up their old ways of living, and start a new life with new ways of living and new ways of doing things. It felt like they had to start their life from the beginning. It was not easy for anybody, especially for the older people. It really was a big and difficult decision to make, to throw all the years of their life away and to start everything from the beginning. I think that it was not so easy for people to move from one city to another city, especially to move from one country to another country.

My grandfather wanted to go to Palestine, but my grandmother did not want to leave her house and her business that she did very well in. She definitely made up her mind that she would not leave everything behind, and besides that, she still had a daughter, my mother, and her son, my uncle, in Poland with their families. On the other hand, my grandfather did not give up his dream and his dream was to die in Palestine. Finally, after some time, my grandfather wrote to his son, stating in his letter that he was ready to come to Palestine.

My uncle sent my grandfather the papers for emigration to Palestine. He did not want to leave my grandmother behind, but his obsession was to die in Palestine. No matter what anybody said to him, nobody could convince him that he was not doing the right thing by leaving everyone behind. No matter how hard everyone tried to talk him out of it, it did not help. He felt very strongly about it and was determined to see Palestine and die there. My grandfather left in 1936, shortly after my father died. He kept on writing to all of us, especially to my grandmother, to leave the anti-Semites behind and come to Palestine. Everyone promised to come later. The later never came and we never went to Palestine.

My grandfather died in 1939, a couple months before the war broke out in Poland, but after all, my grandfather's wish came true and he did die in Palestine. My mother felt very depressed and sorry that she did not see her father for almost four years before he died and when he died she could not even go to his funeral. My grandmother and her other son, my uncle, with his family, felt very badly about it, also, but there was nothing that they could do. In a way, they were happy that my grandfather saw Palestine before he died and his wish came true.

# CHAPTER V
## MY FATHER'S FAMILY

My father, Boruch Moshe, was born in 1904 in Wlodzimierz Volynski, Ludmir (in Yiddish) in Poland. It was about 30 kilometers from Hrubieszow, where my mother was born. My father's family consisted of his mother, his father, one brother and him. My father's parents were strictly Orthodox Jews, and they raised their sons the same way. My father always took an interest in the strict Jewish traditions and religion.

My father's father was a very well known member among the Orthodox Jews. As my father and his brother grew older, they started to think about what they would like to do with their life. In spite of the fact that they had to do what their father wanted them to do, this did not stop them from dreaming and making all kinds of plans in their mind, even when they knew for sure that their opinion or decision did not count with their father.

My father was the oldest child and of course, his father put more pressure on him than on his younger brother. In order for my father to learn higher Judaism, his father sent him to the Yeshiva. Finally, my father finished studying and came home. Right away, he got a position and he started to belong to the Gmeana –Kehilla, which was a religious organization.

From the beginning he was a ritual schoichet, a Jewish man who learned to slaughter animals in a religious, ritual way. This type of work affected his health, and after continuing with his studies, he became a rabbi.

My father's brother was never interested in learning higher Judaism, but his father, my grandfather, had the last word about this and my uncle had to do what his father wanted him to do. That was the way it was in the older days. The father made all the decisions for their children. When my grandfather died, my father's brother, right away, gave up his studying Judaism.

He thought that he already knew enough to be a good Jew, instead of being a very religious, strictly Orthodox Jew. He thought that whatever he learned was enough for him to know about the Jewish religion and traditions and he was perfectly happy with it. When my father's brother got married, his wife kept kosher, they went to synagogue on Shabbos and holidays, but they both were not very strict, religious Jews. Apparently, they both had the same idea about it.

I never knew my grandfather, my father's father. He died before I was born. After my grandfather died, my grandmother kept on living in her house by herself. She did not want to live with any of her sons because she wanted to be independent and besides that, she said that her children had their own lives and their families to take care of and she figured that she would be better off staying in her own home. In spite of everyone trying to talk her into getting married again, she always said that she was okay being by herself. It seemed very clear to everyone that she made up her mind never to get married again. My grandmother never had time to be lonely, either, because she was always surrounded by her family and she always kept very busy.

My father and his brother were very close to each other, but they also were very different from each other in every way. My father was very much involved in studying the Torah and he had a religious position, and my father's brother, my uncle, was always involved in business. He and his wife owned a little grocery store and they both worked together in the store, like a team. My aunt was a very organized person and everything had to be in its place. She was mostly in charge of the store.

My uncle did not mind it at all to take orders from his wife. He did exactly what his wife told him to do. I think he liked it this way, because he did not have to carry any of the responsibilities on his shoulders. He was like a helper and he was happy with his position. My aunt, on the other hand, was a different type. She would not be too happy to take orders from anybody, especially from a husband. She was altogether the opposite of him, so by having one leader and one follower, both of them were happy and it really worked out very well for them.

I remember that it was a little grocery store, but even in a small grocery store, in the older days, they were always busy. When for instance, we wanted to buy a bottle of oil, we had to bring our own empty bottle, because the oil was delivered in a big can, about ten gallons of oil in a can.

When we wanted to buy groceries, like flour, sugar, rice, peas, and many other items, we had to bring our own bag or some paper and they would fold the paper like a cone, or we could bring a napkin that we could tie. They would weigh, on a scale, the amount we wanted to get of the item, and they put it into our so-called bag. Most items were delivered to the store in large quantities, like one hundred kilo sacks. Nothing was ready pre-packed. In my days, paper was very expensive, and so was glass. That was why everyone was saving their newspapers, bottles and pieces of cloth in order to have it when we were going grocery shopping.

In the older days, in Poland, the cities and towns had mostly small stores and every store had certain items for sale. Most of the time, we had to go grocery shopping to a couple different stores, because the stores were specializing in one certain category of items, only. For instance, when we wanted to buy bread, rolls, challah, bagels, pletzel, we had to go to a bread store or a bakery where they were baking all of these things. When we wanted to buy cake, cookies and different pastries, we had to go to a pastry store. When we wanted to buy groceries, we had to go to a grocery store. When we wanted to buy milk, cheese, butter or other dairy products, we had to go to a dairy store. When we wanted to buy meat, chicken, turkey, or goose, we had to go to a kosher butcher. When we wanted to eat lockschen (noodles) we had to make them ourselves because, in the older days, this item was not sold anywhere.

My father's brother, my uncle and his wife, my aunt, did not have any children, but they were happy together. My parents had four children, two daughters and two sons. My uncle and aunt treated us like we were their own children. They always gave us nice presents, and whenever we came into their grocery store they gave us candy and they were always happy to see us because they really loved us like their own and we really loved them, also.

# CHAPTER VI
# OUR FAMILY

I was born on January 15, 1929, in the shtut (city) of Wlodzimierz Volynski, Ludmir, Poland. My family consisted of my mother, my father, two brothers, one sister and me. I was the oldest child in the family. My father was a rabbi, and because of this, we children were raised in a very strictly Orthodox, Jewish way. We learned to observe our religion and all of our traditions. My parents were quite well off and they raised us in a very extravagant way. We had everything that we possibly wanted and needed. We were raised in a very happy and loving atmosphere.

My mother grew up in her parents' home, where they always were in business. At an early age, she started to learn about the business world, and she began to have a special feeling for it and liked it. Very shortly after my mother got married, she decided to open her own business and take care of it. In spite of the fact that she worked very hard, she was happy with it and did not mind it at all. When my mother saw that the business was already organized and it started to run smooth and was doing very well, she opened a second store with the same items that she had in the first business.

My mother was working and because she was away from home for a whole day, so in order to take care of us children and the household she hired help. This way she could do what she liked and was good at doing. She was always involved in business and that was what she liked, being in the business world. In the end it worked out very good for everyone around and everyone was happy with it.

We had a live-in maid, a Jewish woman who helped with the household and she took good care of us children. We liked her very much, and in a way she was like a second mother to us. The fact was that we saw her more than our mother. We saw our mother in the morning, before we left for school, and in the evening when she came home from work. It was okay because most of the day we were in school anyway.

My mother had to work all day and take care of her two businesses. I remember that besides the maid, we had a woman who washed our clothes and did our laundry. We had a steady woman who delivered to us, everyday, fresh pletzel with onion and poppy seed, and fresh, big braided bagels. She already knew the amount that my mother ordered. The woman baked all night, all of these things, and in the morning when she came to us, everything was still warm. She really worked very hard and this was her way of making an honest living. I still remember how delicious the pletzels and bagels were. The woman had her steady customers and everyone liked her pletzels and bagels.

My mother used to bake every Thursday night. She baked bread, challah, (white bread), cakes and cookies, but nothing else. Of course, my mother could bake pletzel and bagels also, but she wanted to give the woman a little business, even if it was more expensive to buy from her than for my mother to bake it herself. My mother really did not mind it at all. Besides that, the woman baked her pletzels and bagels fresh every day, but my mother baked only once a week.

We also had a steady Gentile man who carried water for us from the brina (water well), like a water pump. He had so called cromisles, which looked like a long board. In the middle of the board he put a little padding in order that it should not rub his neck when he put the cromisles on top of his shoulders. On the end of each side were wires with hooks and that was where he hung the water buckets. I still remember that on one side of our kitchen, in the corner, stood a big wooden barrel, so the man filled it up with water once a week and if we needed more water at the end of the week, we went to the brina (water well) ourselves to pump the water and we carried it home. The man was always paid every week and this was his way of making a living. He also carried water all week for other people and he really worked very hard.

In the older days, usually, we had to start school when we were between five and six years old. I learned to read Polish when I was four years old, so I started elementary school when I was not quite at the age of five years old. In the elementary school, they taught us only Polish. Some children attended elementary school and after school, twice a week, they went to Cheider.

A Cheider was a Yiddish (Jewish) school to learn Jewish and Hebrew, but the Cheider was only for the boys and no girls were allowed to attend the Cheider. My parents, especially my father, wanted my sister and me to know all the Jewish traditions and about the Jewish religion, they wanted us to know Yiddishkeit (Judaism). They decided to hire for us girls a Melammed, a Yiddish teacher, and he came to our home twice a week to teach us Yiddish and Hebrew. In the older days, this was the only way for girls to learn Yiddishkeit (Judaism).

I really learned a lot when my father was alive and when I was very young, only a child. I still remember most of the things that I learned in my childhood years. Looking back at these times I realized that in my short childhood years, I learned an awful lot by just listening and obeying my parents and most of all, by trying very hard to learn whatever I could. I remember every morning, just about six o'clock in the morning when my mind was clear, I walked over to the park with my schoolbooks and I rechecked my homework. It was very peaceful in the park then, and the air was clean and smelled very good from the flowers and the pine trees. Nobody was around and even on the hottest days, the park was nice and cool, especially early in the morning. After a while, I went back home to get ready for school.

I remember that before I went to school, my mother said that I had to have breakfast. I was always a very picky eater. My mother made me eat breakfast and drink cocoa every morning. The cocoa was made out of very rich milk, straight from the cow, with a lot of cocoa and sugar in it. I still remember that after my mother came home from work I went with her a few times a week, to a woman who had two cows and she sold the milk from them. We went to the woman's house and my mother got the milk right after the woman was done milking the cow. The milk was still warm and I drank some right away because I liked plain milk, but not cocoa.

My mother knew very well that I did not like cocoa, but she did not care if I liked it or not. She kept on saying to me that it was good for me and I was going to drink it. I still remember that my mother was holding the glass to my mouth and she practically poured the cocoa into my mouth and all of the time while I was drinking the cocoa I really was very upset and I kept on crying. I did not have another choice, but I had to obey my mother's wishes even if I hated cocoa. Another thing that my mother always made me do, was to take lunch with me everyday, so I had to take it. When I saw on our lunch break that some children did not bring lunch with them, probably because their family was poor and they did not have enough food to eat, I always gave them my lunch.

I remember that I used to stand in front of a long mirror and look at myself and when I did not like how I looked because I was very fat, I became very upset and miserable. We were all fat children in my family. My mother paid special attention to our eating habits. She always tried to fatten us up. In the older days, in Europe, everyone wanted to be fat. The way they looked at certain things was, that when we were fat, we were healthy, and when somebody was skinny, everyone thought that this person was sick and they called him Musulman. It means skeleton man and everyone was very sure that this skinny person would die very soon.

They even had an expression that "until the fat one would get skinny, the skinny one would die," and everyone believed in it. In the older days a lot of superstitious beliefs were going around, not only between the Jews, but between other nationalities also. I have to admit that I, myself, adopted quite a few superstitious beliefs that I believed in, and I would not do them because I was and still am sometimes telling myself that it would be bad luck. Over all, I thought that I had mazel (luck) in my life.

In my childhood years, I always felt in more ways than one that I was very fortunate to be surrounded by my loving family and to have everything that I needed in my daily living. We all lived a very normal, happy life, the kind of life where we children ate on time, we had enough fresh air, we played with our friends and my whole family was happy, content and healthy. The only child that had a little problem with his health was my brother. He had stomachaches all the time and he always felt nauseous. He could not eat too much, because he always felt sick to his stomach. A lot of times he ate and after he finished eating he vomited everything out and then he was hungry again, but he was always scared to eat because of his vomiting.

My mother took him to the best doctors, but none of them knew what was wrong with him. At that time we did not have x-ray machines to see what was going on inside his body. The doctors tried to guess what was wrong, but all the medicines that they prescribed did not help at all. On the contrary, he got worse instead of better.

In my days, the doctors did not know enough to help him. They were not too advanced in their field of medicine and they did not have too much knowledge of different diseases because they did not learn enough about certain things. That was why their skills in medicine were very primitive in many ways.

My brother suffered with his nauseousness and stomachaches for a long time. In the older days, people believed in old-fashioned remedies. They grew all kinds of herbs, and they made different medicines out of them. When somebody got sick they knew exactly which herb to use because they were reading up on it. They also believed in supernatural power because in the older days the people were more superstitious than they are now.

One day a man came to our city to settle down. Very shortly after he settled down in his place he started to get to know people. When somebody complained of having some pains he just suggested something for it. After awhile he started to get to know more and more people and he gave them some homemade remedies for their pains and aches and it helped them a lot. In no time he became better known.

People in our city started to say nice things about him. They even said that he knows more than the doctor. He was healing the sick by using all kinds of remedies. In a very short time he became very famous, and they gave him a nickname. They called him witch doctor. He started to heal people with his homemade medicines that he prepared himself. My mother heard about him, also. Since my mother had tried everything else, she figured that she did not have anything else to lose, only a few zlotys (Polish money) for his fee, so she took my brother to the witch doctor. I remember that I asked my mother if I can go with her and she said yes, so I went with them.

In my days, there was not too much of a choice of transportation available. In our city we had horses and buggies for a certain fee, but we had to wait on the street corner to catch them. My mother decided that it would be better for us to walk to the witch doctor, so we walked. It took us a while and finally we arrived at the witch doctor. He examined my brother and right away he told my mother what was wrong with him. He said that my brother's stomach was full of tapeworms and that was why he was so nauseous. I still remember that we were both sitting, as if we were stunned. I started to think and wonder how the worms got into his stomach. I looked at my mother, but she was sitting without saying a word. Finally, the witch doctor said to my mother, "Don't worry, I will try to help him get rid of the tapeworms". I really remember every detail, even now, how it happened because it still stays in front of my eyes.

He took a big shisel (pot), and filled it up with milk, then he put it in the other room and he called my brother in. My mother and I were sitting and wondering what was going on in there. Finally, they came out of the room with the pot of milk full of big worms. The worms smelled the milk while my brother was sitting on the pot, like you were sitting on a toilet, and then the worms started to crawl out. He told my mother to do the same procedure in our home a couple of times and she did. Finally, my brother totally got rid of the tapeworms.

In the older days, the Jewish people believed in the "evil eye" so mostly when a baby was born they put a red ribbon on the baby's wrist, in order to prevent everyone from giving the baby an evil eye. I really did not know if this was another superstition, or if it was our tradition, when somebody was moving into a new home, we had to bring into the home, bread and salt before they were moving in. It meant that we were wishing them that they should never be hungry. Also, when somebody was saying to us that we looked good or healthy, right away, we thought that they gave us an evil eye and something bad will happen to us, so we were knocking on wood in order not to get the evil eye and we were saying pu, pu, pu. I forgot to mention that we were not allowed to walk under a ladder because it was not lucky. I did not know why, but that was what everyone said not to do.

People believed in many more superstitious things, but I cannot remember all of them. Until this day I still believe in certain superstitious sayings and doings, no matter how old-fashioned they sound now, but I never forgot them, I guess because I was hearing them for so many years during my childhood.

I was the oldest child in my family, and that is why I always knew whatever I would do, my sister and my two brothers would try to do it, too, so I had to be careful not to do anything wrong in order that they should not copy and learn bad habits from me. As small as I was, I started to develop my own personality and style of doing things. I learned to evaluate everything and decide which things were more important than others.

According to my thinking, I came to a conclusion that time was the most important and most precious thing in life, because we never can bring back the lost time of our life. In order not to waste our time we have to use it very wisely and always make the best of it. I started to adopt a philosophy in my life, that when I was doing something and I was spending time to do it, why not do it the best possible way. Eventually, I started to push myself to be the best in everything that I did, and most of the time I succeeded.

I was the best student in my class. I remember that everyone in school had to wear black uniforms, buttoned in the front with white collars. I was wearing a black uniform, only in silk, with a white collar and white cuffs, because I liked to be different. I still remember in my school class everyone was writing with a blue pen and my teacher wanted to kill me, because I wanted to write with a black pen. I liked the black pen better. I got away with a lot of things because I behaved very well in class and I was very good in learning. I was a pain in the neck, but in spite of it, I think in a way they liked me for my stubbornness and persistence. As long as I can remember I was never a follower.

I was the best in drawing, knitting, embroidering and as a matter of fact, we had an art class and my drawings were hanging in the school hallway. I also was very good in crafts, and once a week we had a craft class in school. I remember that I sewed a dress by hand, because in my days, we did not have too many sewing machines. After the dress was finished, I traced a flower design on the dress and I embroidered it with a cross-stitch. I made different colors of flowers all over the dress. One time, we had an international show from arts and crafts and my dress was hanging on the wall among other things. To my surprise, that I really did not expect this to happen, I won the first prize.

I still remember that the dress was made out of a very sheer white material, percale. It had a yoke in the front and the back, with puffed short sleeves and cuffs. It was a full dress with pleats and it had embroidered flowers on each yoke, flowers on the cuffs of the sleeves and flowers on the bottom of the dress all the way around. After the craft show was over, and I got the dress back, I was wearing it on our holidays or when I went to a party. Everyone loved this dress, including me. I really put a lot of work into it, but it really was a beautiful dress and I always felt sort of proud wearing it.

# CHAPTER VII
## OUR HOME

Our family had a very nice, big house made out of wood and bricks, which was located on Zamkova Ulica (Zamkova Street) in Wlodzimierz, Volynski. We lived in a Jewish neighborhood near a synagogue and a produce market that was called a Green Market. It was also situated near a park and the Luga River. The neighborhood was known as a very good and religious neighborhood and there was a very nice class of Jewish people.

Our house consisted of four big rooms. We had a big kitchen, two bedrooms and a sitting room like a living room. In the older days in Poland, none of the children had their own bedroom. Sometimes the boys slept any place, like in the kitchen on a coffer or in the sitting room on the sofa. Mostly, all of the children slept in one room and the parents slept in the other room. In the older days, the parents' room had to have two beds, so a lot of times the children sneaked in to sleep with the mother or with the father. I remember that the floors in the house were painted red except the kitchen floor. In the kitchen we had a plain wooden floor. We had curtains on the windows and also pretty furniture, like antique furniture.

Most of the furniture was from my grandmother, my mother's mother, because when my grandfather left for Palestine, she moved into a smaller house and did not need as much furniture. My grandmother was happy that my mother wanted it, because when she came to visit us she could see it in our home. Sometimes I heard my mother and my grandmother talking about certain pieces of furniture. I thought that it held special memories for them and some pieces of furniture had some sentimental meaning to them, also.

We had old pictures, silver and a lot of valuable things in our home. We had a big kitchen, which was the biggest room in the house. It had the best view and the most windows. There was a big table standing in the middle of the kitchen floor with chairs around it. On the opposite side of the kitchen there was a china cabinet with dishes in it. It seemed to me that everyone liked to be in the kitchen best. On the other side of the kitchen there was a big stove for cooking our meals, and an oven for baking. We also had an oven to heat the house, which we used wood and coal in it. The coal gave out a lot of heat and the house was always warm in the wintertime. Our house had a big wraparound porch with furniture, so we children played on the porch most of the time.

We also had an attic and we stored everything there. Because we did not have too much closet space, we had to try to manage somehow. In the winter we put our summer clothes up in the attic and in the summer we put our winter clothes there. We also stored all of our Passover dishes, pots, pans, and silverware. We put everything into a big, straw braided coffer and it stayed there all year long until we needed it for the next Passover. The attic was very useful and we could put all kinds of stuff there that we did not need right away.

It was very seldom that anyone had a shed in the center of the city. Most of the people used their attic for storage, like we did. We also had a big cellar and we could put a lot of things in the cellar. In my times we did not know about refrigeration, among the other things that we did not know and did not have. Mostly, we used the cellar for keeping cold all of the cooked food, and all of the perishable things. In the summer at the highest heat, the cellar was very cold, just like a refrigerator today. None of the food got spoiled, but it was not too convenient to climb steps for everything that we wanted to bring up from the cellar, but we managed. Of course, there were a lot of mice in the cellar, so we had to put a heavy stone on top of each cover, in order to prevent them from moving the cover from the pot. We also had a couple cats and most of the time they stayed in the cellar.

A lot of households had iceboxes in the summer season and they had to buy ice every so often. Most of the population in Europe did their shopping everyday. They bought only for one day what they could use and the next morning they bought everything fresh and that was why most of the people did not stock up with perishable goods.

Behind our house we had a couple of fruit trees and a big vegetable garden. In the garden we grew tomatoes, potatoes, onions, scallions, radishes, carrots, cucumbers, cabbage, dill, parsley, sunflowers and poppies. We grew practically everything in the vegetable category.

Our fruit trees were apples, pears and little brown pears that we called gneilkes. I remember them because I loved them. We also had plums, cherries, and sour cherries. Besides the vegetable garden and the fruit trees we also had bushes of strawberries, raspberries, agras, womperlach, which were growing against the fence.

I remember that twice a day before I went to school in the morning, and when I came from school, I had to water the garden by hand, of course. I was carrying the buckets of water from the water well. This was one of my daily chores. As soon as I woke up early in the morning, about five o'clock, my responsibilities started.

We never had to buy any vegetables because we had more than enough for us. A lot of times my mother gave some vegetables to our neighbors and they appreciated it. We also gave them fruit. Our neighbors did not have any space to make a garden, but we had a big back yard and a fence around it. Besides that, two of our next-door neighbors had permission from us to take as much as they could eat and they did. They never had to buy any fruit or vegetables, either.

When the fruit got ripe we had plenty of fruit for the whole summer and after the summer we stored some fruit in wooden crates and we had fruit for the whole winter long. My father put the crates in the attic and covered them with straw, and most of the things that we did not use summertime from the garden we stored, also.

Our next-door neighbors were very nice, they also had small children, and I played with them after school all the time. Both of our houses were very close to each other and we could see directly what was going on in each other's homes. We did not even have to go into each other's houses to keep in touch. When we wanted to see or talk to each other we just had to stay by the open window and we could talk. I talked to the children as soon as I came home from school.

Sometimes in the morning, before my mother went to work and she had a little extra time, my mother and the neighbor were also talking through the open window and they were telling each other different kinds of happenings, mostly my mother was asking the neighbor about this one and that one. The neighbor knew everyone and everything that was going on in our neighborhood. After all, she was not working, and in order to do something she may as well be a yenta (busybody) and collect all the news in order to keep my mother up to date with the latest news. She knew that my mother was busy working and my mother had no way of knowing all the gossip, if she would not fill her in. The neighbor felt that this was her responsibility to collect news for my mother.

I was very curious and for a while I was listening to all the stories and all the gossip that they were telling each other, but after awhile I had to leave them because I did not have too much time to waste, and I started to get ready to go to school. I had my daily routine, like watering the garden, picking the ripe fruit and vegetables and taking them into the house, hanging up my school clothes, and helping my sister and my brothers with whatever they needed help with. Sometimes I did a little extra work so I had to do my homework in the evening by a kerosene lantern. That was how we lit up our houses. I always felt an obligation to help my sister and brothers because I was the oldest child in the family.

In one way, it made me feel important and sort of special because the children always looked up to me, and they clinged to me like I was their protector. Even though I was only a child myself, but with me close to them, it made them feel safe. Even when my parents were around they still stuck with me. In spite of it that I always bossed them around and told them what to do and what not to do they always listened to me anyway. I still remember that my mother used to say that the children were more afraid of me than of her and she was probably right.

# CHAPTER VIII
# OUR BUSINESS

My parents owned two businesses near the market on one of the nicest streets in our city. The street was called Warshawska or Warshawa Ulica (Street). Both businesses were variety stores, like five and ten cent stores. The buildings belonged to us, also. Because my father was employed, and he had a position, my mother took care of the businesses. She had some hired help, but she worked very hard herself. After we children left for school, my mother left also. She went to open the stores.

In Poland, they did not have a specific time when to open or when to close the businesses. Every storekeeper used his own judgment. There were no regular hours. If they did good business they stayed open a little later, and if not they closed earlier. My mother sometimes came home later and sometimes earlier. We children already knew when the business was good and when it was bad. Even when she had a slow business day, she was still happy to come home earlier, just to be with her children and we children were happy to see her, also. Wintertime, when the days were shorter and the nights were longer, we saw our mother more.

In wintertime, it was very cold in Poland, and when the winter started it was below zero degrees everyday of the week for the whole winter. My mother tried to bundle up with a lot of warm clothes and warm boots, but it still did not help too much. There was no heat in the stores and it was freezing cold. In order to keep her hands, feet and face warm, my mother had a little pot filled with burning coals. Every storekeeper did the same just to keep a little warmer. It felt good to stay near the heat. I remember that my mother kept on moving her arms, feet, and her whole body just to keep warm and most of the time even this did not help too much.

Besides staying in the store in the wintertime and freezing, there was no business at all. Nobody came in to buy anything and everyone tried to stay home, especially when they did not have to come out in the frost and snow, they felt, why should they. Most of the storekeepers opened their stores even if only for a couple hours to see how business will turn out. The way the winters were below zero degrees, the summer climate was not much better.

When the summer started and it got very hot, the heat did not make us so comfortable either, but no matter what, how and when, nobody complained and whatever it was, we knew that we had to accept it and live with it. Just like in the cold winter days, people were not coming out too much, the same was for the very hot summer days. Most of the people were trying to stay away from the heat by either staying home or going to the lake. So you see, in the winter and in the summer, nobody did too much business, including my mother, but in the spring and in the fall it was better and all the storekeepers made up for the lost time.

After school, on my way home, I always stopped in the store to see my mother. I had to pass the whole street of stores to get to my mother's store. Everyone knew me and I knew everyone. Usually on a slow day everyone was sitting in front of their stores and talking to each other. When they saw me walking by, everyone tried to grab me and kiss me. I was a very cute and friendly child, even if I say so myself. I always had a big smile on my face and I was always polite and that was why the storekeepers loved me.

In the older days, everyone had the greatest respect for the law and they obeyed the orders of the leaders in their community, and this was the policeman. The police were very strict in our city. Every community had their policeman patrolling the neighborhood, especially the business section. The policeman, who patrolled Warshawa Street, where my mother had her stores, was the same person since I could remember. He also looked the same and acted the same. In plain words, he was always the same very mean person and everyone was afraid of him.

This policeman who everyone was scared of, used to walk around with an angry look on his face all of the time, and with a rubber club in his hand. He was tall and fat, and he never smiled at anybody. He looked and acted like he owned the world and when he gave an order everyone was jumping, but when he saw me walking by, he picked me up and gave me a big smile and a big hug and a kiss. I think this was the only time that somebody saw a smile on his face.

I kept on walking along Warshawa Street until I finally reached my mother's store. When I came into the store and I saw that my mother was very busy and she needed help, I helped her for a while. I tried to sell things to the peasants, like for instance, ribbons, tread, buttons, and all kinds of little items that they needed for sewing. I remember that the best selling items were ribbons. The peasants always wore full long skirts and on the bottom of the skirts they had about twelve rows of different colors of ribbons all around the skirt.

I spoke Ukrainian well, so the peasants liked the way I showed them how good the colors would look together. They really thought that I was right and eventually they made up their mind and bought a lot of items from me. My mother used to say that she was doing better business when I was around. In a while my mother did not need me anymore and she also knew that I was tired from being in school all day, so she sent me home. Our house was about ten minutes walking distance from my mother's business. I passed the Green Market on the way home, and sometimes I stopped to talk to the children who lived nearby, and finally I reached my home.

The maid always reminded me to take off my school clothes and hang them up, so I did. I had something to eat and shortly after, I walked over to the empty lot where the children were gathering right after school in order to play. They played different games that they liked. Our neighborhood had a lot of young children. They got along good with each other and they played together very well.

I played with my girlfriends and we played jump rope, marbles, hide and go seek and we also played in the sand by making an outline of little boxes and we jumped into each box and then we turned around and jumped back to the front, like hopscotch. The streets were also full of children, and since we did not have too many cars in my days, the children used the streets as a playground, also.

Sometimes the children got out of line and they got carried away and did things that they were not allowed and should not do. They threw stones at somebody's house and broke a window and without permission from anybody they climbed through somebody's fence and pulled out the vegetables from their garden. They climbed the trees and pulled the fruit off and threw them all over the yard without even realizing that they could fall off the tree and break their neck. In other words, they were very wild. Even when they knew that they were not allowed to do such things, this did not stop them and they still did it anyway.

These children were called loubas (wild) and of course, they got punished by their parents for doing these wild things. I remember my little brother had an obsession to break our neighbors windows by throwing stones into them and my parents had to pay for every window. It seemed to me that everyday someone came with a complaint about a broken window by my brother.

The girls were more settled than the boys. They hardly did things without their parents' permission. Most of the boys were more on the wild side. My mother never got upset with my brothers' behavior, especially with my little brother. She always used to say that boys will be boys. I remember that my father most of the time let my mother discipline the children, the way she thought was best. I also remember when my father got good and angry, especially with my brothers, he took his big strap that he got in the army and kept on hitting my brother with it without stopping. My mother had to pull my father away from my brother. After that, my brother remembered whatever he did to make my father so angry, he made very sure not to do it anymore.

To tell you the truth, sometimes I am wondering myself how I remember these incidences that happened such a long time ago, when I was only a young child. I remember good happenings and bad happenings, but all in all I am very thankful for my childhood memories because these were the most memorable and best years of my life.

# CHAPTER IX
# THE JAIL or PRISON IN WLODZIMIERZ VOLYNSKI

Our city had two jails (prison), one little jail and one big jail. To the little jail, they sent people who broke the law by doing little things, like not obeying an order of a policeman, not paying the bills, not keeping the street clean and for doing things like this, they got a fine to pay and if they did not pay the fine the police put them in jail for a couple days.

The big jail was for real criminals, people who committed serious crimes, like killers, rapists, thieves and many other crimes. These people had to serve long sentences and they remained in prison for years and years. The prison was surrounded with hills and no prisoner could escape from there. The buildings where the prisoners were kept were all the way in the back of the jail property. They were surrounded with barbwires and it was a very tight watch. In the front of the prison grounds, between two hills, they had an iron gate, which was locked all the time. On the other side of the gate were a couple of prison guards. The warden's house was very close to the gate.

We lived only about three blocks from the prison and between our house and the prison was a big empty lot where the children played. By me staying in my bedroom, I just had to look out of the window, and I could see the gate of the prison and what was going on there.

Every Monday the family members of the prisoners were allowed to visit them. The prison guard checked everyone's identification and when it seemed to be in order, the guard let them through the gate. The visitors could see the prisoners through the barbed wire fence only.

The empty lot near the prison was our playground. Everyday, when I played with the children, I always looked at the gate. I started to think and wonder what was going on there, and the more I thought about it, the more fascinated I became by it. I was also very curious to know what was on the other side of the gate. One day I made up my mind to be there every Monday, on the visiting day, so right after school I was ready to try my luck.

I only lived a few blocks from the prison so it did not take me too long to walk over and wait for my chance to be able to sneak in and get to the other side of the gate. Finally, one Monday I got my chance that I was waiting for. I got in through the gate and I kept on walking with the other people. The warden's daughter saw me right away, and she came over to me and asked me if I wanted to play with her. I said, "yes". We played for a while, and then she took me into her house. When her parents saw me all by myself, they were very surprised. Besides that, children were not allowed to come through the gate.

Her father started to ask me all kinds of questions. I remember that I really got scared and I did not say anything, but he kept on asking me what I was doing here. Finally, I told him the truth that the reason I sneaked in was because I wanted to see the prison. I still remember how I felt. I looked at them and they started to smile. The daughter was not interested about what happened. She kept on asking her parents over and over again, if I was allowed to come everyday and play with her. Her father said, "Okay" and he took me back to the gate and told the prison guard that whenever I would come he should let me through.

Since that time, the warden's daughter and I became very good friends. I saw her every so often and we played together very good. We were both the same age and we really got along very well. I was happy with her and she was happy to have somebody to play with because she was not allowed to have anybody come in there. I was the only friend and I had not been invited, either. I was there by accident only because I sneaked in, but no matter how it happened, it worked out well for both of us.

I always went to her home and her parents treated me very good. They always wanted me to eat there, but I explained to them that the Jewish people eat only certain kinds of food and they had to eat only kosher food, so I thanked them and I said I was sorry that I had to refuse.

They knew that I was Jewish, but they did not care and they seemed to like me anyway. Their daughter loved to play with me, and sometimes we stayed near the gate and we watched the other children playing together on the empty lot, which was our playground. They were laughing and shouting and it seemed that they were having a good time. She always looked at them and I could see on her face that she was really lonely by not having sisters or brothers and being the only child in the family. On top of it to be isolated from everyone just because her father was a warden. In a way I started to feel sorry for her and by the same token I really felt very lucky and happy that I had a sister, two brothers, friends and I was free to do whatever I wanted to do.

# CHAPTER X
## BUSINESS ACTIVITIES IN OUR CITY
## WLODZIMIERZ VOLYNSKI

## THE MARKET

Our city, Wlodzimierz Volynski, was always a very lively city. We had a lot of activities going on, especially in the business world. People came from the small towns and villages to do their shopping in our city. The reason for it was because we had a better variety of goods and better prices, also, then in the small towns or in the neighborhood stores.

We also had a lot of business sections, with all kinds of goods. Some stores were more expensive than others. Certain people did their shopping anywhere, because they just did not care about the prices, but the majority of the people looked for good quality of merchandise and less expensive prices. They looked for bargains, so in order to get bargains they had to buy at the market.

The merchants who were selling at the market were bringing their goods with them in their wagons or trucks, then they were renting out a couple of tables, which they were getting from the owner of the tables for a certain rental price. Next, they were putting out their merchandise on the tables. After everything was set up in order, they were ready to start to do business.

The reason that the market merchants could sell everything for much cheaper was because they were not paying high rent and their expenses were low. These kinds of merchants had to set up their merchandise every morning and they had to pack it up at the end of the day. It was not so easy for them to make a living and they had to work very hard to make ends meet, but nobody was really complaining and they thought that as long as they were healthy and they were able to do it, they were happy to be doing it.

In our city, we had two markets open everyday. The first market had all kinds of fruits, vegetables, chickens, fish, herring, and seafood, everything that was edible in the food department. Most of the people of the city came to this market to buy the goods there. This market was called the Green Market and it was located a few blocks from our home. I remember in the Green Market they had pickled apples and pickled pears. It was in a big bucket with all the pickled sauces. I always bought these apples and pears because I really loved them a lot. They had a very good taste. They were pickled with all kinds of spices. In the Green Market we could see a lot of peasants who lived close to our city. They were coming for a couple of hours, with some of their fruit and vegetables, in order to sell it and then buy things that they needed right away.

The second market was located in the center of the city in the business section. This market had only clothes, mostly working pants, jackets, shirts, shoes, belts, hats, sweaters, and everything that a workingman needed to wear to work. Most of the customers were the peasants. They always needed a lot of work clothes because the work that they were doing on the farm wore out their clothes in no time and they had to buy new clothes constantly. This market had steady merchants who came everyday and they had the same tables all year round and most of the time they also had the same steady customers.

I still remember that when I came out of my school, I had to pass the second market in order to come to one of my mother's stores. Being the curious child that I always was, and knowing the Ukrainian language, a lot of times I was standing and listening and watching, in order to see what was going on.

One particular time stuck in my mind and when I think of it, until today, I am still amused by it. Once I stopped near one of the stands and I watched a merchant selling a coat to a peasant. He put the coat on the peasant and the coat did not fit him. It was much too big on the peasant. The merchant did not have a coat that was the right size for the peasant, but the merchant was very determined to sell a coat to the peasant. After all, he came there to do some business and in spite of not having the right size coat, he still did not give up yet because he really did not want to lose the sale. The merchant took the coat that was twice as big as the peasant needed, and he put it on the peasant. He buttoned the coat in the front, and then the merchant stood behind the peasant and he held the extra material from the back, so the coat looked like it fit. When the peasant looked in the mirror, he thought it looked nice and he bought the coat. Finally, they were both happy for the time being. I walked away laughing and when I came into the store and my mother asked me why I was laughing, I told her what I just saw, and she laughed, too.

Everyone had their own way of dealing and wheeling. It amounted to the same thing, that everyone was trying to make a living the best way they could, no matter "if it even was by hook or by crook".

# YAHRITH (Bazaar)

In our city, besides the two markets that we had everyday of the week, we also had the yahrith (bazaar), which was open twice a week, every Monday and Thursday. The yahrith (bazaar) started early in the morning before the sun came out. On the yahrith (bazaar) days the peasants came into the city with their wagons.

They brought their products and they started selling everything from their wagons. After they sold their goods, they did their own shopping in our city. They had a special big square near the Green Market where they traded all sorts of merchandise there. The peasants were selling their agricultural products and they were buying city goods. In the summertime, the peasants arrived with their wagons, but in the wintertime, they came with their sleds in order to get through the snow.

Because nobody cleaned the snow off the roads in the villages in the winter, the snow was very deep there. Every farm had to take care of the road and clean the snow off in order to be able to come to the city. When the peasants came they were dressed warmly. Everyone was wearing high rubber boots and warm fur coats with fur hats and fur gloves and a wool shawl on top of their hat.

These wagons or sleds were packed full of different things, which they grew on their farms. The peasants, with their wagons or sleds filled with all kinds of fruits and vegetables, usually arrived earlier than others to make sure that they got a good spot, in order to sell their produce before it got spoiled. In the summertime, when it was very hot in the city, everything was getting spoiled very fast. In the wintertime, they had to take care of the produce, also, because the cold was not too good for it and they had to see to it that it would not freeze. The best thing was to cover it with something, which they usually did.

The square was filled with a lot of booths and stands and they sold all sorts of merchandise. Wagons or sleds of peasants kept on rolling in all day long. In the summertime, the peasant women were walking beside their wagons, barefooted, carrying baskets of cheese, butter, eggs, chicken and many more items.

They also brought to the bazaar all kinds of wheat, grain, corn and more. They sold their goods all winter long because they stored whatever they grew and did not sell in the summer. In wintertime, they took it out of storage and little by little they brought it to the yahrith (bazaar) in order to sell it. This way they had a steady income all year round. The bazaar in our city was situated in two places, one place in the big square, and the second place where the peasants were bringing their livestock.

This place was almost at the edge of the city. Some peasants had an animal farm so they brought livestock, like horses, cows, goats, sheep, calves and more. The bazaar was also the place where the butchers were getting their meat.

The butchers, who were selling only kosher meat, first bought the animals. Then the butcher was taking them to a place, called a jatke (slaughter house) and there, in a ritual method, shchitah (slaughtering), they were killing the animals. They had to go through all the procedures to make the meat kosher. The shchitah (slaughtering) of an animal had to be done according to our religious laws. A special Jew who finished the studying in order to become a shoichat had the authority of doing the slaughtering. Finally, the meat came to the kosher butcher and we could buy the meat there.

To get the best prices, everyone had to know how to bargain. The way they did it was that the seller set a price and they started to slap each other's hand and kept on negotiating. The seller's price was coming down and the buyer's price was going up. Each time they were saying a price, they were slapping each other's hand and shouting. They kept on bargaining with each other until hopefully they would reach an agreement of the selling price. In Europe they did not have any steady prices, especially on yahrith (bazaar) days, so that was why everyone was bargaining with each other.

After bargaining for a while and when both of them finally agreed to a certain price and the transaction was made, everyone was happy with it. While they were bargaining with each other, they drew a big crowd. Everyone was watching and shouting and laughing and I used to watch them, also. I really looked forward to the bazaar because I always liked excitement, and this made me very happy.

Right after school I ran from one wagon to the other, especially where I saw a crowd and I heard loud voices. I remember my mother used to say to me, "Whenever I need your help, you're never around," and she was right, because on the yahrith days she was always very busy. I knew that she really could have used my help, but I had a better time, though, being where the action was instead of being cooped up in the store. To me, the bazaar was more interesting.

I always liked big crowds, and loud voices always fascinated me. I liked to watch them bargaining with each other and I thought, in fact I knew, that it was very interesting to me. Most of the day I was at the bazaar instead of helping my mother or even playing with my friends. Of course, my mother was not too happy when I did not help her, but I was happy by doing something that I liked better. I liked all of the excitement then, and believe it or not, I still do, even until today. Getting back to the good old days it seems to me now, that we really enjoyed just being alive. We were always thankful for everything, and we always tried to make the best of it and appreciate all of the things that we had.

Some peasants had a poultry farm, so they brought to the yahrith (bazaar), chickens, turkeys, geese and all kinds of eggs. They brought white eggs, brown eggs, goose eggs, and turkey eggs. All the city people came to the yahrith (bazaar) to buy from the peasants, because everything was much fresher and the prices were much better than at our daily market or in the stores. Some people really waited until the days of the yahrith to do their shopping in order to get everything fresh and save some money, also.

In spite of the fact that the peasants were not able to read, write or count, they did pretty well for themselves. They counted on their fingers and they kept their money in the corners of their kerchiefs. The way they did it was that they took a corner and put the money on it and then they rolled up the corner of the kerchief with the money in it and they made a knot. They did this to all four corners of the kerchief. They wore their kerchief on their head all the time so nobody could steal their money.

After the peasants sold their goods, and with the money that they took in, they bought whatever they needed, like shoes, boots, material for dresses, oil, vinegar, sugar, salt, herring and many more products. Twice a week, no matter how noisy it was with all the wagons and all the people, everyone was happy, especially the storekeepers because our city was booming with business. The owners of the stores, booths, and stands, were busy selling their merchandise to the people, especially to the peasants because the peasants were always buying a lot of goods and they were easy going customers. Most of the time they came to buy, not just to look. In general, the city people liked to buy in the city stores with better quality of goods.

When the peasant men and women were ready to do their own shopping, most of the time they did it in the Jewish shops. The reason for it was that the Jewish storekeepers sold their merchandise for a much better price. They wanted to do as much business as they could. Even when they sold their goods for a much smaller profit than the other stores, they were still happy. They were not greedy, and the Jews always said, "Live and let live." They also had another philosophy. The Jews used to say that a small profit was much better than no profit at all. So they figured that the more they would sell, the more profit they would make. In the overall picture, they were right because when they added up a lot of little profits, the bottom figures were more than when they added up just a few big profits.

I have to state a fact that the Jews were always very good in business and they were always successful in it. They always had and still do have a good business head on their shoulders and that was why the Jews were most of the time doing very good business.

The peasants were wandering around from shop to shop looking for the best bargains. All the merchants were calling customers to buy from them. The shops had everything that the peasants usually needed. They always bought a lot of goods. After they sold their own products at the bazaar they bargained for the city goods with the storekeepers in order to buy their goods for a good price. The clothing industry was always very important, especially on the yahrith day. The peasants got their working clothes and this was the most needed item for them. The women bought material for dresses, skirts, and blouses and material for men to make pants, shirts and jackets.

A lot of peasant women knew how to sew so they were making clothing themselves. The peasant women were always wearing bright colors, mostly flowers, sometimes stripes. They were wearing very full, long skirts with fitted blouses and large kerchiefs with a floral design on their heads. They always went barefoot in summer, and in the winter they wore heavy boots. In the villages the snow laid all winter long and the peasants had to walk in the snow to take care of their farm, mostly of their livestock.

On bazaar days everyone was doing business, including the Jews. The Jews had a lot of steady customers who liked to deal with them and it was good for the Jews, because they sold a lot of merchandise and did very good business. In spite of them having to work very hard in order to be able to make a living, they were still happy and content with it.

The anti-Semitism started to get worse. They saw that the Jews were doing well on yahrith days because a lot of people wanted to deal with the Jews, so the Polish government decided to hold the yahrith (bazaar) on Friday's and Saturday's, which was the Jewish Shabbos (Sabbath). They knew that the Jews would not work on Shabbos and that was why they did it, just to take away the parnuse (livelihood) from the Jews. They also knew that the Jews on yahrith days were doing good business because they were selling their merchandise for a very small profit. When they made the yahrith (bazaar) on these days, most of the peasants did not want to come on Friday or Saturday because they liked to buy from the Jews and many of the peasants boycotted the Shabbos yahrith (bazaar).

The reality of it was that the peasants were not so dedicated to the Jews, only to their low prices. They liked to pay as little as possible for the things that they were buying. The reason that the Jews could sell everything for such low prices was because they bought the merchandise in the factories for a good price and they sold it to the customers for a good price, with only a little profit. That was why the peasants liked to buy from the Jew. Like everyone else the peasants liked a bargain, also.

The community council saw that their plan was not working too well for them. In fact, it worked against them because when the peasants did not come with their wagons, the council was not collecting any fees for wagons and stalls. The government changed their mind very quickly and they went back to the old yahrith (bazaar) days.

Our city was surrounded with villages and the peasants brought in a lot of business into the city. Our part of Poland, the Ukraine area, was famous for the best and richest topsoil in the world. They called the soil, schwartze earth, which means black topsoil. The soil was very rich in minerals and whatever a farmer wanted to grow on his farm he could and he always had the best results in quality and in quantity.

Volyner state was known for being a big agricultural state, where the farmers grew all kinds of fruits, vegetables, wheat, grain, cotton and more crops. They always got the best results and the finest quality that you could find. Poland had enough food for their population, and besides that, they exported a lot of their products all over the world.

# THE BIG FAIR IN OUR CITY

Our city, Wlodzimierz Volynski, was a city of the Volyner state. We always had some activities going on there. One of the many things that we had in our city was the big fair. The fair was like a festival and it took place once a year. The peasants came from all around the vicinity and it was very lively. At the time of the fair we had a lot of excitement in the city. The music was playing very loud, they had all kinds of games for children and for adults, and whoever played the game and won, got a prize. They auctioned off different kinds of things and the people kept on betting and buying a lot of nice and useful items that they really needed for their households or their farms.

Mostly, everyone from around the vicinity came to the fair in order to see all of the activities that were going on. On the days of the big fair, we had a lot of different entertainers, like singers, acrobats, clowns, trained dogs, and trained chickens for the races. They also had different kinds of musicians playing their instruments. After these groups were finished with their performing, they collected money from the crowd that was standing around and watching them, and another group started with their entertainment performances.

There was also coming to the big fair a special entertainment group, and these were the gypsies. They came in their covered wagons, like the pioneers, with their whole families. They always lived in their wagons, this was their permanent home, and they wandered from place to place. That was why they were called gypsies (wanderers), because their way of living was not to settle down in one place. They liked to see the world and they were going from one place to another place, because they were born and raised as free spirits and they always liked it this way.

They lived without any worries or responsibilities to anyone. They went wherever they wanted to go, and they did whatever they wanted to do. It was their life and they lived it the way they chose to live it. Most of the time they set up their camps in the outskirts of the cities, in the woods. In the evenings they were sitting around the fire and were singing all kinds of songs. We saw gypsies in our city all year long. Apparently, these were the local gypsies who lived in the outskirts of our city.

The most interesting and the most entertaining people were the gypsies. Their way of dressing was very similar to the peasants' way of dressing. They were dressed in very loud colors, big prints, full skirts, and short sleeve tops. They wore kerchiefs on their heads and they wore a lot of jewelry, like big hoop earrings, a lot of strings of different colors of beads, and a lot of bracelets. They did not wear any shoes either, just like the peasants. The gypsy men wore mostly black pants, black shirts, and black shoes. On their head they wore a black kerchief, tied in the back. The men wore a gold earring in one ear and some gold chains. The gypsy children were dressed like their parents were, and they had the same way of behaving as their parents. I guess they were taught to follow in their parents' footsteps.

The gypsies were making a lot of noise to get attention from everyone. They were dancing with tambourines in their hands, they were singing very mellow and sad gypsy songs, and they drew a big crowd for themselves. Some of their children walked in the crowd between the people and collected the donations that the people gave them. All the gypsies were fortune-tellers. They were born with this talent. Some read the palm, and some read cards. They did all these things for a fee. These were the ways they made a living.

The gypsies were very talented in their performance. They also were very talented in doing a lot of other things, which they should not do. They were thieves and kidnappers and that was why they got their reputation of stealing money from people's pockets and kidnapping children. Everyone was very careful and they watched their pockets and held on to their children's hands when the gypsies were around. My mother kept on telling me that I should not talk to the gypsies, and I should watch out for them because they were thieves and they would steal everything that they could. I could not understand why my mother was saying such things about them, because they looked to me like they were very friendly people.

I thought that everyone was accusing them of something that was not really true. I kept on believing that the gypsies were very nice people, until one time, on fair day, something very unexpected happened to me. I still remember this incident. At this time I was very young and very naïve. I remember once my mother gave me an extra job to do. My mother told me that before our Shabbos (Sabbath) I should take everyone's shoes and polish them for the Shabbos. I gathered together everyone's new shoes and lined them up on the front step of the house. Then I went back into the house to get the shoe polish. It did not take me even more than a couple of minutes of getting the polish and when I came back out I was standing with the shoe polish in my hands, but no shoes were on the front step. The shoes were gone.

Right away, I started to think about what my mother always told me about the gypsies, but I did not pay enough attention to my mother's advice that she gave me to be more careful. In spite of it, that she kept on telling me over and over again not to trust the gypsies, unfortunately, I did not listen to my mother and I got into big trouble. I believed what I wanted to believe, that the gypsies were not thieves. I remember that besides losing all of our shoes I was very disappointed with the gypsies because I really liked them before this happened.

My mother knew that I felt very bad about the whole situation. The shoes had to be made by a shoemaker. It took him a long time to make the shoes and everyone was very upset with me because there were no more holiday shoes. Everyone had to go to the shoemaker to get new shoes made. They had to be made special for everyone's size and this took at least a couple of months because the shoemakers were always very busy.

In the meantime, everyone had to wear their everyday shoes on the holiday and on Shabbos. I felt very guilty and I was very upset about what I had done because it really was my fault. I blamed myself for it and I kept on saying that I should have listened to my mother and I should have known better. I knew that the gypsies were in our city, and I also knew what everyone was saying about them, including my mother, that they were really thieves, but I still did not think that they would steal in a few minutes time.

The only explanation that I thought of about how it happened was that they were watching me and the minute that I walked into the house they grabbed the shoes and disappeared. From then on I knew that everyone was right about what they thought of the gypsies. That was why everyone was very careful by watching the children, their pockets and their possessions. When my mother told me that they were thieves I guess I really did not want to believe it, but after what happened to me with the shoes I knew it was true what everyone was saying about them.

In the meantime, everything was going along and the fair went on for three days. I tried to be at the fair everyday and see as much as I could. I still liked to hear the gypsies singing, and I watched them dancing, but from then on I knew that I would never trust them again and when they came to our city I never talked to any of them.

From then on, no matter how friendly they pretended to be I knew better than to believe them. After everyone sold everything, they were on their way home. The city had their workers to clean up and in no time the city was back to normal again.

# CHAPTER XI
# THE CELEBRATION OF OUR TRADITIONAL HOLIDAYS

## ROSH HASHANAH-The Jewish New Year

In our Jewish religion, our New Year started with the holiday called Rosh Hashanah. It was and is one of the most holy holidays of the year and it was observed more or less in September. This was the day when our New Year was starting. Rosh Hashanah was the Day of Judgment. The holiday started in the evening, at sundown, as all of our Jewish holidays were starting.

On Rosh Hashanah, every Jew, even the ones who were not as religious as others, still were coming to synagogue for prayers. The next day, the davinnen (prayers) started in the morning until late noon. Everyone was praying for a good New Year. The rabbi and a special chazen (cantor), the leader in the davinnen (prayers), who was called Boal T'fila, was hired only for the high holidays in order to lead the services.

On Rosh Hashanah, God was deciding the goyril (destiny) of every Jew, for instance, who will live and who will die, who will be rich and who will be poor, who will be healthy and who will be sick and on and on. Every Jew was praying and asking God for forgiveness for their sins. When the praying was over, a special Jew was blowing the shoifer (ram's horn), and very shortly after, the whole congregation walked down to the lake. Everyone was making a brucha (prayer) and they threw in pieces of bread into the water. It meant that we were throwing all of our sins in, and this special ceremony was called "Tashlich".

After that the rabbi made a brucha (prayer) over the challah, and we had challah dipped in honey, which symbolized having a sweet new year. Finally, all of the traditional ceremonies were over and everyone was wishing each other a good and healthy new year. Now, everyone was ready to go home and have a festive meal. Later in the day, usually only the men returned to synagogue and they were davinnen (praying) minhah. Minhah they davinnen (praying) before sundown and before the stars were coming out and Marif prayers they davinnen (praying) after sundown when the stars were already out.

# YOM KIPPUR - The Day of Atonement
# YOM-TOV (HOLIDAY)

The most serious holidays of the year in our Jewish religion were Rosh Hashanah and Yom Kippur. Yom Kippur holiday was ten days apart from the Rosh Hashanah holiday. In the older days, I remember in the morning before the holiday started, my father took a live chicken and held it in his right hand, then he swung it around, over my, my sister, and my two brothers heads, three times. While he was swinging with the chicken, he said a brucha (prayer), then he took the chicken to a special place called a jatke (slaughter house) for the shchitah (killing) and a special Jew called a shoichat killed the chicken in a ritual method. This ceremony was called "kapores".

It was only performed before Yom Kippur and it was a ritual and symbolic transfer of the sins. Maybe it sounds a little strange now, but when I was brought up, this was our way of doing certain things. Besides that, this was our tradition, which we always observed. What the ceremony meant was that if the children committed some sins in the past year, my father was sacrificing the life of the chicken for those sins. The other tradition was that everyone was wishing each other a good and a healthy new year. It did not matter if they were talking to each other during the past year or not. Before Yom Kippur holiday everyone was making up with each other and saying the New Year was starting and let the bygones be bygones.

Everyone was hugging and kissing and crying and wishing each other the best and healthiest New Year. Finally, everyone was going home to have their meal. I remember that we did not eat foods that were too salty before Yom Kippur started because salty foods made us thirsty. My mother had prepared the meal the night before. After supper, everyone had to drink tea in order not to be thirsty and to be able to fast for twenty-four hours. The adults were not allowed to eat or drink during the time of fasting.

The fasting was starting after sundown until the next day after sundown. Small children only fasted a half of a day. Babies did not fast at all. Sick people did not have to fast if they could not. The Yom Kippur holiday started after sundown. The Jewish people came to synagogue in the evening in order to hear Kol Nidrei prayers. This was a special davinnen (praying) for Yom Kippur. Only the chazen (cantor) who was the leader of the prayers was saying Kol Nidrei. The cantor who was called Boal T'fila, wore a white, long robe, which they called a kittel, he was saying Kol Nidrei in a singing neegun (melody). It sounded very special and different from the other prayers and it felt that we were in a different world, like the walls were shaking when he sang Kol Nidrei.

I still remember when I was sitting in synagogue next to my mother, and when the cantor kept on praying, his voice and the melody carried into everyone's heart and the tunes, which came out of his mouth sounded holy. It felt like we were in heaven talking to God and asking him for forgiveness for our sins, because on Rosh Hashanah God was making up the list and on Yom Kippur God was sealing it. This was the verdict of God for everyone for a whole year, from this Yom Kippur to the next Yom Kippur.

After Kol Nidrei was over, everyone felt almost sad and preoccupied with their thoughts. Nobody knew what laid ahead for them in the coming year and everyone just hoped for the best. Some Jews stayed for a while and told each other how they felt and most of the Jews, right after the prayers were over, were on their way home. The next morning, the young and the old Jews were again coming to synagogue to pray.

On Yom Kippur we were not allowed to ride any vehicles, so everyone had to walk to the shul (synagogue). We were not allowed to eat or drink, make a fire, or carry money with us and much more. Some Jews were getting a room near the synagogue for the night and some Jews lived near the synagogue. A lot of times, the Jews who lived in walking distance to the synagogue invited some friends to stay with them for the night and it worked out very good. The prayers started in the early morning.

Everyone in the synagogue was dressed in their yomtovdik (festive) clothes and everyone was very involved in praying. After so many hours, about high noon, we had a break. On our break time most of the Jews were staying around and talking to each other, and some were taking a walk around the synagogue for a while. After a certain time, everyone came back and the chazen (cantor) was continuing with the services.

On Yom Kippur we said "Yiskor". This was a special prayer for the dead, to show them that we did not forget them and their spirit lives with us forever. Before the holiday was starting we also were lighting Yahrzeit (remembrance) candles. It means that they should have a lit up heaven. In the older days the Jewish people believed that after death, we were going to another world. After "Yiskor", when the prayers were over, a special Jewish man was blowing the shoifer (ram's horn).

The shoifer was made out of a ram's horn and gave out different tones when he was blowing it. The man who was blowing the shoifer had to do it according to what was written in the siddur (prayer book). Finally, the services were over and the stars were coming out. It meant that we could break the fast. Everyone was happy that after twenty-four hours of fasting we finally could eat now. Everyone was wishing each other a happy and a healthy new year. They had prepared, in the synagogue, all kinds of drinks, cakes, and challah, in order to break the fast. After a while, we were all on our way home to have a light meal. We ate mostly dairy food because after twenty-four hours of fasting, it was better not to have a heavy meal.

## SUKKOT YOM-TOV (Holiday)

Every year we celebrated the holiday of Sukkot. Every holiday that was observed by the Jews always brought different kinds of joy and excitement to our lives. The Sukkot holiday comes out sometime in October. This holiday was the Festival of the Tabernacles, and it was traditional to celebrate the journey of the Jewish people wandering through the desert. On Sukkot we also celebrate the harvest season and the Jews showed their gratitude for a good and successful years crops.

I remember that my father was holding a bunch of long weeds, I think it was called etrog and lulov. He was shaking it and he said a brucha (prayer) in order to keep evil spirits away. This holiday lasted for seven days. Sukkot was a holiday when religious Jews ate their meals in a Succah. I remember my father made a Succah next to the house. It looked like a shelter. It had three regular walls, with an open top. My father put some sticks on top of the Succah and some long weeds. On the fourth wall, he hung a big sheet to cover the hole. Inside he put a table and chairs. It was like a big open shed without a roof. For seven days we had our meals in the Succah. On the Sukkot holiday everyone was allowed to work and to go on with their daily routine.

I remember that my mother worked all day and when she came home, she had to warm up the food and then bring it into the Succah. It took a while before we started to eat, because my father had to say some bruchas (prayers). In the meantime, the food got cold and we had to eat cold food. This was our tradition.

## SIMCHAT TORAH YOM-TOV (Holiday)

Simchat Torah was celebrated sometimes in October, on the eighth day of Sukkot. On the Simchat Torah holiday, the Jews were rejoicing the Torah. In our traditional way, on Simchat Torah, in the synagogue, they started to read the end of the Torah and then they went back to read from the beginning of the Torah again. It was a cycle every year to read the whole Torah, a different portion every week until Simchat Torah.

Simchat Torah was a very happy time for us. All of the Jewish people were coming to synagogue with their children and their friends in order to celebrate Simchat Torah together. I remember coming to synagogue with my whole family and it was very exciting and lively. Everyone had a good time, especially the children. The rabbi, with a couple members of the congregation, walked around with the Torahs and everyone tried to get as close to the Torahs as possible because they were very anxious to touch the Torah.

Most of the people tried to touch the Torah with the corner of the siddur (prayer book), which they held in their hand. After touching the Torah, they kissed the siddur, (the prayer book), and it made them very happy. In the Jewish religion, kissing the Torah was a symbolic act and according to our tradition it was a mitzvah (a good deed). The children walked around with feindlach (flags) and on top of the flags was a red apple and in the middle of the apple was a burning candle.

Everyone in the synagogue was singing and dancing and laughing and it really was a very enjoyable time for us. In a while, the whole congregation walked out of the synagogue carrying the Torahs. They walked all the length of the street, and very shortly after, the whole neighborhood of people, Jews and non-Jews, joined them. The crowd got bigger and bigger by the minute, and everyone was having the best time of their lives.

## CHANUKAH HOLIDAY- The Festival Of Lights

The holiday of Chanukah was celebrated in the winter, sometimes in December, and it lasted for eight days. In the Jewish religion every holiday that we celebrated always had a specific traditional meaning to it, and there was always a story behind it. The way I was taught about Chanukah was that when the Jews recaptured the temple in Jerusalem, they came into the temple and they found a little oil in the lantern. They lit the lantern up, and it was enough oil to burn for one day, instead, the oil lasted for eight days. Because of this miracle, we were celebrating the Chanukah holiday for eight days. It became a tradition to light candles in a Chanukah menorah (candle-holder) for eight days. The candles were placed in the menorah and a ninth candle was used to light all of the others. On the first night, one light was lit and each night a light was added, until all of the eight candles were lit. The adults made a Chanukah party, and the children got Chanukah gelt (money) and dreidlach (a spinning toy) and everyone gave each other a Chanukah present. My mother used to make potato latkes (pancakes) for our home and for the synagogue because Chanukah would not be a holiday without potato latkes (pancakes). That was the Jewish tradition. Everyone made a point to celebrate the holiday with their families and friends. We sang Chanukah songs and we were all enjoying our holiday together.

## PURIM HOLIDAY-The Story Of Queen Esther

The Purim holiday was celebrated in late February or early March. On Purim, the synagogue was full of Jewish people and their families. Everyone came to hear the reading of the "Megillah". This was the scroll of Queen Esther. The children made a lot of noise with their gregers (noisemakers) as soon as they mentioned the name Haman, because Haman tried to talk the King Ahasveurus into killing all the Jews.

Haman did not succeed, thanks to Queen Esther and her cousin, Mordechai. On Purim we baked special cookies. It was a Purim pastry that looked like a triangle cookie because Haman wore a hat with three corners, that was why they named this cookie after Haman. The cookies were called hamantaschen and they were filled with poppy seeds, apricots, or prunes. On Purim, we ate kreplach (dumplings) filled with ground meat and we also had many other Purim dishes.

Every Purim, in the synagogue, they always had a Purim spiel (play) about Queen Esther. Everyone in the group, who took a part in Queen Esther's play, wore costumes, like in the older days. In spite of it, that the children were not professional actors, they put on a good play and they told the whole story about the Purim holiday and Queen Esther. Everyone in the synagogue was very pleased with the play and they liked it very much. After the play was over they had some refreshments, like drinks, hamantaschen and fruit. It was also traditional to give each other shalachmones, a treat of different edible goodies. After a while everyone was on their way home. I felt very content and happy to be together with my family and share the joy with them.

## PESACH (Passover Holiday)

The Passover holiday was celebrated in the springtime at the end of March or early April. Pesach was a nice holiday, and it was the time for the Jews to remember the slavery and suffering that our Jewish people went through for thousands of years. It was also a time of celebrating because God freed the Jews from the slavery in Egypt. In my days, the way I was taught the story of Passover was that after the Jews were freed from Egypt they started to wander in the desert.

They kept on wandering and looking for food, but they could not find anything to eat and everyone was very hungry. Suddenly, they saw, falling from the sky, white flakes that looked like flour. The Jews called it Manna and they thanked God for sending it to them. Out of the manna, which they mixed with water, they made flat pieces of dough like pancakes and they baked it in the sun. That was why, on the eight days of Passover, we ate only matzoh instead of bread. The matzoh reminded the Jews of the time when they baked the flat pieces of dough in the desert, that looked like matzoh.

I remember that for Passover my parents, mostly my father, organized people to come to our home and bake matzoh. In the older days, the strictly religious, Orthodox Jews on Passover ate only one kind of matzoh, which was called Shemurah matzoh. This matzoh was round and was made out of wheat flour. I remember that my father made, out of two stands and a long board, a table, and the women were standing next to each other on one side of this table and they were welgering (rolling) out the matzoh and a man put the matzoh in the oven to be baked.

The matzoh dough that was baked for Passover, no matter if it was shemurah or plain matzoh, had to be mixed according to our religious tradition. In order to make the right dough for the matzoh, they had to make a few samples of dough and get to know what the right amount of flour and the right amount of water was that should be used. This was the traditional way of baking matzoh. After putting a certain amount of flour, only once, and a certain amount of water, only once, we were not allowed to add any more flour or any more water, because it would not be kosher and we could not use it for Passover.

I remember that one woman was sitting in the kitchen mixing the dough and my father was watching her all the time, just to make sure that she would not put any more water or flour in the dough. The woman made the dough and she gave it to the other women and they rolled it out. After the matzoh was rolled out it was baked in the oven, over the flame and then it had to be turned over to be baked on the other side. I still remember the night they baked the matzoh in our home, I did not want to go to sleep. I was sitting in the corner of the room and I was watching what everyone was doing.

I remember that before the Passover holiday my parents made a lot of preparations in order to have everything kosher for the holiday. It meant that we were not allowed to have bread in the house for eight days. For Passover the Jews, especially the Orthodox Jews, had to have a separate set of dishes, pots, pans and silverware. We had our Passover dishes stored in the attic. When the house was clean from chumitz (leavened bread), which meant that we did not have any bread in the house anymore, my father then brought down the Passover dishes from the attic and he put our everyday dishes up in the attic.

It was a lot of work to do all of these preparations, but this was and still is our tradition and we observe it. I remember that I helped the maid with the cleaning. We had to get out every little piece of dust and the crumbs of bread from between the cracks of the chairs, table, and from every corner of the house. We did it for weeks because most of the furniture had carving. My father supervised so we had to do a good job. I did not think that my mother would care too much if it was done perfect or not. She was religious and clean, but not as much of a fanatic as my father was.

All the bread, flour, rice, beans, and many more items, that had any starch in it, were considered as bread and they were called chumitz. These items were gathered in one place in the kitchen corner. I remember my father walked around with a lit up candle all over the house and he said a brucha (prayer) and when I asked him what he was doing, he told me that he was burning the chumitz.

The whole house had to be cleaned from top to bottom. In the morning before the Passover holiday started, we could eat bread until noon, and then we had to get rid of the chumitz (leavened bread). I remember that a Gentile man, who was called, Yom-tov Goy, was coming to our house and according to the Jewish religion, my father sold the chumitz to him. This gentile man was supposed to give my father some money for it and take some food from him. This was the Jewish ceremony.

The Passover holidays started after sundown. Everyone went to synagogue to pray. When the praying was over, everyone was on their way home to start to celebrate the Passover holiday. On Passover, we had two Seders and we read the Haggadah. The Haggadah was a special Hebrew book, which told us in which order the Passover Seder had to be conducted. It also told us the whole story about the Pesach (Passover) holiday. The youngest child always had the job of asking the father the fear kashes (four questions).

After the religious ceremony was over, everyone waited to have their yomtovdik meal (festive meal). I still remember that on Passover, the table was set with the best dishes and silverware and in the center of the table were brass candlesticks with lit up candles and everyone in the family, including our guests, sat around the table, ready to begin to eat. I have to mention, that it was proper and traditional to have on Passover, non-Jewish guests join us who were our friends and they were very glad to celebrate our Passover with us. They came and they were happy to learn about our traditions. They always said that our ways of doing certain things were more complicated than their ways and they were right.

Finally, we started our meal. First, we had a glass of wine in order to drink L'Chaim, which means, to life, and then we had chopped liver, boiled potatoes with onions and eggs and gefilte fish with horseradish. We also had charoses made from apples and nuts. It was all chopped up in a shteisel (mortar), then we added a little wine and when it was all mixed together we ate it on a piece of matzoh.

After everyone was done with these dishes, my mother served a bowl of chicken soup with kneidlach (matzoh balls). After that my mother put out platters of chicken, roast, potato kugel (pudding), matzoh meal latkes, (pancakes), carrots with prunes and sweet potatoes. Finally, we were ready for desert, which consisted of sponge cake, honey cake, cookies, candy, tea, and wine. I remember that we did not drink coffee, but we drank something like coffee that was called cecorria. By the time we finished our Seder, the children started to get very tired.

Everyone said a prayer to thank God for everything, and we all sang the traditional Passover songs. My father hid a couple pieces of matzoh. This was called urenkoimet. After the Seder the children ran around to find the matzoh that my father hid and whoever was lucky enough to find it, got some money from my parents. My father also filled up a glass of wine for Eillehunueve (Elijah or Messiah), the prophet, and then he opened the door for the Eillehunueve (Elijah or Messiah) to come in.

This was our tradition. Now the first Seder was over. The next night we had the second Seder, and it was conducted in the same way as the first one. The very religious Jews went to synagogue everyday. Other Jews went to synagogue just the first two days of Passover. None of the Jews worked the first two days. On Passover we were allowed to do things that we were usually doing during regular weekdays. For the rest of the days of Passover, we had our regular meals. The only difference was that on Passover we were not allowed to eat bread for eight days, we had to eat only matzoh, and all of the other food items that we ate on Pesach had to be under rabbinical supervision and inspected by a rabbi. It had to say kosher for Pesach, and then it was known to be Passover food.

## LAG B'OMER YOM- TOV (Holiday)

Lag B'Omer was celebrated, sometimes in April or in the beginning of May and it was a one-day holiday. Lag B'Omer was a holiday of celebrating the forest. A lot of Jewish people hired horses and buggies with a driver in order to get to the forest. The forest was not too far from our city. It was right on the outskirts of the city. I still remember that my parents made an arrangement with a man who owned horses and a buggy in order to take our next-door neighbors family and us to the forest. The man dropped us off at the forest, and at the end of the day he picked us up at a certain time and took us home, for a fee that they agreed to.

I remember that the maid got us ready and she made us wear good walking shoes and comfortable clothes. My mother packed a good lunch and we were all ready to be on our way to the forest. Everyone sounded happy and all the time on the way to the forest, we were singing the traditional Lag B'Omer forest songs. The road to the forest looked like a long caravan. Almost everyone celebrated the Lag B'Omer holiday. In springtime the weather was warm, but not hot. Everything was starting to bloom and it looked and felt like everything came back to life again. After a long and a very cold winter that we always had in my days in Europe, everyone was happy to be able to enjoy the good weather and the happy holiday.

Lag B'Omer was a family holiday. The children were looking forward to this holiday. They knew that they would have a good time in the forest. When we came into the forest it was very nice. The pine trees smelled very good. The air from the pine was very healthy for our lungs and everyone tried to take a deep breath. After we settled down, it was time to have lunch. It felt like we were on a picnic, only better, because it was in the forest. After lunch, my parents and our neighbors took a walk and we children ran around. We picked strawberries, blueberries, and mushrooms. Without even rinsing them, we kept on eating everything that we picked, because they tasted fresh and delicious.

After a short walk, my parents and the neighbors came back and they were happy just to sit and relax for a while, especially my mother. She enjoyed being with her family and she also enjoyed the company of our neighbors. They were a very nice family and we played very well with their children. My parents liked them a lot. In fact, my father always talked to the neighbors about all kinds of happenings that were going on in our city and they always had a nice conversation together.

When it got darker, and the sun went down, we packed up and we waited for our ride. Very shortly after we got ready, the man came to pick us up. Everyone climbed into the buggy and we all were on our way home. Everyone was tired, but it was a lot of fun and enjoyment for all of us. We felt very content and happy and we all thanked God for this wonderful day.

# SHAVUOT YOM-TOV (Holiday)

The Shavuot holiday was celebrated sometime in the end of May. It was a harvest holiday and this was the season to cut down the crops. On the Shavuot holiday, it was customary to eat dairy food so everyone's meal was dairy. We ate kreplach (dumplings) stuffed with cheese, cheese blintzes with sour cream, cheesecake, lockschen kugel (noodle pudding) with cheese, raisins and nuts, and many more dishes made out of dairy products. The house was decorated with little green branches, green flowers, and all sorts of green bushes. It was fun to see all the greenery in the house. The more it was decorated the more we got into the yomtovdik (holiday) spirit.

We probably had a lot of other holidays, but I cannot remember them because they were not as noticeable to me. I guess the reason that I do not remember the other holidays was because we did not have to prepare for them in any special way. I am sure that they were traditionally just as important as the other holidays were, but the most that I really do remember were all of the big holidays, when everyone, including my mother, had to make all kinds of different and extra preparations to make the holidays in our specific, traditional ways. I always got involved in helping my mother prepare everything, even though I was very young at the time, but I always liked to know and do a lot of things and most of all, I liked to be my mother's little helper.

In the older days, everything that we did was never simple or easy. On the contrary, it was always a big procedure with everything that we had to do. In my times, everything that had to be done had to be started from scratch. In these days, the life and the conditions were very primitive, but in spite of everything, we tried our very best to make the most of it. Because we did not know anything better in my times, that was why we were happy with what we had and we managed the best way that we could.

# CHAPTER XII
## OUR TRADITIONAL RECIPES AND ITS CUSTOMS

In the older days, we did not have any ready cooked food items. Any kind of food that anyone wanted for everyday for the Sabbath or for the holidays had to be prepared by them from scratch, and they had to cook it themselves. Of course, it always was a big procedure to make a meal. That was how it was in my days, but everyone did their very best to keep up with our ways of living. In those days, everything also had to be done according to our religion and our customs. Like for instance, before we cooked the meat in the Jewish religion, chicken, turkey, meat and other animals, had to be made kosher and this was called kashrut.

First of all, we had to buy the meats at a kosher butcher. After we brought the meat home our procedures started. First, we had to put the meat in a big special pan filled with water to be soaked for half an hour. By the way, this pan was only used for soaking the meat. Then we took the meat out of the water and we laid it out on a wooden loosely braided, big tray, so that the rest of the water could drain out. Next we sprinkled coarse salt on each piece of meat in a way that every side of the piece was covered with salt. It looked like rain pouring on the meat. Then we let it lay in the salt for one hour. When the hour was over we poured water on each piece of meat, separately. After the whole procedure was done, the meat was kosher and ready to cook. I have to mention that in order to be kosher, we had to have one set of dishes for milchicke (dairy) food and one set of dishes for fleishicke (meat) food.

The Jewish traditions were not so easy to observe, but this was our religion and we were and still are used to them for thousands of years.

## THE RECIPE FOR CHALLAH (White Bread) AND PASTRIES

In the older days, it was known that all week we ate bread, but on Shabbos and on our holidays it was customary to eat challah. I remember when my mother came home from work on Thursday, before she even had her supper, she mixed the dough for the bread and shortly after, my mother mixed the dough for the challah in a big shishoul (pot).

The ingredients for the challah were flour, yeast, a little salt, a couple eggs, a spoon of sugar, a couple spoonfuls of oil, and enough water to make the dough not too loose and not too hard. She covered the pot with a cloth and let the dough rise. After it rose, she kneaded it a little and let it rise again. When it rose the second time, she divided the dough into pieces and each piece was used to form a challah.

She made one braided challah from five or six pieces of dough, I do not remember exactly how many pieces. Next, she made long strips out of the pieces of dough, braided them, and let it rise a little. When all of the challahs were in the pan, she beat an egg and with a little brush she spread the egg on the top of each challah. The reason for it was that after the challahs were baked, the top of it looked nice and golden brown. Finally, the challahs were ready to be put into the oven in order to be baked. I remember that my mother, before she put the challahs in, she always threw a little piece of dough into the oven first, and she made a brucha (prayer).

My mother also could use the same dough for making pletzels and bagels, but the reason for using this dough was to make the challah. Besides baking bread and challah, my mother also made another dough, which was much richer than the challah dough. It was made with flour, butter or oil, eggs, sugar, some extracts, orange juice and some yeast. With this dough, she could make all kinds of pastries, like cookies, rogalach filled with powedle (marmalade), fruit cake, Polish babke (coffee cake) filled with cinnamon, raisins, poppy seeds or anything we liked. She also made apple cake filled with apples, raisins, and nuts. I remember that all of the pastries that my mother baked were delicious.

Every Thursday she also baked bread for the whole week, but I have to admit that I really do not remember the ingredients of it. In the older days, especially in summer when it got very hot, everything got stale, including the bread, but we ate it anyway. In a way everyone was happy that they had something to eat.

I still remember that most of the time when we had bread, everyone liked and ate it in many different ways. One of the ways was like this. First, they cut off a slice of bread, then they rubbed the hard part with garlic and on top of the slice they put on goose fat or chicken fat with griven (crispy skin), which we got after cooking the pieces of skin of the chicken, goose or turkey. My mother let the skin cook long enough and the skin got nice and crispy. Everyone loved the bread with a lot of griven (crispy skin).

My mother used to cook and bake all night long. I do remember that a lot of times when I woke up in the middle of the night and everyone else was asleep, my mother was still up, doing something. In the morning she had to go to work, but I never heard her complaining. She always looked happy. I think she was happy to do what she was doing. In a way it made her feel good to do things for her family. No matter how hard it was for her, it seemed to me that she enjoyed doing it.

## THE RECIPE FOR GEFILTE FISH

This was the recipe the way my mother made the gefilte fish. First she filleted the fish, then she chopped up the meat of the fish with onions, a little salt, pepper, a pinch of sugar, a couple of eggs, a little matzoh meal and a little bit of water. After everything was chopped up very good, she let it stay for a while. Then my mother put into a pot, some sliced onions, sliced carrots, salt, pepper to the taste and some water. When the water with all of the ingredients in it started to boil, she made little fish balls and put them into the boiling water. It cooked on a small fire for about three hours. After it cooled off she took each piece of fish out of the pot and placed them on a platter. Next, she put a slice of cooked carrots on each piece of fish to make it look nice, and it did. This was the traditional recipe for gefilte fish.

## THE RECIPE FOR CHOPPED LIVER

In the way that we had to make the meat kosher, we had to make the liver kosher, also, only this was a different procedure. The way my mother made it kosher was, first she put the liver on burning coals, like a grill. In a while she turned it over because in the Jewish religion, the blood of the liver had to be burned out, then it was considered to be kosher. When the liver was done, she cut it up in little pieces, and put it into a bowl, together with the other ingredients which were a couple hard-boiled eggs, onions, a little salt, pepper and a little chicken or goose fats. Then she chopped it up very thin, like a paste. Finally, the chopped liver was done and ready to eat. I have to mention that in the Jewish religion we were not allowed to cook liver in a pot before making it kosher and by burning out the blood from it, the liver became kosher.

## THE RECIPE FOR NOODLES

In the older days we could not buy ready-made lockschen (noodles). I remember that we had to make the noodles ourselves from scratch. I always liked to do it, so I made the noodles. On Thursday, when I came home from school, I started to make the noodles. First, I made the dough from flour, a little water, and eggs. Then I rolled out a thin round bletelle (sheet) with the valgerholtz (rolling pin) and I let the sheet dry for a while. After the sheet got a little dry, I put a little flour on top of it, and spread it out with my hand. Next, I rolled up the bletelle (sheet) very tightly and with a very sharp knife I cut slices as thin as possible, like we were slicing meat or onions, only thinner.

Then I put a big pot of water on the stove, adding a little salt. When the water came to a boil I put the noodles in, and let them cook for about ten minutes, stirring occasionally. After the noodles were cooked, I spilled the noodles into a doorshlach (drainer) and I poured cold water over them. Now the noodles were done and ready for Friday's dinner. This was our tradition to have chicken soup and lockschen (noodles) on Friday, for Shabbos dinner. It was a lot of work, but these were our good old days and we did not mind it at all.

## THE RECIPE FOR CHULENT

By the Jews it was a tradition every Shabbos (Saturday) to eat chulent. I still remember the recipe for the chulent that we had on Shabbos (Saturday). I used to help my mother put it together. The chulent consisted of potatoes, onions, lima beans, flanken (beef) marrowbones, kishka, and sometimes barley. We both put all of the ingredients into a big pot and we filled the pot up with water. We added a little salt, pepper, and a pinch of sugar and on top we put a little flour. After the preparations for the chulent were done, we put it into the oven on Friday before sundown. The chulent cooked all night long until lunchtime on Shabbos. The house smelled very good from chulent.

I was a child, but I still remember on Friday some of our neighbors, maybe perhaps those who did not have an oven in their home, or for some reason or another who did not want to burn their oven all night long only for the chulent, made their chulent ready in their pot and then they took it to the bakery. For a certain fee the bakery would put the chulent in their oven, on Friday before sundown, in order to be cooked. On Saturday, after the prayers were over, they went to the bakery to pick the chulent up. No matter how anybody chooses to do it, the main thing was that every Jew on Shabbos ate chulent.

## THE RECIPE FOR DRELIS
## (Yiddish) or GALARETTY (Polish)

Sometimes we had a dish called drelis or galaretty. This dish was made from cow or calves feet. The procedure of it was that first we washed the feet and then we koshered them just like we did with the meat. After the feet were made kosher, we had to cut them into little pieces. In a big pot filled with water, we put the pieces of the feet in, adding a couple diced onions, carrots, some salt, pepper and garlic. We let it cook for a couple of hours until the meat of it was tender. When the meat was soft, we took it off the stove and let it cool off for a while. Once it got cool, we took the meat off the bones and chopped it up into little pieces. After it was all chopped up we put it back into the broth that it was cooked in, stirring everything together. Next we poured all of the ingredients into a big, glass square dish like a baking pan and we let it get cold. Before it was completely cold, we sliced up hard-boiled eggs and put the slices on top of the ingredients, next to each other. In a while, when it was completely cold, it formed a firm gel and then it could be sliced into square pieces. This was called drelis or galaretty.

## THE RECIPE FOR POTATO LATKES (PANCAKES)

In a big bowl, first, we grate one large peeled onion, and three pounds of peeled potatoes, preferably baking potatoes. Then we add to the mixture two eggs, ½ cup of flour, salt, pepper to the taste and mix the ingredients together well. Next, we put oil in a frying pan and let it get good and hot. When the oil is hot, we drop tablespoons of the batter in the oil, next to each other. We have to keep on repeating this procedure until the frying pan is filled with the latkes (pancakes). After they get brown on one side, we turn them over and let them fry for a while until they get brown on the other side. When they are done, we place them on paper towels in order to remove the extra oil. We repeat the same procedure until we are done with the batter. They can be served with sour cream, sugar or plain.

## THE RECIPE FOR MATZOH MEAL LATKES (PANCAKES)

This is the way my mother used to make matzoh meal latkes (pancakes). In a big bowl she put in three cups of matzoh meal, with a little salt, pepper and the right amount of boiling water, in order to make a batter, not too hard and not too loose. She then let it cool off for a while. After the batter was cool, she put three beaten eggs into it and combined all of the ingredients together so it would be nice and smooth. Next, she made little balls from the mixture and flattened them, like a pancake. When the oil in the frying pan got very hot, she put the latkes in, to be fried. After the edges around the latkes got brown, she turned them over to the other side. When they were done, she placed them on paper towels to remove the extra oil. She repeated the same procedure until she was done with the batter. The latkes can be served plain or with sour cream, sugar or jelly.

## THE RECIPE FOR POTATOES, EGGS AND ONION DISH

As long as I can remember, on the Passover holiday, in my parents' home, we always had this special dish. After the war, when I got married and I had my own family, I started to cook the same dishes that my mother used to make. One of these dishes was the potatoes, eggs and onions. In my family it almost became like a tradition that every Passover we had this dish. It is a very simple procedure to follow. The ingredients are three pounds of potatoes, five hard-boiled eggs, one cup of oil, three diced onions, and a little salt and pepper to taste. First, you peel the potatoes and put them to be boiled. After they are done cooking, drain off the water. You let them cool off for a while. Next, you put into the potatoes the peeled and chopped up hard-boiled eggs, oil, the diced onions, salt and pepper. Then you mash all of the ingredients together. Now it is done and ready to be eaten. This dish can be served as a side dish, warmed up or cold on a piece of bread or matzoh.

# CHAPTER XIII
# THE BEGINNING OF THE SHABBOS
# (SABBATH) ON FRIDAY NIGHT

Our Shabbos started on Friday, after sundown. On Friday, most of the women were busy with cooking and baking and making everything ready for Shabbos. My mother was busy with her business and she did not have time to cook on Friday or any other day of the week. The maid did the cooking the whole week, but for the Shabbos, this was the only time that my mother really liked to cook and make the Shabbos as special as she possibly could. In order to do so and make everything as good as she wanted to, she had to start ahead of time because there was a lot of cooking and baking to be done. She started to prepare everything and cook most of the things on Thursday night when she came home from work.

I helped my mother with whatever I could, and so did our maid. There was plenty to do for everyone, but it got done, somehow. On Friday, my mother closed the business earlier than usual and she came home to get done with the rest of the cooking. Even though she did not have too much of the cooking to do because she did a lot of it on Thursday night, she still worked a lot of hours to have everything done before our Shabbos was starting.

When all of the cooking was done, and the table was set, then my mother changed her clothes and she was ready for her family. I remember that the house smelled very good from all of the cooking and I felt very safe and happy because I loved my family. In the middle of the week, we never ate supper together because my mother came home different times and my father did not have steady hours either, so the maid gave us children supper and whenever my parents came home they ate.

The only time we had our meals together was on Friday night and we had all of our meals together on Saturday and sometimes on Sunday. I remember on Friday, before sundown, my mother lit candles in the candelabras (candle holder). The tradition of the orthodox Jews, was that before a woman lit the Sabbath candles, she had to put on a white shawl to cover her head. She lit the candles, and swung her hands towards herself three times in front of the candles, then she put her hands over her closed eyes and said a brucha (prayer) over the candles. After the brucha she opened her eyes and said, "Git Shabbos". It means, a good Sabbath.

After lighting the candles, my father went to synagogue to attend the Friday night prayers. Sometimes he took my brothers with him. Almost no women went to synagogue on Friday night. My mother did not go, either. When the davinnen (praying) was over they came home and they said, "Git Shabbos everyone." I remember that my father walked over to the table and poured some wine in everyone's glass, then he made Kiddish, which was a special prayer over the wine and everyone drank a little wine. He then made a moitze, a prayer over the challah and gave everyone a piece of challah. Now all of the traditional parts before dinner were over and we were ready to have our meal.

My mother started to serve the meal. On Friday night, it was our tradition to have chicken soup with lockschen (noodles), which was and still is called to this day, Jewish penicillin. We had brisket (roast), chicken, potato tagachts (kugel or pudding), compote (desert) cooked from all kinds of fruit, babke (cake), cookies, baked apples and tea with hard square pieces of sugar. In the older days, we did not have loose granulated sugar in a bowl. We only had square pieces of sugar, which we bit off a piece and held it in our mouth until it dissolved by drinking our tea. When this piece of sugar dissolved, we bit off another, and another piece of sugar until we were finished drinking the tea. This is how we drank our tea.

After supper, my father went back to synagogue for a while and my mother and us children stayed home. On Friday night and on Saturday, we were not allowed to wash the dishes until Saturday after sundown. The maid took off the dishes from the table and put them into a big basin filled up with water. My mother helped her put everything away. When the kitchen was all cleaned up and everything was done, finally, my mother sat down and started to relax a little.

My mother always got a few Jewish papers delivered to the house everyday. I remember that she got two Jewish newspapers, one was called Unser Leiben (Our Life) and the other was called Der Tag (The Day). We also had all kinds of Polish papers in our city, but my mother liked to read the Jewish papers and find out all the news from them. My mother did not have time all week to read the papers, so Friday, after supper, she took out all the newspapers that she saved from the whole week and she read them. Of course, the news was already one week old and it was not new news anymore, but it was old news. My father used to tell her to get a paper when she had time to read it right away, but she did not care if the news was new or old, she read it anyway.

I remember that she used to joke about it, and she said, "So, I'll hear the news a week later." She read the papers out loud in order for us to hear and we children sat around her and listened to the news. Of course, most of the time we did not understand too much about what the papers said, and what they were writing about, but it felt good to be close to my mother. Finally, it started to get to be our bedtime and my mother told us to get ready to go to sleep.

Because I was the oldest child in the family, I was always in charge of the children and I saw to it that they got ready for bed. When everyone was in bed, I got ready to go to sleep, also. I have to admit that after getting up at five o'clock every morning and doing some chores before I went to school, then after coming home from school and having to do all the other chores, at the end of the day I was all worn out and very tired. I remember, after we were all in bed, I was happy and I felt very comfortable, finally, to lie down. After all, I was only a child myself, but being the oldest child made me have more responsibility than the other children in the house. That was how it was in Europe in my days.

After we were all settled in bed, my mother came into the room and she sang us a lullaby in Yiddish and very shortly after we fell asleep. My mother had a beautiful voice and I loved to hear her singing. She could sit and just sing without even thinking about if somebody was listening or not. Most of the time she sang Yiddish (Jewish) songs. She also knew Polish and Ukrainian songs, but she liked Yiddish songs the best.

## SHABBOS (SABBATH) Saturday Traditions

In the Jewish religion, Shabbos was our most important holy day of each week. On Shabbos a Jew was thinking about nothing else, but only that he was a Jew and he got into a spiritual mood, like he was devoting the time to God. The fact was that all week every Jew was always busy with a lot of their daily routines and everyone's mind was usually preoccupied with other thoughts, like trying to make a living for the family, taking care of everyday problems, and worries about this and that. When Shabbos came every Jew made themselves forget all of these things from the whole week and they only concentrated on Shabbos.

The Jews knew that Shabbos was the time to acknowledge our religion and direct our thoughts to God. I think that Shabbos did not only have a religious meaning, but it was good in other ways, also. It gave us a chance to recuperate from a whole week of hustle and bustle and by breaking this circle, our mind and our body was rejuvenating and we were ready to start the new week fresh.

In the older days, the Jewish people observed Shabbos every week and they did not work from Friday after sundown until Shabbos, after sundown, no matter how religious or not religious they were.

When God created the world, he worked six days and on the seventh day, Shabbos, was the day of rest. Saturday morning, every Jew was going to synagogue until noon. On Saturday morning my parents were not allowed to eat before prayers. They could eat only after the prayers, when they came back from the synagogue, but we children ate breakfast. My mother put out our yomtovdik (holiday) clothes, which we wore only Shabbos (Saturday) and on the holidays. They were our best clothes that we owned and we all got dressed. Everyone felt and looked good in their nice clothes.

The whole week my mother was wearing a shawl on her head because by the strict Orthodox Jews, the married women were not allowed to show their hair, but on Shabbos she was wearing a paruck (shaitel- wig). After the prayers were over, everyone was on their way home, including my family, in order to have the traditional Shabbos meal. I remember that before we left the synagogue, my father looked around and when he saw strangers still sitting there, right away he knew that they would not have their Shabbos meal. It seemed to him that nobody was inviting them, so my father decided to invite all of them to our home in order for them to have a Shabbos meal.

Like every Jewish husband, so was my father, the head of the family and the king of the house. He was officially in charge of being able to do whatever he wanted to do. My mother agreed with my father on everything, because in the older days men were more valued than women.

The husbands never asked the wives for any opinion or permission. They made all the decisions themselves and the rest of the family had to follow them. My father never mixed into the business, but when it came to his religious statutes, he had the first, the last and the only word. Sometimes we had three or four Jewish people for Shabbos. These people were called hoyrach for Shabbos.

The reason they were stuck in our city was because they could not make it home before Shabbos. A lot of times when the Jewish men traveled like peddlers to look for business, they were gone for weeks and weeks at a time. They traveled from city to city, from town to town, from village to village in order to sell their items that they were dealing with. Sometimes they lost track of time and before they knew it, the sun was down and by this time the Shabbos started and it was too late for them to travel in order to reach their home, because the Jews were only allowed to travel until Friday before sundown. These peddlers had to stay over in the place that they arrived before our Shabbos started. They stayed there until Shabbos ended, which was after sundown and after that they could travel back home.

Besides not being allowed to travel on Shabbos, we were not allowed to make a fire or light a lamp. Our family hired a Polish woman who came in on Saturday morning to do these jobs for us. In order to warm up the food, the Polish woman made the fire and she put the food on the stove to keep it warm until we were ready to eat. They called these people who did these jobs, Shabbos Goy. This was done for a fee, of course. It meant a non-Jewish person who helped Jews on the Shabbos.

We had the same woman for years and years. She was happy with us and we were happy with her. My mother did not even have to tell her what to do, she knew herself. Besides that, in the Jewish religion we were not allowed to tell anybody to do anything on the Shabbos, because by telling somebody to do something on Shabbos was like we were doing it ourselves, and it still counted like we were committing a sin. The Polish woman was with us long enough to do everything the way my mother liked it.

When we all came home from the synagogue, everyone washed their hands and said a brucha (prayer) and then it was time to have our meal. Everyone sat down at the table and my mother started to put out the food. First she put a bottle of wine on the table, and then she put out the chopped liver, herring, and challah that my mother had baked Thursday night. She put out gefilte fish with homemade horseradish that she cooked on Thursday night, also. My father made Kiddish (prayer) over the wine and a moitze (prayer) over the challah and everyone started to eat and drink L'Chaim (to life). After everyone was done with these dishes she started to put out hot food, like warmed up chicken, and carrot tzimmes, which was made with carrots, some meat, a little sugar and cinnamon. Tzimmes could also be made with prunes, carrots, potatoes or sweet potatoes.

I remember that we always had carrot tzimmes during our Shabbos meal. Now, the best thing was yet to come. This was the chulent. Every Jew loved chulent. By the Jewish people, Shabbos would not feel special without chulent. I remember that I could not wait until lunchtime to eat chulent, especially the meat and the kishka from the chulent. It tasted very delicious.

Finally, it was time to have desert. For desert, we had all kinds of fruit, cakes, and applesauce cooked with prunes. When we finished the meal everyone sang Smearos and thanked God for everything. This was a special song for Shabbos. We also sang Jewish songs and everyone was happy. After the meal was over, our guests got up and they said to my parents that they really had a good time with our family. By the strictly Orthodox Jews when somebody was doing something for somebody else, they did not say thank you. Instead, they said you did a mitzvah. It meant you did a good deed and God will repay you. That was what the Jews always believed, in doing good deeds for others. The guests left and my mother and father started to get ready for whatever they wanted to do.

My father had his routine. Right after the meal, on Shabbos, my father always took a nap and my mother got the children ready to take a walk. We walked on the main street, which was like a promenade. It was called Fahrna Square. Saturday, after lunch, we could see all of our friends there. It was like a gathering place. Everyone was still dressed up and they were looking forward to seeing each other.

In the older days, this was the only way of keeping in touch with each other. I still remember on the corner of Fahrna Square there was a beautiful, big church. At the time I was taught not to look at the church, but I always looked at the people who went into the church. They were Polish people and I liked the way they were dressed and the way they behaved. Most of the women wore loud colored clothes summertime and they were holding on to their husbands arm.

As we were walking, we met a lot of our friends and together we walked and talked and everyone had a good time. My mother caught up with all of the gossip from the whole week. We children walked in front of the adults, holding each other's hands. We could hear everything that the adults were talking about. In the beginning, it was interesting to listen to their conversation. After awhile, it started to get boring and we started to talk about things that interested us.

A lot of times, the adults felt like walking off the square, so we children kept up with them and we walked down on Koshara Ulica (street). It was a nice street, too, and it was not as crowded as Fahrna Square, so it was much easier to walk a little faster. The sidewalk was all cemented. They had some stores on this street also, but we were not allowed to carry money with us on Shabbos, so we could not buy anything.

At the end of the business area, there was a residential section. Nobody paid much attention to the surroundings because everyone was busy and preoccupied with talking to each other. In no time, we found ourselves out of town, near the koshare (army base) and as I remember, the 27th Polk Battalion was stationed there. It was called AK (Armia Krajowa). This means the army of the country.

In the older days in my times, since nobody had a telephone and the people did not have any way of communicating with each other in other ways, except by getting together personally, everyone saw to it that they met at least once a week, in order to be in contact with each other. The women who did not work gathered together in the park everyday and everyone had a story to tell. They talked about cooking, baking, and they always praised their children, no matter how good or bad they were. These women, most of the time, were not too interested in more important things and they only wanted to gossip, criticize and talk about everyone.

Mostly, they talked about their neighbors. I remember that during the week, I would look out of the back window of our house and see the women sitting on their benches in the back yards and they were talking and laughing for hours. They would sit with their legs spread out wearing full skirts and telling each other all kinds of stories. Many of the women were heavyset. They would gossip all day, and would not get any work done. They considered gossiping to be their job. My mother did not have time the whole week because she was working, so on Saturday, after lunch, was my mother's time to catch up with all of the gossip. My mother did not care what the other women were doing all week. She figured that this was not her concern and she was on good terms with everyone. They all could not wait for Shabbos and Sunday to fill my mother in with the latest news. My mother did not mind this at all. She never talked about anybody, but if somebody told her all the happenings, she was interested in hearing about them.

I always listened to what the grown-ups were talking about, so I knew what was going on in our city, but I never mixed in on their conversations. Instead, I pretended that I did not even hear because in the older days children were not allowed to hear what the older people were saying to each other. Whenever or whatever I heard, I never repeated to anyone. I figured if I will tell somebody what I heard, and they will tell my mother, she would never take me anyplace with her again. I knew that the best thing would be not to say anything to anybody. After a few hours of walking and talking, we children got hungry and tired and we wanted to go home. My mother left her friends and she took us home. When we came home, we relaxed for a while and after having a snack we went out to play with our neighbor's children in our yard.

Summertime, when it was too hot to take a walk on Saturday, after lunch, sometimes we went to the lake where it was nice and cool. Some people were in the water, some were sitting on the grass and they were just relaxing and some people were paddling kayaks in the lake.

While we were at the lake, we sat down on the grass for a few hours, also. We were sitting and watching people riding kayaks. Sometimes, we children talked our mother into renting a kayak. It looked like a boat or a canoe, and it was long and narrow. On Saturday, we were not allowed to handle money or ride a kayak. My mother explained to us that we could not go in a kayak on Saturday, because it was against our religion, but she promised us that we would come back on Sunday and we did. After we got the kayak, everyone was happy. My mother and my brother were paddling for a while, then they got tired and my mother decided to stop at the other side of the lake in order for her to be able to relax. We, children, wanted to go swimming for a while and my mother was happy with this because she knew that we would enjoy it and have a good time.

After a couple of hours of swimming and being in the sun, everyone came home very tired, but it was fun. Sometimes our mother gave us a treat on Sunday, but not too often. She said that we had to rest up a little because Monday was a school day, and she was right.

I remember that sometimes on Saturday, after lunch, when it was raining and we could not go anywhere, my mother read a Yiddish (Jewish) book to us, with different kinds of jokes. We all sat around and listened to them. Most of the jokes were about our life and our way of doing things. In other words, the jokes were on us. The Jews always made a joke out of everything because they always had a good sense of humor.

The jokes of our Jewish comedians were really funny. Even we children could understand them and we laughed when hearing them. I still remember one of the Jewish comedian's names was Herschele Stopooler. This comedian was very famous for his jokes.

My mother also went to the library to take out some Jewish books. She always loved to read and she read every chance she had, even if only for an hour. She read her newspapers, her books and anything else that interested her. Besides reading she really took an interest of knowing what was going on in the world. She had a lot of intellectual acquaintances that she talked to, and by having discussions with them she always found out a lot of news. My mother was a very knowledgeable person and whatever free time she had, she used it wisely. The best thing that she liked to do was to read and talk to people. This was her relaxation.

On the other hand, my father was only interested in studying the Torah with the Chassidim. He was educated in our Jewish religion and he was happy in his own world. When it got a little darker, I remember that my father went back to synagogue to davinnen (praying) Minhah and Marif. When they finished with praying, everyone wished each other a gutte woch, it means a good week. The Shabbos was over and everyone went home to have their evening meal.

The custom was, that after eating the meal, with meat, the adults had to wait for six hours in order to eat dairy, and the children had to wait three hours only. After having a dairy meal, adults and children, had to wait only three hours in order to be allowed to have a meal with meat. The Shabbos evening meal was called melaveh-malkah. After the six hours of waiting were over, it was time to eat dairy.

We had borscht made out of beets or schav (like green leaves). It also could be made out of cherries and blueberries. We had boiled potatoes, herring and sour cream. We ate mostly dairy food and then we drank hot tea. I have to mention that this is how it was in the older days and it is still our tradition, when Shabbos is over we have a melaveh-malkah, especially by the Orthodox Jews.

## THE JEWISH ENTERTAINMENT WORLD

On Saturday evening, after the melaveh-malkah meal (supper), my mother and her women friends had made plans to go out for the evening. My mother waited all week and looked forward to Saturday evening to get away from her weekly routine to forget everything and just enjoy herself.

My father did not have any interest of going to the entertainment places, so he went back to the synagogue to study or to talk to other members of the synagogue and discuss the Torah among other things. We children stayed home with our maid. Our city was filled with Jewish life. We had a Jewish theater, Jewish gatherings, Jewish speakers and many more Jewish entertainment activities.

I remember we had a big hall in our city, and every Saturday evening it was packed full of mostly Jewish people because all week most of the Jews worked or took care of their businesses. Saturday evening and Sunday, usually, most of the Jews went out to be able to relax and to have a good time. In my time, we did not have any movies in our city, and the only entertainment that we had was with real live entertainers. They put on concerts with Jewish singers, dancers, comedians, and musicians. We had Polish entertainment in the city, also, but the Jews liked the Jewish music better and besides that the Jews had another reason for it, also. In the older days, we did not have any telephones in Europe, so in order not to lose track of each other, and to be able to communicate with each other, there was no other way than to meet personally, face to face and have a conversation with each other.

That was the main reason why most of the Jews came to this hall to socialize and bring all of their family news up to date. They met and gossiped for a while, because this was the only way of keeping in touch with each other. The Jews saw to it that they met every week in the same hall, which was the Jews meeting place.

I remember that the most popular group of Jewish music in Europe were the Klezmer musicians. Everyone loved them. They played mostly Jewish songs and it was the traditional and spiritual Jewish music of my parents and my grandparents. The Klezmer were very well known all over Europe. You could hear Klezmer music at the festivals all throughout Europe.

Sometimes, my mother took me with her because she knew that I loved to see and hear all kinds of entertainment and she also knew that I did not mind staying up late at all. I loved to go with my mother because everything was very interesting to me, and I was sure that I would get a lot of enjoyment out of it. I used to observe everything and it stuck in my mind. Now, a lot of times I do not remember what happened yesterday, but most of the things that happened when I was a child I still remember. These were my childhood years, which were my best years of my life, but to my regret they were very short years. My childhood years and my happiness ended with the beginning of the Nazi occupation. They took everything away from me.

I remember that we had a lot of talented entertainers in Poland, but it was very well known that most of them could not even make ends meet. In Europe, especially in Poland, being in the entertainment world was not considered a job, or a profession. Nobody looked at the fact that entertainers had a gift and they made people happy with their performances, instead they were treated like their talent was not important enough in order for them to be recognized and acknowledged.

It looked like all of their talents were not important to anybody. On the contrary, it was really ignored by everybody, and it was not appreciated by anyone. Even when the people came to see or to hear the performers, they paid very little for the admission to go in. These groups of entertainers were trying in their worst way to make a living. They used to travel to different cities and entertain people in any way they could, only to get by.

I remember the streets in Poland were always filled with singers, dancers and musicians. They played all kinds of instruments and people were standing around them, and when they finished playing everyone gave them some money. That was how most of the musicians made a living in Europe. They really did not live a normal life and they really did not have a steady income. They only lived from day to day and they tried their best to exist. This was the life of the talented entertainers in Poland.

# CHAPTER XIV
## OUR CLIMATE AND THE SEASONS OF THE YEAR

## WINTERTIME IN POLAND

Our climate in Poland consisted of four seasons of the year, winter, spring, summer, and autumn. When a season started, from the beginning of the season until the end of the season, the temperature stayed more or less the same. The climate was very steady in Poland, in fact, we did not need a weather report. We always knew what the weather would be the next day and everyday after until the next season began.

Wintertime in Poland was very cold. In my days, when the winter started, mostly everyday was below zero degrees. It was good in a lot of ways because in wintertime all of the bacteria died and when spring came, we started with clean and fresh air. The other good thing was that our body adjusted to one temperature during the season and that was why most of the population stayed healthy. The people in Poland were used to this climate and it did not bother them too much. In the other way, it was not too good because all of the business and the traffic in the city during wintertime slowed down a lot.

No matter what, life was still going on anyway. All the businesses were open and people went where they had to go. Of course, some older people would try to stay home in the warmth, instead of coming out in the freezing cold weather, but the children did not care about the freezing cold. They came out anyway. They had too much energy and they were eager to use it up. They ran around throwing snowballs at each other and doing what they liked to do.

Our house was located near a brina (water well). Because nobody in the older days had water in their house, everyone from the neighborhood came there to get the buckets of water from the brina (water well). It was on a long back street and to go down the street was like we were going down a hill.

The well was located in the beginning of the street, on top of the hill. Every time somebody pumped water from the brina (water well), a little water was spilled and went down the hill and it froze right away. The spilled water formed an ice pad down the hill. Because the children did not go to school on Saturday or Sunday, they could play and do whatever they wanted to do and they did. In spite of the bitter cold weather, they still came out in order to join the others. The children were gathering near the water pump on top of the hill, sitting on their shliten (sleds) and waiting for their turn to slide down the hill.

We could see a lot of boys, and some girls there. They were waiting impatiently because there were a lot of children and everyone was in line waiting for their turn, next. The children made a lot of noise. They hollered at each other when they lost their patience, and they started to get nasty. Mostly the boys were not afraid of this sport, because they were boys. Usually the boys had more nerve to do more dangerous things than the girls did, and a lot of times they tried to show off in front of the girls. When we stood on top of the hill and we looked down the hill, it looked a little scary, so a lot of the girls were really afraid to slide down and they did not want to take a chance of hurting themselves.

Many girls were too scared and they decided not to do it, so instead of sliding down they stayed and watched the other children. They did not take a chance themselves, but they still wanted to watch. Sometimes the girls came with their mothers and they slid down together.

I was like a tomboy, and I was never scared of trying to do something that looked a little scary. No matter what the boys did, I tried to do it, also. I tried to think positive and I was always between the children all of the time. Most of the time, the sleds turned over and the children fell on top of each other. They slid down without the sleds and the sleds slid down without the children. It was not a gradual, smooth hill, instead it was a sharp and bumpy path, so we could not control where we were going. Everyone was bundled up so much, that when they did turn over with the shliten (sleds), they did not hurt themselves. We could not even see their face that was how much the children were bundled up.

Once they were on the bottom of the hill, they had to struggle to get back to the top of the hill, but somehow they made it and they started all over. They were again standing in line and waiting for their turn. After sliding down the first time, the second time was not so bad anymore, because the children had more confidence in themselves and they realized that they could do it.

## SPRINGTIME IN POLAND

After a very long and cold winter, we welcomed the spring. This was one of the nicest seasons of the year. The weather in spring was nice and it started to get warm. The whole city was coming back to life again. Everything started to grow again and the flowers started to bloom with different colors and it looked very nice all over. Finally, we saw a lot of people on the streets. I was sure that they were glad to come out of their homes and see the world again. Everything in the city looked and felt clean. In springtime the temperature was warm, but not hot, and it was very comfortable. This season did not last too long, just about two months, until the end of May. Then the summer season came and with it came the heat.

## SUMMERTIME IN POLAND

The summer in Poland started with high temperatures right away. It became very hot and humid during daytime, but in the evening the temperature dropped and it cooled off a little. I remember in Poland, in the summertime, when the heat was high and, of course, we did not have any fans to cool off, we used to make a fan out of a piece of paper by folding it like an accordion and it served more or less, the purpose of a fan. It blew some air on us and it helped a little bit, but not too much.

In spite of the fact, that we did not have too many cars in our city, the air still was not clean enough to breathe. The air in the summertime became polluted because of a lack of sanitation. Most of the people tried to get out of the city in the summertime. The parents tried their very best to take their children to some kind of resort place in order for them to breathe clean air, so they would be able to enjoy their summer vacation.

When school closed for our vacation in the summer, my parents always rented a place in the same village on the outskirts of the city. In general, a village consisted of a lot of farms, farmhouses and barns. The village houses in Europe had straw roofs, and all the houses had a wooden fence around them. Every farm had a couple of dogs, cows and horses. The peasant's fields were not far from their houses. All the villages had only dirt roads, and when it rained the horses and the buggies got stuck in the middle of the road, and the neighbors had to help pull the stuck wagons out of the mud.

The Ukrainian peasants who we stayed with had a big farm, and we children were happy to spend our vacation there. My parents and we children knew them for a very long time. They were very nice to us, and they treated us very good, and we liked to go there. There was a big pine forest nearby, which smelled very good and the air was healthy and clean.

In the back of the house was a little lake, and it was deep enough for us children to be able to swim. We loved to be in the water. I remember we splashed each other with water and we had a very good time. The whole place was very nice. We were happy that we stayed with a private family, and we could do whatever we wanted to. Next to the farm where we stayed was a development. It looked like a summer camp and it had all of the advantages of a camp.

It was a datshe (summer resort) and they had a lot of little bungalows for rent for the city people. A lot of people from the surrounding area used to spend their summer there. Other families came with their children, also, so we played together and we really had a fun vacation.

Some people came to the resort for health reasons. The fresh pine air was very good for them and it also was good for us children to breathe fresh clean air. Our maid took very good care of us and she watched us every minute of the day. We ate very healthy food. The Ukrainian peasants cooked and we had our meals together with their family and all of their workers, who worked on their farm. They had a lot of workers, working for them. Some worked in the fields, and some were taking care of their livestock, and they also did many other jobs on the farm that had to be done.

The farm was very big, they had a lot of fruit trees and vegetable gardens. We, children, picked the fruit straight from the trees and the vegetables straight from the garden because we were told by the owners that we had permission to do it. We stayed there almost the entire summer vacation.

It was only about seven miles from the city but there was a very big difference in the temperature. We did not even feel the heat in the country, maybe because we were surrounded with a lot of trees and water. I thought of my parents, who were in such a heat in the city instead of being here with us, and I started to feel a little guilty, but that was the way it was. I guess that they had responsibilities and obligations that they had to take care of, so first things came first.

Our parents came only for the weekend. On Friday, my mother closed the business earlier than usual, and my father also worked half of the day on Friday and then they got ready to come and spend the weekend with us. They stayed from Friday afternoon until Monday morning. I remember they brought their own cooked food with them because they ate only kosher food. They could eat a lot of fruit picked from the trees and vegetables from the garden. They also brought their own dishes and pots with them. In our home, everything was kosher and we never ate anything else, only kosher food. When we children were away, we ate what the Ukrainian people fed us, except we had no ham or bacon.

My parents observed our traditional religious ways all of their lives and they never ate anything else except kosher food. I saw these ways of living and doing in my parents and in my grandparents' homes. Even though, I am not so religious now and most of the time I do not observe our traditions, I know them and until today I still remember them because I was born and raised with them. It feels like it was drilled in my memory because everything that I learned in the early years of my life, I still remember well.

Very rich people spent their winter vacation in Zakopane, far from our city, Wlodzimierz Volynski, and they spent their summer vacation in Krinica. These were the most famous resort places in Poland. My parents could not go there because, first of all, it was too expensive for them, and the second reason was that my parents did not have the time. They really could not go so far away from home, leave everything behind, and worry if things were going right or not. My mother thought that by worrying and by concentrating on anything else except the vacation, she would not enjoy herself anyway.

My mother always thought in her mind that when she was away things would not be done as well as when she was there. She had her people working for her for many years, and they knew everything that they were supposed to do, but my mother always worried that it would not be done the way she liked it. She was far from being a perfectionist in our home, but when it came to the business, everything in it had to be arranged and displayed in perfect order. She used to say to me that if it will not look appealing to the customers, they will not buy it and she was probably right.

Besides this, she had steady customers and they wanted to deal only with my mother and not with the help. They were also storekeepers that bought a lot of merchandise from my mother and usually she sold the goods to them for a small profit. They were happy because everyone liked to make a good deal. My father had his job, also, and he had to take care of it. He had his everyday functions as a rabbi and he had to fulfill them.

## AUTUMN IN POLAND

Finally, after so many months of summer heat and all of this humidity, most of the people were happy that the summer was coming to an end. Everyone came back home from their vacation and very soon the children would go back to school because the school vacation would soon be over. When the summer season ended, the temperature changed from very hot to warm. Spring and autumn were the nicest seasons of the year in Poland. In spring, everything came back to life, and in autumn, it looked like everything was getting ready for a deep winter sleep. Nothing grew anymore, the leaves were falling off the trees, the days were getting shorter and it started to get colder, but all in all it was a very nice time of the year. Little by little, the people were starting to prepare themselves for the long, cold winter. In the meantime, everyone tried to enjoy every day of the autumn season for as long as it lasted. We could see a lot of people in the streets before the winter crept up on us, because everyone knew that the cold weather would come very soon.

# CHAPTER XV
# THE LIFE IN POLAND BEFORE THE WAR

In the older days, in Poland, when I was born, the people lived in the dark ages and they tried to manage their lives the best way they could under these circumstances. Looking back to these old times, how people lived, and managed their everyday lives by putting in a lot of time, effort and strength in order to get something done, now it would seem to everyone to be impossible.

Apparently, it was possible and in spite of all of that hard work, they were still happy to do it, without any bad feelings or complaints about it. It looked like people in the good old days were much more thankful for what they had instead of being miserable for what they did not have. Besides this, the people did not even think that they were missing something. The only thing that they knew was to accept everything that came along, make the best of it, and be happy.

Looking back to these times, I really believe that these were the good old times, in spite of the fact that it was such a hard life. People really worked very hard, and everything was very primitive. There was no water in the homes, no electricity, and everyone had to cook on a woodstove. When the wood was wet the house was full of smoke and when they heated the house with coal and wood, the gases from the coal gave everyone a headache. In a way we were lucky that the homes were not airtight and the gases from the coals could escape through the cracks of the house.

We had to carry the water from the brina (water well) and we lit up the house with a kerosene lantern. We could hardly see what we were doing because the light was very dull and the kerosene smelled very bad, but all in all people were still thankful for everything they had, even if they really did not have too much of anything to begin with. According to their way of looking at life, all of the material things were not as important as their health and they thought that when they were healthy, they had to be happy and thank God for it.

Because my mother was working, I remember that she had to hire people to do certain things for us. When we had to wash clothes, we had a washwoman, who came to our home once a month. That was her way of making a living and this was her parnuse (livelihood). I remember that the whole house was full of wet clothes. She washed every color separate and the bundles laid everywhere for a whole week. Of course, all of the laundry had to be done by hand. The way she did it was, first, she put everything into a big balli (washtub), filled with warm water that she had to warm up on top of the stove. She then scrubbed the laundry with a washboard. Next, in a big kettle filled with water, she put in the laundry and let it boil for a while. The reason we had to do it this way was to kill the bacteria in order to stay healthy.

After it cooled off, the washwoman took the laundry out of the kettle and she went to the lake to rinse the laundry. She then brought back the heavy, wet laundry and hung it in the yard on the clotheslines to get dry. The washwoman did all of this in the summertime. In the wintertime the clothes washing procedure was the same except for the rinsing. Because in the winter she could not go to the lake to rinse the laundry, so it had to be done in the house. It also had to get dry somehow. The washwoman spread some clothes in the house and we had nothing but wet laundry lying around all over the house. She also hung some clothes on the clothesline in the yard. Of course, on the clothesline in the wintertime, the clothes froze and got so stiff that we could not even move them from the line, but somehow it worked out.

In these days, whatever we did was a big procedure, which was why the clothes had to be worn many times before washing them again. I remember that my father used to wear a shirt a whole week and everyone else did the same. My father was wearing white shirts only, but by the end of the week the shirt did not look so white anymore. We all had to be very careful not to make our clothes too dirty because they had to be worn by us from one Friday until the next Friday. Then we would again get clean clothes for the whole week.

When we children came home from school, in order to go out to play, we had to take off our school clothes, hang them up and put on our play clothes. I remember on Friday before sundown, everyone got clean clothes for the Shabbos. I washed my school uniform myself. My school uniform had white cuffs and a white collar that could come off.

I remember that I was very fanatical about my cleanliness and I wore sparkling clean white socks, which I washed everyday. If anyone of my brothers or sister would touch my clothes, I would scream at them.

My mother used to say that I was worse than the malhamowas (devil). My sister and brothers were more afraid of me than of my mother or the maid. My father never interfered with what anybody was doing. He was a very easy-going person. On the other hand, I was more demanding and bossier than anybody in the family. Being the oldest child, I knew that I had the responsibility to take care of certain things, especially of my younger brothers and sister. That is how it was in the older days. Come to think of it, I do not remember a time in my life that I lived without any responsibilities or without any obligations.

I remember that sometimes our maid did not wash the floors right and it did not look too clean according to me, so I would wash the floor over again. We had to scrape each board of the floor with a knife in order to make it clean. After it was rinsed, the whole floor was covered with rags until the next day. When the floor was dry, and the rags were taken off, the floor looked clean and yellow. I also remember that I worked quite a lot of hours in order to do it the way I liked it, but when I looked at the floor, I was very happy with the results.

When my mother did her baking, she always baked more than we needed because poor people from our city used to come to our home every Friday morning, and my mother gave them bread, challah, and cake. It was called a mitzvah (good deed). My mother always said that she was very thankful to God that she could do it, because she always had consideration for others and she always felt sorry for those who had less than she did.

As I mentioned quite a few times, life in the older days in Europe was very hard and everything had to be made from scratch and women were working day and night to get some things done. All in all, the Jewish people had certain values, which made them very happy and content because the reason for it was that between us there was always friendship, dedication, love, togetherness, acceptance and appreciation for everything that we had. This was why we were happy and content with everything and we always thanked God for giving us our health and happiness.

My father was a strict Orthodox Jew and he was very educated in the Talmud. He performed religious ceremonies and he did everything that he was taught in his profession to do. Because my father was a rabbi, he belonged to an organization named Kehilah or Gmeana and he was paid a salary every week. Only people who had a religious position could belong to this organization. It was a religious, Jewish organization with many benefits. Every member of this organization had a policy, that in time of his death, his salary was still paid, to his family every week, by the Kehilah.

I remember that my father, after supper, every night, used to go back to the synagogue to study the Torah with other Orthodox Jews. My father studied with Jews who were his match and knowledgeable enough for him to discuss the Torah with. He also valued their ways of understanding certain things that were written in the Torah.

I used to ask my father why was he studying the Torah so much, and he told me that he wanted to know everything about the Jewish religion and the more he would study the more he would know. I remember that from time to time, I kept on asking him if he knows enough already. Once, to my surprise, he said to me that he thinks that the more he was studying the Torah, the less he knew. Of course, it did not make any sense to me what he said because I remembered that he told me a while ago that the more he would study the more he would know. I started to think about it and I became very curious. One day, I decided to ask my father if I could go to the synagogue with him and I promised to be quiet, but he always had some reason and excuse not to take me. Mostly, my mother did not think that it was such a good idea for me to stay up so late on school nights. I did not give up and I kept on kvetching (whining) to my father and finally he gave in to me and agreed to take me with him. I always felt, not like a child, only more mature and my mind was very settled, so I was happy that my father took me with him because I was always curious to know how he was studying the Torah.

I went with him and I remember that I was lying under the table in the synagogue and I listened to him and his study group of Jews, studying together. Every one of them said something different by expressing their way of thinking and understanding certain statements of the Torah. Each of them understood the Torah differently because everyone's mind works, thinks and understands in a different way. Every person had their own unique way of thinking and understanding certain things. From what I heard, they did not come to a final conclusion.

I laid and listened and my thoughts, in my mind, were wandering around because I listened to their discussions and all the questions which they asked, "Why was it so and why does it have to be this way and not the other way?" and they kept on asking each other these questions and none of them could figure out any answers, because in the Torah there were no answers, only statements. The Torah was only telling them how it has to be, but there was not a direct explanation for it. The Torah was only making a statement and we Jews had to accept it without asking why. In our religion, most of the Jews in the older days accepted whatever the Torah taught us. Only the very religious Orthodox Jews who were highly educated in the Talmud, wanted to know more and more about Judaism.

They discussed and discussed and could not figure out any answers. Finally, I got very tired and I would fall asleep and my father had to carry me home. A lot of times, I was wide-awake until my father was ready to go home. On the way home, on the same street next to the shul (synagogue), there was a bakery and they baked bread and challah all night long. I still remember that in the middle of the night, when my father and I were on our way home from the shul, sometimes we stopped in the bakery and we got fresh bread straight from the oven.

They baked all kinds of different breads, like pitlova bread, which looked white, Russian bread, which was very black, and rosava bread, which looked like dark rye bread. My mother baked bread every week, but she only made one sort of bread. It was very good, but not as good as the bread from the bakery. This bread, which we brought home, was even a treat for my mother. The next morning I had to get up very early because it was a school day. I really did not mind that at all, because I loved to hear my father studying the Torah and I loved to be around my parents any chance I had. Maybe this was because in the older days, the parents were the children idols and maybe because I really loved them very much.

Suddenly a big tragedy hit our home. In 1935, when I was only six years old, my father was diagnosed with lung cancer. He took sick and suffered for over a year. All the time while he was sick I kept on saying to him, do not worry, you will get better. I, myself, did not even worry because for some reason or another in my mind I told myself that for sure my father would be okay. My mother never told me how sick my father was, even when she knew that there was no hope for him to get better. After a whole year of suffering, the doctor could not do anything for him anymore and my father died. It was in the year of 1936.

He was only 32 years old. Even being the oldest child, I could not understand and face the reality that my father was dead, and that he was not going to be here for me when I would need him. I just could not believe or accept the fact that I would not have my father in my life anymore.

For a very long time, I pretended that I watched my father putting on his tallis (prayer shawl). The prayer shawl looked like a long shawl and in the four corners of the shawl it had fringes that were called tzitzis. I kept on telling myself that I saw him standing in the corner of the kitchen with his yarmulke (skullcap) on his head where he used to stand and pray when he was alive. I pretended that I saw him putting the tefillin (phylacteries) on his forehead. The tefillin looked like a square little box with two leather straps hanging out and he wrapped his arms around with them and then he was ready to pray. When he was alive, he used to do his morning prayers at home and then he had breakfast and shortly after, he left in order to take care of his obligations.

I kept on pretending as long as I could, but in a while I had to face the reality that my father was dead. My sister and my two brothers did not understand too much. They were too young to have any emotional feelings about anything, but I knew what happened and right away I changed. From me being a very happy child, after my father's death, I became very moody.

I was not the same child anymore. I became very withdrawn and very serious about everything. My personality changed completely. I felt like I was not a child anymore and my childhood years suddenly ended. I told myself that now I have to behave like an adult. I did not want to play with children anymore and I felt the responsibility of helping my mother with whatever I could. In a way I worried about my mother and I wanted to see her as often as I could. After my father's death, I always felt like I was not sure of anything anymore and this scared me a lot.

After school, I went straight to the store, to see if my mother was okay. For a long time I could not shake off the feeling of fear that I felt inside of me. I always imagined that something bad would happen again. I never let my mother know how I felt, instead I told her that I came to see if she needed me to help her with anything. She was happy to see me and I was happy to see that she was okay and taking care of everything. I really did not know how she felt, but she seemed to be herself.

In our city, we had a wholesale magazin (store) that all of the little businesses could buy merchandise from. My mother used to go to Warszawa four times a year to the factories to get merchandise for the stores, but when she needed a couple of items right away, she got them in the wholesale store in our city. Most of the time she asked me to get the couple of items for her. She gave me the list of the items and some money, and I went to get them for her. The wholesale place was not too far from my mother's stores. I walked very fast, and sometimes I ran and in no time I was there. I knew that she really needed these items as soon as she could get them. A lot of times, I saw that the customers wanted something that she was out of, so she told the customer that I would bring it in ten minutes. These were my mother's steady customers and they waited for me to come back with the items that they wanted.

I remember when I came into the wholesale magazin (store), there were always a lot of people waiting for their turn to be next. I pushed myself through the crowd and in no time I was in front of the counter. Everyone started to get angry with me, but when I gave them a big smile and I said that my mother needed the items right away, they started to laugh. The owner and the employees loved me and they always paid special attention to me. As a child, I was very alert, always smiling, with big red cheeks, black eyes and black hair and everyone touched me, pinched me and kissed me. They really loved me.

My grandfather, my father's father, died before I was born, and I never got to know him, but I was very close with my grandmother. I saw her all the time. After so many years of her living alone and taking care of such a big house, one day she decided to try to sell it. For a long time she could not find anybody to buy the house. Finally, she got a customer and she sold her house, together with all of her furniture. After that, she moved in with my father's brother, my uncle and his wife. They had a big house and there were just the two of them, so my grandmother had enough space and she was quite comfortable there.

My grandmother had a little store near my mother's store where she sold pottery. She made enough in her store to cover her expenses and it kept her busy. I think it was very good for her to see people all day long.

I saw my grandmother everyday. When I came from school I stopped to see my mother and I wanted to check with her to see if she wanted me to do anything for her, then I stopped to see my grandmother.

I still remember the way she looked. She was very short and tiny. She looked very young and whenever she saw me she gave me some spending money. She always told me that everyday she was waiting for me to come and hoped that I really would come to see her, and I did. My father's brother and his wife had their house on the same street near us and we were very close to each other. In my days, the closest people to us were our family members.

The family would do everything for each other, no matter what kind of help we would need, we could always depend on the family. They would always be there to give each other support in any way they could, financially, emotionally and in many other ways.

Some of our family members lived in different cities, like in Hrubieszow (Rabeshoiw in Yiddish), Lutsk, Kovel, Rovno, Chelm, and Warszawa (Warsaw). We did not see them as often as we would have liked to, because everyone was busy taking care of their businesses or their jobs. Besides that, in order to get together, we had to travel. In the older days, the transportation was not good at all. The trains were never on time and to travel a long distance by horse and buggy would take forever.

My other grandparents, my mother's parents, and my mother's three brothers lived in the town of Hrubieszow. It was not too far from us, it was just about thirty kilometers from our city. Whenever my mother went to see them I went with her, also, and we visited them every so often. Almost everyone in my mother's family was in business. My grandparents, my mother's parents, had a yard goods store in Hrubieszow on Targowa Ulica (street). They did very well in their business.

I think because my mother grew up in business surroundings and she came into her mother's store all the time, so that was where she learned to be such a good businesswoman. I think, as a fact, I know, that she was better in the business world than she was in the domestic world. She even admitted to us that she hated housework. I still remember that one time, she made a statement that she would rather walk ten miles instead of sweeping the floor once, and I knew that she really meant every word of it.

Most of the Jewish people were in business. Besides working in their own businesses, everyone could find a job in order to make a living because our city was an industrial place also. Some Jews who did not have their own businesses worked for somebody else. We also had some small factories in our city. We had a salami factory, candle factory, sugar factory, where they made sugar out of sugar cane, a candy factory, and a mlecharnia (dairy factory). In the mlecharnia they produced sour cream, cottage cheese, pot cheese, cream cheese, butter and sour milk. The dairy factory was right in the city, not too far from Fahrna Square.

I remember after I came back from school, my mother used to send me over to the mlecharnia (dairy factory). I went there twice a week to get all the fresh dairy products because the prices were much better there than they were anyplace else, and besides that, everything was very fresh.

My mother, besides taking care of her two stores, also had a wholesale trade with the Gentile Polish storekeepers. She sold all of the items to them that they carried in their store and she made a little profit. When my mother went to Warszawa to get merchandise for her own two stores, she also got the items that the Polish storekeepers were carrying.

The storekeepers that my mother was dealing with had their businesses in the more expensive sections of the city and they sold a better quality of goods, but my mother carried in her stores only merchandise that the peasants needed and bought. In spite of the fact that our stores were located on one of the nicest streets of the city, and the street was called Warszawa Ulica, the same name like the capital city of Poland, the whole street of storekeepers were catering mostly to the peasants.

The reason for it was that the peasants were very good customers and everyone liked to deal with them. My mother's variety stores were like a five and ten cent store, with all of the trimmings and accessories that they needed.

After the peasants bought their yard goods for their family, in order to make their clothes, they came to buy all of the trimmings in my mother's store. It was very seldom that the city people bought in these stores. Most of the time, the city people liked to shop where they sold a better quality of goods. The people who did not care about the quality, only about the cost, were the kind of customers who did their shopping on the bazaar days for reasonable prices. The majority of the population apparently could not afford to pay high prices and they shopped on the bazaar days, also.

My mother built up her wholesale business very fast. The storekeepers with whom she was dealing with, recommended her to other storekeepers. My mother always worked very hard, but she made a good living and by the same token the storekeepers made a good profit, also. All of her customers for the wholesale business were Gentiles. My mother had connections with the owners of the factories in Warszawa and they sold her the merchandise for a good price just to get it out of the factory because they needed the space. To them, the space was more valuable than the couple zlotys (Polish money) that they got for it.

This merchandise was a closeout, which was of no use to the factory owners anymore. My mother bought the leftovers from the season, like odds and ends and then she sold it to the other stores for a very reasonable price. The factory owners liked to deal with my mother and they always wrote to her when they had a foreclosure. Right away, she made arrangements to go to Warszawa and get whatever she thought was a good item to sell and make a couple of zlotys (Polish money).

I still remember in the evening after I made my lessons, I used to help my mother match up the buttons and sew them on a little carton, because in the factory she bought big sacks of different buttons, different sizes, and different colors. She bought it for next to nothing and my mother and I matched them up and we sewed at least six matching buttons on a carton, then she sold them for a good price. It was a lot of work, but she did very well with them, because these buttons were very expensive to buy at a regular price. My mother paid practically nothing for them and took in good money when she sold them. The factories were glad to get rid of their leftovers because they were ready to start manufacturing the new line of clothing. Everything that my mother thought she could sell, she bought, and of course, with a little work and a little effort she got good results out of it and made a good profit.

My mother used to go to Warszawa at least four or five times a year to buy merchandise, but a lot of times she just went for a couple of hours to see what the factories were discontinuing and maybe she could use the item in the stores or in her wholesale business. I remember that she always came back with a lot of bundles.

All the Gentile business owners liked my mother and they loved to deal with her. She used to sell to them for very low prices and they liked it because this way they made more profit in every item, and they really appreciated the way my mother was taking good care of their needs.

# CHAPTER XVI
# THE ANTI-SEMITISM IN POLAND

In 1935, the anti-Semitism in Poland started to become very bad. Before that time there was plenty of anti-Semitism in Poland, but it was not so obvious because the Gentiles still behaved a little better and they hid their bad feelings towards the Jews. It used to be that the Polish and Jewish flags were side by side and the orchestra played the Polish National Anthem and a Jewish hymn. The Polish people hired Jewish bands, like fiddlers and Klezmer bands.

These bands were very famous and well-known musicians and they played all kinds of music, including Jewish, Polish, Gypsy and Russian songs. They were hired by everyone to play at all kinds of occasions, like weddings, birthdays, anniversaries and other festive events. They played music for dancing and they played happy melodies and sometimes they played sad tunes. They played whatever anybody liked to hear and they knew all kinds of music.

When the Polish president, Joseph Pilsudski, who was against anti-Semitism, died, and the other president named Ignac Moscicki, with his foreign minister, Jozef Beck, came to power, the anti-Semitism started to become very open for the Polish goyim (prejudiced Gentiles). They started to act as they really felt towards the Jews all of their lives. Poland was and had always been anti-Semitic, but it got much worse with the new president in power. Jewish children were forbidden to sit with the Polish children in school. The Jews were called names like parshywy Zyd, which means rotten Jew and the Jewish children were beaten up in the streets by the Polish hooligans (hoodlums).

No matter how bad it was before President Pilsudski died, now with the new president, who was a Jew hater himself, the anti-Semites took the authority to do whatever they had wanted to do to the Jews all of their lives. The law was on their side and nobody interfered with their actions and their brutality towards the Jews.

The Polish Parliament voted to forbid the Jews to perform the shchitah, which was a Jewish ritual ceremonial way of slaughtering animals. I think the reason for it was to chase the Jewish katzifs (butchers) out of their businesses. The religious Jews stopped eating meat or they slaughtered the animal the ritual way in secret. My mother lost all of her wholesale customers. Most of them were very nice people, but they told my mother not to come into their stores anymore, and the reason for it was that they were afraid of the anti-Semites because they were warned by them, not to have any contact in any way with the Jews.

The Polish storekeepers did not want to deal with Jews anymore. Poles did not buy from the Jews. The Polish and Ukrainian anti-Semites boycotted the Jewish businesses, and all kinds of Jewish establishments. Little by little they took over the businesses and the Jews could not make a living. The only customers that the Jews had were the Ukrainian people, the peasants. It was true that they were good customers and they were buying a lot of goods and they liked to deal with the Jews, but all in all it was not enough business to make a living.

It was not even enough to cover the expenses and in a very short time our life started to change from bad to worse. The Jews in our city had a private free loan organization society, which they organized themselves. These Jews who offered to belong to this society knew everyone in the city. They knew who could afford to lend money to the needy ones and they also knew which Jews were in need of their help. All day they were busy making these transactions. They borrowed money from one Jew and lent it to another Jew. The political leaders did everything that they possibly could to make it very difficult for the Jews. It was practically impossible to get a loan in the bank. Even when the bank had dealt with the Jews for years and years, they still refused to give the Jews a loan. It was very obvious that they had orders from the higher authorities not to help the Jews survive.

Instead they did everything possible to get rid of the Jews. The Polish leaders made all kinds of restrictions for the Jews. They raised their taxes, they boycotted their businesses and eventually they succeeded to chase the Jews out of their businesses. The Jews were left without an income and without any way of being able to make a living for their families.

The anti-Semitism grew day by day and there was nothing that we could do. Our troubles started long before the war began. The Polish people did not consider us as being a Polish Jew, they only thought of us as being a Jew, in spite of the fact that we were Polish citizens. I think that the Jews were doomed from the minute they were born. They were always labeled as a Jew and they were persecuted for it. No matter what they did or what they did not do, they were discriminated against, criticized, and accused untruthfully. For no good reason everyone disliked them, only because they were Jews and believed in a different religion and they had a different culture, and spoke a different language. The Jews also had different dietary laws, and kept up with the Jewish tradition of eating only kosher foods. The Jews celebrated different holidays and did not work on Shabbos because according to our religion, Shabbos was a day of rest.

Just because the Jews had a different way of living, the hateful anti-Semites made up all kinds of lies and they accused the Jews of being evil and superstitious. They also said that the Jews were cheaters, bloodsuckers, parasites, lazy, unfriendly, and they could not be trusted. The anti-Semites said that all that the Jews cared about was money, nothing else, because they were money hungry. All these things that the anti-Semites accused the Jews of, were of course, false. The Jews could not convince them that all of these accusations were not true, so the anti-Semites kept on hating the Jews unreasonably.

The anti-Semites always said that the Jews did not blend in with the local population, in other words, they did not follow the crowd, especially the religious and the Orthodox Jews, who were identified, mainly because they wore different clothes than the others.

Why did this matter? Where did it say that everyone had to dress alike or believe in the same religion or live their lives according to others and follow others rules and regulations in order to blend in with the rest of the people? Where did it say that anybody had to blend in with everyone else? Why couldn't people live the way they wanted to, and the way they felt comfortable with, and worship the religion that they were born into, and dress the way they choose, and manage their life the way they felt that was best for them?

After all, it was their life and I think that nobody, especially all of the prejudiced anti-Semites, even when the Polish government gave them the authority to treat the Jews any way they wanted to, according to my thinking, they were wrong and they did not have the right to condemn the Jews for being different. They should have behaved more civilized.

The Jews had their own way of living and that was why the anti-Semites hated the Jews, because the Jews did not follow anybody. They were putting a label on the Jews and they said that the Jews were not one of them.

These common anti-Semites, who did everything in their power to belittle the Jews in any way they could, were determined to do anything just to break the Jews spirit, and they were angry that they could not succeed. The ignorant, hateful, anti-Semites always had one thought on their mind, to hate the Jews. That was all they knew, to hate, rather than to love. They did not even try to get along and accept one another, and most of all to respect each other's differences.

I always thought and I still do think that no matter what kind of clothes a person was wearing or what religion they believed in, and what their race, or language was, we were, and are all God's people and all of us must be treated with equal dignity, respect and freedom. I also think that we should love each other instead of hating each other.

I also know for a fact that in a home with a family and a certain amount of children in it, every child will be different, and they will have different characters, different habits, different ways of dressing, different ways of talking, walking and more. This does not give the parents a reason not to love them the same and not to treat them equally, just because they may all be different. I am sure that this would not be right or fair to anyone, to be categorized because of their different way of living and doing certain things.

# PART TWO

# CHAPTER XVII
# THE BEGINNING OF WORLD WAR II IN 1939
# AND THE RUSSIAN OCCUPATION
# OF THE EASTERN PART OF POLAND

The first tragedy for me was in 1936 when my father died. The second tragedy happened when I was not even ten years old and the war broke out. It started in September 1939. I felt that the whole world around me collapsed, and all of our lives fell apart in minutes. I remember that I went to my girlfriend's birthday party, and I came home very late. As soon as I came home I went straight to sleep and because I was very tired I fell asleep right away.

In my sleep I felt like I was having a bad dream or a nightmare. I heard loud pounding and funny noises. Suddenly, I felt somebody near me. I opened my eyes and I saw my mother leaning over me and shaking me. She kept on hollering, "Wake up, wake up". I still thought I was having a nightmare, but the nightmare turned into reality. When I saw everyone running around in the house without knowing what to do, right away I started to get scared. I jumped out of the bed. My mind was not too clear yet and I was very confused. I could not understand what was happening, and to hear the loud noises of the planes made me more scared.

We children really did not know what was going on, but my mother already could figure it out that this was the beginning of the Second World War. We all ran over to the windows and we saw the German planes, the Luftwaffe flying over our heads. They were flying so low that we could see the pilot. The planes made a big loud noise and in a couple of minutes they dropped the bombs. This was the first time in my life I heard such a loud noise and so much commotion.

It was a big surprise to everyone, because nobody suspected that there was going to be a war. Even the Polish Army was not ready for it. Besides that, they could not put up enough resistance to fight the planes, which were flying and throwing bombs. The Germans attacked Poland by air. We did not see any German soldiers in our city, we only saw German planes dropping bombs all over the city. The first bomb that they dropped was very close to our house. They were probably trying to bomb the jail, which was a few blocks from our house. Instead the bomb fell on the house next to ours and it exploded. This house was demolished in seconds and right away our house caught on fire.

Everyone got scared and confused. I remember that my mother pushed us out of the house without any clothes on our backs and she said to me, "Take the children and go into the synagogue with them", but none of us wanted to go anywhere without our mother. The synagogue was about three blocks away from our home, but we did not move from our house. We stayed near the door and we waited for our mother, after all, we were only like babies, ten years, eight years, six years, and four years old.

I remember it very well, we all kept on crying without a stop and because I was the oldest child I tried to calm them down and tried to keep them together, but I also could not stop crying. We were all very scared and confused about the whole situation. The noise of the bombs, the fires, and staying outside without any clothes on, and being barefooted, made us even more scared.

My mother grabbed some clothes and after she ran out of the house we followed her. I still remember that she gave each of us some clothes to put on, and while we were running we tried to dress. It was a big commotion. Everyone kept on running and crying and screaming and the bombs kept on flying over our heads. Finally, we ran into the building, which was the synagogue.

Everything still stays in front of my eyes until today. A lot of our neighbors were killed from the bombs right away. A lot of our homes, stores, buildings, workshops, and factories were demolished. Everyone was running in different directions. In no time the entire synagogue was filled up with people who were lucky enough to have survived the bombs. The bombing did not last too long. We still could hear the planes flying, but from a distance. In a while we had heard the news on the radio that the Germans occupied the western part of Poland, but nobody yet came to our city, which was in the eastern part of Poland. We were all wondering what was going on. We kept on having trouble on top of our troubles. Now we did not have a place to go home to, we did not have any clothes to dress with, and we did not know what to expect next and for sure we did not like the situation that we were in.

My mother tried very hard to keep calm and I tried to do the same. In a while everyone calmed down and the children started to relax more freely, but in my heart I felt very badly about not having our home anymore. I remember that I was standing on a chair near the window of the synagogue and even though it was three blocks away I could see the fire very clearly. I was watching our house burning to the ground and I felt very sad and depressed. I still heard the blast of the bombs in the city, but from further away.

The Ukrainian and the Polish hooligans (hoodlums), who were always anti-Semitic, saw that they now had an occasion to use their talent of being common thieves and wild animals, very freely and without any interruption from anybody. They knew that now they could act very openly. They also knew that nobody would stop them from doing anything that they always wanted to do to the Jews. It looked like they were waiting for this moment to show the Jews how much they hated them.

We knew all along that they were not our friends, but until that time when the war started on September 1, 1939, they were a little more discreet and they acted in a more civilized way. Some even pretended that they liked the Jews, but when the war broke out, right away they started to show their real colors. Until then they were not openly anti-Semitic. Now, since they were free to do what they wanted to do, they thought to themselves, why not. They figured this was their chance to grab whatever they could, and of course, they used the occasion to the fullest and did everything that they wanted to do all of their lives.

They broke into the Jewish houses and stole their belongings. They called us all kinds of dirty names. They made fun of us and treated us like dirt and they said that we did not belong in Poland and we should go to Palestine. This was all said in spite of the fact that we, too, were Polish citizens. The Jews really did not pay too much attention to their insults. We knew that they were nothing, but low class hoodlums. There still were some nice Polish and Ukrainian people who did not behave this way at all. In general, we always got along very well with all the other nationalities, including the Poles, and the Ukrainians. They lived their lives their way and we lived our lives our way and it was okay with everyone.

After the bombing stopped, we walked out of the synagogue, to see what had happened. It was a disaster. I asked my mother where we will be going to live from now on and she said to me, "I don't know." Then my mother left me in charge to look after my brothers and sister and she went to see if the stores were still standing. Luckily for us, the two buildings of the stores were okay. At least we had a place to go into. In the back of the store there was like a little kitchen, with a table and a few chairs in it, and that was all.

I helped my mother with whatever I could. We moved into one of our stores. Whatever we could salvage from our burned home, we did and we took these few belongings to the store. No one came to us yet. We still did not know what was going on, and everyone was very confused with the situation that we were in. The only thing that we heard on the radio was that the war had started. It was the year of 1939 when the Nazis came into Hrubieszow (Rabeshoiw). This was the western part of Poland where my grandmother and my third uncle with his family were still living.

My mother got very upset because she knew what the Nazis were doing to the Jews. She read the newspaper and she knew that Hitler started with killing the Jews in Germany in 1933 and that was why she was scared for her mother, her brother and family. We still did not know what would happen to us, who would be coming in, if it would be the Germans or the Polish or the Russians or who else?

After the bombing, a few days later, we heard on the radio that the Russians were not too far from our city. On September 17, 1939, the Soviet Army, the Russians, occupied the eastern part of Poland, including our city. They sent their troops into Poland from the east. When the Russians came into our city, it started to get busy. They came in with their katchushas (tanks), army trucks with soldiers and it became lively. Everyone was very happy that we got the Russians, instead of the German Nazis, because everyone knew what the Nazis were doing to the Jews. With them around it was a sure death for us, but with the Russians at least our lives were not in as much danger as it would be with the Nazis. That was why the Jews were especially happy with the Russians. They hugged the soldiers and many Jews believed that the Russians were our Messiah. It seemed to everyone that it was the best thing that could happen to us and I thought so too. At least our lives were not threatened and no matter what the Russian Communists will do at least they were not killing Jews like the Nazis were.

Very soon everyone started to have doubts about Communism. The people started to resent the Russian politics and their ways of doing things. For instance, the very first thing that the Russians did was to open the doors of the jail and let the war prisoners out. Of course, every prisoner claimed that he was a war prisoner, so after releasing all of the ferbrechers (criminals) such as, killers, rapists, thieves and others, everyone was scared to walk the streets. The other thing that the Russians did was that they organized peoples police units to control the people in the city. They had a lot of volunteers, right away, mostly young boys who were very excited to carry weapons and boss everyone around.

Some people, especially the poor, were extra happy with the Russians because they knew that the Russian Communists did not like rich people. They called them burzuje (rich). The poor people saw that now they had a chance to get a good government job in order to feel and become important. They volunteered for the peoples police. They walked the streets of the city with rifles on their shoulders and they were very proud of themselves and very happy that instead of having to take orders from others, they could now give orders and the others had to obey them.

The Russian Commissar ordered everyone to register for Russian citizenship and if they did not want to become a Communist and refused to take Russian citizenship they were sent to Siberian labor camps or they were put in jail. Some people were sent to build new bridges and roads. If the Russians suspected somebody of being involved politically and not being loyal to them or being burzuje (rich), they were either put in jail or sent to Siberia.

The Russians ordered the Jews to give up their Jewish identity, their religion and culture and become a Russian and a Communist citizen. It did not take too long for the Jews to change their minds that the Russians were not the Messiah, after all. Instead, they were only dictators and they had the authority and power to carry out their plans and their ideas the way they chose to.

The Russians liquidated and closed all the synagogues and the

Jews were not allowed to pray publicly, just because the Russians did not believe in God. According to them, nobody was allowed to believe in God. That was what Communism meant, we had to do what the Communist dictators wanted us to do. In spite of all these restrictions the Jews organized little groups, especially the religious, Orthodox Jews, and they prayed secretly. They met in houses, cellars, and attics and in other hidden places that they could find in order to davinnen (pray) and somebody always stood on guard. The Jews had to have at least ten men in a group to be able to pray. This group was called a minyan.

The Jews used to meet secretly in the synagogue. They met not only to pray, but it felt better to get together and they felt not so lonely when they met with other Jews. They talked about their lives and how the routine of their living had changed from good to bad. The Jews were depressed and worried by not knowing what the outcome of this war would be. Every Jew knew that it was no good with the Nazis because our life was in danger every minute of the day. It also was no good to live with the Communists, either, because we did not have a life of our own and our life did not belong to us anymore. Only the Communists had the authority to control our lives for us, the way it fit them and was to their satisfaction.

After the closing of the synagogues, the Russians closed Hebrew-Yiddish schools, the Yiddish kindergartens, and fired all the teachers. They also closed all the Jewish organizations. Everything that had to do with religion and was observed by the Jews were forbidden by the Communists. This was the way that the Communists were taking care of religious beliefs, in other words, religion and Communism did not go together.

Our lives and our future did not look so bright, but we had to accept it because we did not have another choice. We thought, after all, at least they did not kill us. No matter how bad the Russian system was, we still tried in the worst way to tell ourselves that whatever their policy was they were still a lot better than the Nazis. The Russian people loved to sing, dance, and drink vodka (samogan in Russian). They also drank a lot of chai (Russian word for tea). They boiled the water in a big samovar (tea kettle) and they drank tea all day long. They liked to make everything look and feel lively and right away they opened entertainment halls with singing and dancing. A lot of people attended these evenings almost every night. The hall was packed with people. Even the peasants came to see what was going on there, especially with no admission charges to go in. Besides that everyone was curious to learn about the Russians and of their Communist ways of living.

In general, the Russians were very friendly and happy people. Every night the hall was open and the Russians had all kinds of entertainment, with singing Russian songs and playing different instruments and dancing different dances, including a Russian Cossachka. By the Russians, a Cossachka dance was their specialty. The Cossachka was only danced the best by one of them, and almost every Russian was dancing this dance.

When the Russians went to the dance, the women dressed up in nightgowns that they had bought right after the occupation. They thought that the fancy nightgowns were party dresses. When the Russians occupied the eastern part of Poland and their wives came shortly after to meet their husbands, they bought all kinds of items, including the nightgowns.

A lot of people from our city went to the hall to see the Russian entertainment and I went, too. We saw the Russian women dressed in their nightgowns. Of course, it looked really funny to us, but the Russian women did not know any better. They thought they were really nice evening gowns. In Russia they did not have too many fancy items, especially fancy nightgowns. In Russia, the Russian people lived on cards, which were like money. That was how they got paid for their weekly work. The wages that they earned every week was hardly enough to buy food. They really could not afford to buy luxurious things that they could manage without.

The Russian soldiers did a lot of shopping in our city. They bought a lot of watches, shoes, rugs, jewelry, furs, hats, lingerie and whatever they could find. The storekeepers were forced to stay open and sell off their stock without replacing it and the Russians took the money away from them. After the storekeepers did not have anything left to sell, the Russians liquidated the properties. Besides the fact that the Russians did not believe in religion they also did not believe that people should have the right to manage their own life and their own belongings. According to the Communists, everyone and everything had to be controlled by their government, which was the Communist party, and the Communist way of doing things.

For a while we were happy with the Russians in spite of what kinds of unreasonable things they did to us financially, and religiously. At least we felt that with them our lives were not in danger like it would be with the Nazis. That was why we were not complaining too much and we tried to be happy with everything that came along, but the happiness did not last too long. The Communists in no time at all had control over us. Nobody was allowed to make a move without their permission. After they took care of all the people's belongings in the cities they started to take care of the farms. They got the farmers to agree to their rules and regulations. Very soon the government had control over all the farms and they made out of them, kolchozes (cooperatives), it meant that everyone was working collectively together.

The peasants were working on the farms, but they did not have any legal right to them. The Russian government took away their farms and they managed them the way they wanted to. This was their way of running a country. They were Communists and there was nothing that we were allowed to do or say.

In the time of the Communist occupation, we had to live and obey all their rules and regulations. All in all, everyone felt like they were in a prison and they were scared of their own shadow. Nobody was allowed to say a word because the Communists had a lot of spies in the city. From September 17, 1939 to June 22, 1941, we were under Communism and it was very hard for us to get used to it. We had to get adjusted to a very different way of life from what we lived before. They took our buildings and the stores, with the merchandise, away from us. Because our house burned down, the Russian government gave us permission to live in the store for the time being.

After the Russians took everything away from us, the Jews used to make jokes about it. The Jews said that by the Nazis we would be sent to death, but by the Russians we were sentenced to life in prison. The Russians divided the Jews into three categories, those who were already in prison, those who were now in prison and those who would soon be in prison. The Jews called them Bolsheviks (Communists). Everyone tried to accept everything the way it was, no matter how it looked good or bad and every Jew was hoping and praying that it should not get worse. Most of the Jews, especially the Orthodox Jews, used to thank God for everything, like for instance, "if a Jew had an accident and he broke one foot, he thanked God that he did not break both feet".

Very soon after the Russians occupied our city, they opened a Russian school. Anybody who wanted to learn Russian and had good grades in elementary school could attend this school. The school was called Desatiletka. It means it was a ten-year school. The classes were taught in the Ukrainian language. If anybody knew the Polish and Ukrainian language, it was much easier for them to learn Russian. The Russian language was a very nice language, but it was very hard to learn Russian because the way they wrote Russian was not the way they were speaking or reading it. I also signed up for the classes. It took me almost a year to learn to read, write and speak Russian.

No matter how anti-Semitic the Russians were, they did not allow anyone to use dirty language or name calling against the Jews (Yevrei-in Russian). If somebody called a Jew parshywy Zyd, (dirty Jew), it was illegal and they were given a jail sentence. The Russians kept on saying that they were our friends. In Russian they called us towarishche (it means my friend).

We lived under Communism and under this system nobody owned anything anymore. The outlook for the future was not too bright. We were living without any rights to anything, like refugees. We were not allowed to say anything because they had a lot of secret police, like the NKVD and the city police. If they did not like what we said or what we did, they would send us to Siberia or to prison without a hearing. This was the Communist way of doing things. The rich people were sent to Siberia and they took everything away from them. They called them burzuje (rich) in Russian. The others who they thought had committed a political crime, no matter what nationality they were, Poles, Jews, or Ukrainians were also sent to prison, or to Siberian labor camps.

The Russians were with us about twenty-one months, but the prisons were overcrowded with the so-called guilty ones. Most of the people were sent to Siberia. At the time of the Russian occupation we did not have any private businesses open to be able to buy certain things. The only place that we could get anything was in their magazins (stores) that were under their control. If I remember correctly they were called lawotchka, in Russian. In order for us to be eligible, and to be able to buy there, we had to register with the Russian authorities. After the registration they gave everyone a card to get food. They did not have too many magazins like this in our city, so, of course, the lines were very long. In order to get into the magazin in the morning, we had to stay in line all night long, so hopefully we would be able to get some food.

Everyone in our family stayed in line the whole night. A lot of times, when it was our turn to be next, they were out of everything. This happened a lot of times to a lot of people. After a whole night of staying in line, we came home without any food. Everyone was very disappointed, tired and hungry. Even my mother did not know what to do and she could not figure out how to buy anything. From the beginning nobody had any connections with anybody who knew where we could buy some food. My mother thought that even if some people did know where to buy any food they would be scared to say anything because with the Russians nobody trusted anybody.

In a while, the people started to form a black market. The dealers of the black market were buying their food illegally, and they sold it the same way. When they started the black market, from the beginning, the dealers of the black market sold some food only to people who they knew. They were very careful and they did not want to deal with everyone because if they would be caught they would be sent either to prison or to Siberia. They figured that all of their business would not be worth risking their freedom. Because in our city we had a lot of collaborators who reported to the Russian authority, whatever was going on. The black market dealers tried not to deal with just anybody, in order to protect themselves, and avoid all the danger.

My mother was very worried because we children did not have enough to eat and my mother did not have a source to be able to buy anything. Finally, she decided to look around and tried to get in contact with somebody, and eventually she got to know some people who dealt in the black market. From the beginning my mother bought a lot of items from them. Of course, the prices that they charged were very high, but she did not have another choice than to pay what they were asking for in order to have some food for us children. She kept on looking around and eventually she got to know the suppliers and these were the Russians who were in charge of the magazins or lawotchka (stores). They stole the merchandise that we were supposed to get on our ration cards, and they sold our food on the black market. That was why there was not enough food for everyone.

It was not fair what they did, but my mother did not know what to do. She had to decide between buying food from the supplier or letting her children go hungry. She also knew if she would not buy it from them, they would sell it to someone else. No matter how badly she felt about what they did, she thought that her children came first and she started to buy everything that the supplier had to sell, not only food, but she bought clothes, also. She bought for us and for our friends and neighbors because they did not have any connections with anybody and they needed food for their families, too.

I still remember that all of our friends and neighbors looked up to my mother because they knew that she was a businesswoman and that she would always try her very best in order to accomplish what she had to, and usually she always did. She always tried to help people who needed her help and anything they needed she would go out of her way in order to help them. That was why everyone always liked her.

When my father was still alive, he was only involved in his job and in our religion, but my mother was involved in other things besides her own personal life. My mother took care of everything else. Besides being a nice person and a good businesswoman, she was a good mother. No matter how busy she was, she always worried about her family and she always saw to it that everyone had what they needed, especially enough food in order not to be hungry.

Even when it was a big change in our living from a big house to living in the store now, in one room, we all had to adjust and get used to it. Whatever happened my mother always said, "Gamzool - L'tovah", the meaning of it was, "Thank God for what it was because it could still be worse." In spite of the fact that she had to take care of everything and everyone by herself, she was wise enough to know that she had to do it, without expecting anyone's help. I always acted very brave, also, even when there were times that I was really scared to do certain things, but I never let my mother know that, and I always stuck by her side.

Because the Russians took most of our merchandise from our business away, and we hardly had any income, my mother had to find a way to earn some money. She knew some people who had an oil business before the war so she made a deal with them. They gave her oil to sell in order for her to get commission. My mother and I smuggled big cans of oil to Kovel and we made a couple of shillings (Russian money). I remember an incident that happened to us. One time we were sitting on the train and the cans were standing on the side of the seat near us. The NKVD (secret police) came over and they saw the cans.

They asked my mother what it was, so my mother said that she does not know because it did not belong to her. Of course, right away they took the cans away. We turned back home without oil or money, but at least we were not arrested. It was a good thing that my mother made an agreement with the people who owned the oil, that if something like this would happen she did not have to pay for the oil, so it was their loss.

My mother managed to take out some merchandise before the Russians liquidated our two stores with all of the goods. Little by little, she sold whatever she could on the black market in order to have some money and to be able to buy some food for us children. She was really at risk of going to prison or being sent to Siberia. This worried me a lot, because if they would catch her, we children would be left all alone without a mother or a father.

In our city, in my time, there were very few cars. We had to be very rich to own a car. We mostly traveled by horse and buggy or by train. Suddenly, the traffic in our city became unbelievable, like bumper-to-bumper traffic. It was very noisy in the city from all of the cars, which were passing all day and all night long. When the war broke out in Poland, in September 1939, the Jews passed through many cities and towns that were already under the Nazi occupation and they hoped to be able to cross the border. Our city was about 20 miles from the German and Russian border. The border was between Uscilug (Nistila- Yiddish) and Hrubieszow (Rabeshoiw-Yiddish).

When the Germans and the Russians made a non-aggression pact with each other and it was signed by the Soviet and German leaders, they divided Poland by the western part of Poland and the eastern part of Poland. The border between them was the whole length of the River Bug. The German and the Russian armies met near Brest Litowski. The Germans occupied the western part of Poland and the Russians occupied the eastern part of Poland.

September, October, November, and until the beginning of December 1939, the Russians had their borders open. Before closing the border whoever wanted and could run away from the German Nazi occupation did. In the beginning of the war, my mother went to see her mother and her brother with the family. They had a discussion with each other and my mother suggested to them that maybe it would be better to live with the Russian Communists instead of with the Nazis, but they did not want to move. They really did not believe that the Nazis were as bad as people were saying. My mother was a very strong-headed person, but she was not certain enough if it would be right for her to try to persuade them of doing something that she herself was not sure of. Jews from the eastern part of Poland were going west and Jews from the western part of Poland were going east. No one really knew what the right thing to do was.

Some Jews did not want to live with the Communists and some did not want to live with the Nazis. Most of the Jews were very confused and they could not make their minds up what they wanted to do. According to their thinking, no matter what side they would choose, it would not be a good decision and they were right. It was and it looked like they were "going from the frying pan into the fire".

The Jews who came from the western part of Poland by crossing the border, told us what was going on there. We really did not want to believe that the Nazis were committing mass murder and killing the Jews. We really could not believe that such barbarism existed and that this was really the truth. One day my mother and I took a walk to see what was going on in the city. We thought that maybe we would see somebody we knew.

Suddenly, my mother saw a Jewish man walking the street, and she recognized him right away. He was a neighbor of her parents, my grandparents, in Hrubieszow (Rabeshoiw) and he had lived there all of his life. My mother was very happy to see him, and talk to him. She started to ask him how her mother was doing and how her brother and his family were getting along. The man did not answer her, instead he just looked at her with a sad face. She asked him again and finally he told my mother that the Nazis had murdered them right away.

My mother said that it was all her fault, because if she had talked everyone into going to Palestine long before the war even started, they would all be alive now, especially when my uncle who was already there wanted all of us to leave Poland and come to Palestine. She felt very guilty and kept on blaming herself for everything. I think, that even if she had tried harder to persuade them, they would probably not have listened to her anyway. Maybe they would and maybe they would not.

She really did not know for sure if she would have been able to make them do what they did not want to do, but in her mind she was still thinking that it was her fault.

She kept on asking herself all kinds of questions, like why she did not try hard enough to persuade everyone to leave Poland and why did the Nazis have to kill them? There was nothing that she could do for them now and everyone told her that it was not her fault that her family did not want to leave their homes to go anyplace else. Deep in her heart my mother knew that it was not her fault, but she still could not accept the fact that the Nazis killed them. She kept on feeling guilty and very upset about her loss.

Nobody imagined that such an intelligent and educated nation like the Germans would do such inhumane things. Finally, after many months of keeping the border open, the Russians closed the border. When the border was closed and whoever wanted to cross from the western part of Poland to the eastern part of Poland, had to come on their own. They could do it by smuggling themselves over, or bribing the Russian guards to let them pass. The Jews that knew the territory there, and lived nearby had a better chance of passing the border faster. Most of the people left on foot. A lot of the refugees escaped the Nazi occupation by dressing like a peasant (farmer) on the day of the yarith (bazaar). The refugees who passed the border lost themselves in the crowd. They passed, but they did not stay in our city.

Our city was only a transit area because as fast as they passed the border and they came into our city, they made all the preparations to get away from Poland as soon as possible. They could stay in our eastern part of Poland and live under Communism, but they chose not to. Not only did they not like the Nazis, but they also disliked Communism. In order to leave Poland, no matter what kind of transportation they got, or even by foot, was good enough for them.

They took a train or whatever they could find to leave the area, and they kept on going to different countries, wherever they could go and whoever would let them in. Most of the countries did not open their borders for refugees (homeless people) and many had to turn around and come back. Of course, they did not go back to the western part of Poland, so they stayed with the Russians.

Everyone tried to save their own lives. There was a lot of confusion in our city. In a way, we were very happy that we did not have to run anywhere and we could live in our city and in our home, even if it was only in our store. Most of the people did not like the Russian Communism. We all knew that under Communism everything that we owned would be taken away from us. We also knew that the Russians at least would not murder us and that was what made us happy. Besides that, the Communists made the poor people very happy because, first of all, they did not have anything to take away from them and second of all, they took everything away from the rich people, so now everyone was equal. This was the Communist way, nobody was richer than the others, as a matter of fact, everyone was just as poor as the others. Except, of course, the leaders, they all became rich.

I remember one morning, when I got up earlier than usual, right after breakfast I went to the park, which was just four blocks from our store where we were living. I used to go to the park very often, I was sitting on a bench and reading my book. It was always nice and peaceful in the park and I loved to sit and read there. Usually the park in the morning was almost empty. To my surprise, this particular morning, the park was full of people, mostly Jews because it was a Jewish neighborhood. I saw a lot of Jews, gathering in little groups and talking very quietly to each other. Living with the Russians, we had to be very careful what we said because they had a lot of spies and secret police all over the city. Me being so very anxious to know what they were talking about, I walked over to one of the groups and I overheard their conversation.

Everyone was saying something else and they all seemed to be very upset with the news. I still did not know what the news was. Then I overheard one of the Jews in the group saying that he heard on the radio that the Nazis planned to attack the eastern part of Poland. It meant the part that was under Russian occupation was going to be attacked. I rushed home to tell my mother what I heard. She tried to keep calm and decide on what to do. She knew what the people told us in the beginning of the war, that when the Nazis invaded the western part of Poland, right away they started to murder the Jews. That was why whoever could run away from the Nazis did. The Jews finally started to believe the truth that the Nazis were really murdering the Jews. They had already killed, my mother's mother, my mother's brother, and his family. Whoever could, was running away from the Nazi occupation just to try to save their lives if they could succeed.

My mother started to think and speculate about what would be better to do and where we should go. She said maybe it would be better to go with the Russians to Russia instead of waiting for the Nazis to come to our city and kill all of us. Every Jew knew that in order to survive the Nazis, they had to run. Everyone was thinking about it, but nobody could make up their mind fast enough. Actually, the Jews did not like to live with the Communists, either, and most of the Jews were disgusted with the whole situation and they gave up. They said, whatever will be, will be. Before my mother made up her mind about what to do, the Nazis were in our city and it was too late to go anyplace or to do anything. The only thing that we could do was to pray to God and keep on hoping that somebody in the world would help us.

# CHAPTER XVIII
# THE NAZI INVASION AND THEIR OCCUPATION
# OF THE EASTERN PART OF POLAND IN 1941

On June 22, 1941, without any warning, the Nazis attacked the eastern part of Poland, which had been occupied by the Russians since September 17, 1939. The outbreak between the Nazis and the Russians did not last too long. It was not a big battle, but it was a big surprise to the Russians because they did not expect that such a thing would happen. After all, they had made the non-aggression pact between each other, on August 23, 1939 and on September 28, 1939, it was signed, but this did not mean anything to the Nazis. In spite of the pact, the Nazis pushed the Russians out of the eastern part of Poland, and now Hitler occupied the western and the eastern part of Poland.

The Russians did not know that they had made a pact with the devil. They thought that Hitler only hated the Jews, and with his anti-Semitism, hatred and blaming the Jews for everything, the Russians thought that this really did not concern them. Hitler thought of the Jews as being the lowest human beings in the world and he called the Jews untermenschen (subhuman). The Russians were sure that this did not have anything to do with them, either.

Unfortunately, for the Russians, Hitler liked them just as much, and in the same way that he liked the Jews. The Russians found this out, only not soon enough that the joke was on them after all. I was sure that the Russians really were very disappointed that they were not Hitler's favorite people and instead, Hitler hated them just as much as he hated the Jews, in spite of his pretenses that he liked the Russians. The Russians also found out that Hitler only played a very good game with them in order to use them for his purposes and unfortunately for the Russians, they fell into Hitler's trap.

Adolf Hitler was the most evil man in history. He had nothing but hatred in his heart for all humankind, but most of all he picked the Jews to be his victims (scapegoats). The Russians felt very good by thinking that Hitler was their friend.

The Russians did not expect that Hitler would break the pact that they had made together and they would be attacked. Hitler's only reason to sign the pact was to invade Polish territory without interference from Russia, and when Hitler was settled in the western part of Poland, he was ready to carry out his plan that he made from the beginning of the war. He knew exactly what he was going to do. On June 22, 1941, Hitler broke his non-aggression pact with Russia and chased the Russians out of the eastern part of Poland.

The Russian soldiers were surprised and confused and they did not know themselves what was going on. It came so suddenly and unexpectantly that the Russian soldiers did not even receive any orders from their superiors and they did not know what they were supposed to do. Every Russian soldier had to decide for themselves how to act and what they should do. Because they did not have a leader, and they were all on their own, each Russian soldier was forced to make their own decision. Some Russian soldiers ran towards Russia and some Russian soldiers ran the opposite way. They probably lost their sense of direction and a lot of them were caught by the Nazis and they were shot. Some Russian soldiers wound up in the forest.

Now the Nazis occupied our city, Wlodzimierz Volynski, and now we knew what we could expect. Everyone knew it was the beginning of the end for the Jews. On one side we had the Polish and Ukrainian anti-Semites and on the other side we had the Nazis and between both of them we all knew that we never stood a chance of surviving and coming out of it alive. As soon as the Nazis chased the Russians out of the territory and they occupied the eastern part of Poland, the Nazis started to take over.

Most of the people were standing in the streets waiting to see the German soldiers. The Jews were also among the crowd, including my family. I still remember that first, the German patrolmen came in on their motorcycles, and they checked out our city. Then the tanks and the army trucks came in with German soldiers. Their uniforms were sparkling clean and they wore highly polished boots. Looking at their murderous faces, we knew right away what we could expect from them. Everyone was scared of them. Very shortly after, the German army followed them, on foot. Now we were under the Nazi regime and we already knew what would happen to the Jews. We knew what they did to the Jews in the western part of Poland and we also knew that they would do the same here. In spite of knowing this, we really could not help ourselves because we had no way out of this situation.

That same day, the Nazis placed posters all over our city, warning all the people in the city that whoever would help the Jews by giving them food or hiding places would be shot with their families. After this announcement, of course, even Poles who were once our friends were scared to talk to us or help us in any way.

In spite of all of these warnings, the Polish underground organization named Zegota, started to help the Jews. They found them safe hiding places, they gave them money and food and they did whatever they could to save the Jews and tried to prevent them from being murdered. The Zegota organization was against the Nazis. They did not agree or approve of murdering people because of their religion and belief. We also had a second underground group, the AK, and this group was part of the Polish army, (Armia Krajowa), the army of the country. It was a political organization made up of many groups and each group had a different way of acting and doing certain things.

Some groups were against the Jews and some groups helped the Jews by doing whatever they could. In our city we had a minority of Poles who tried to save Jews by taking them into their homes and hiding them until the war was over. They really risked their own and their families' lives by helping the Jews, but they felt very strongly about it, and they did it in order to have a clear conscience. They felt that they had to do what they could in order to save human lives. Others only pretended to be a friend by saying that they would help and after taking all of the Jews belongings, they did not want to know the Jews anymore.

The Jews had a reputation of being very dignified and polite, but apparently Hitler did not think so, or maybe Hitler really knew that it was so. That was maybe the reason of getting rid of the Jews because he was hateful and he thought that the only way to get rid of them was to kill all of the Jews. The Nazis, of course, under Hitler's orders, immediately searched out Jewish leaders, and they killed them. They got rid of professionals like teachers, politicians, writers, craftsmen, judges, nurses, entertainers, lawyers, and doctors.

The way that Hitler acted by getting rid of the intelligent Jewish people, made it very obvious that he had an inferiority complex and by his actions, it looked like he was scared and jealous of the Jews. The other classes of Jews, like the religious and plain working Jews, were left alone for a while. He thought that with the religious group of Jews, the Nazis could amuse themselves by making fun of them, and with the working class of Jews, he could work them to death, so he let them live a little longer and work, until the Nazis would decide that they did not need them anymore. Then they would be murdered. That was how it was with the life of the Jews.

When the Jews could not work like slaves anymore, they were shot on the spot or they were taken out of town to the death pits to be shot. After all, Hitler and his followers were the judge, jury and the prosecutor and Jewish lives were in their hands. Most of the Jews could not imagine or believe that this could or would happen to us. But some Jews were realistic and smart enough to face the reality and they knew that if they would stay with the Nazis they would be killed by them. They decided at least to try to do something about it and they thought that their life was more important than all the wealth in the world and they were right.

No matter how rich or poor some Jews were, they left everything behind, and they tried to save their own lives. They were running away from the Nazis to different countries and different places only to try to survive and by doing this quite a few Jews did survive in spite of Hitler's wishes.

Most of the Jews did not want to leave their homes and businesses behind, and everything that they had worked for all of their lives. I think most of us, especially the Orthodox religious Jews who never believed in violence and murder, really could not believe or accept that such cruel things could and would happen to us and that we would be murdered for no reason at all.

They kept on believing that this cannot and would not happen to us because we were good and honest people and no harm would come to us because God would help and protect us from evil. God would not let anything bad happen to us because we were God's chosen people. The religious Jews also believed that the Messiah would come soon and a miracle would happen and we would all be saved from the Nazi murderers. The Jews never lost their faith in God.

The Orthodox religious Jews preached to everyone that we would not be harmed or destroyed and whatever God was doing, it was for the best. We had to accept everything that was happening, gamzool l'tovah, meaning this, too, was for the best, because this was God's will. Many Jews believed that the blessing of the rabbi would protect them, but some Jews were so scared of losing their lives that they were praying for the Messiah to come and save them and their family from death. Everyone kept on praying for different things, but mostly everyone was praying to be spared from their death. Everyone was talking to God and asking him to help us.

I think that this praying was like a crutch to lean on. They had an expression that "a drowning man will grasp at a straw". I think that the Jews knew and they felt that their lives were in danger, but nobody wanted to admit it, not even to themselves. Instead, the Jews closed their mind to it, and they pretended that nothing bad would happen to them, even though deep in their hearts they felt that all the praying in the world would not change our hopeless situation that we were in. We also knew there was no way out of it and this was our goyrel (destiny) to be killed by the Nazis.

Hitler made his plan a long time ago, to eliminate the Jews and to erase them completely off the face of the earth, he even wrote a book in jail, Mein Kampf (My Struggle), and I still remember my mother talking about it, but I did not understand too much at the time. Even though Hitler told his plan to the world in every detail about what his intentions were to make Europe Judenrein (free from Jews), nobody paid the slightest attention to it. He kept his promise and carried out his evil plan without any interference from anybody.

Since the world existed, nobody and no one before Hitler had tried to murder an entire religious group of people from all over Europe and the world. Nobody was as close as Hitler to succeed in murdering and erasing all of the Jewish population. He had to thank the world and their silent bystanders for not standing in his way and letting him carry out his barbaric plans. The fact was that by not taking an interest in stopping his brutality, this meant that the whole world agreed with him and they were with him and against the Jews. In my opinion they were just as guilty as Hitler and the Nazis. We knew that we were dead before we even were dead. In spite of knowing that we did not even have one chance in a million of surviving, we were still praying to God to help us. We were hoping that God would help because nobody else would, and nobody else did.

My mother kept on saying to us, "Children, keep on praying to God and everything will be okay", and we really believed her. I think we believed her because we wanted to believe her, but I also think that deep in our hearts we were all scared to think otherwise. When Hitler came into power, he started to poison everyone's mind with his speeches, his propaganda and his lies. He kept on saying over and over again and drilling in everyone's mind, that the Jews were rich and they took the wealth away from everyone. He said only one strong leader was needed to run any country and with his lies he succeeded to make everyone believe that the Jews were no good and that they were evil. According to him it would be the best thing for everyone around just to get rid of the Jews. Most of the Jew haters started to agree with him.

Very soon, he had a lot of followers believing him, especially the anti-Semites. There were also other categories of low class, common hoodlums who were failures all of their lives. These kinds of people stuck with the Nazi party because the Nazis gave them wealth and power, and for this they became followers and they really did not care about good or evil. They did not worry about how many Jewish lives they were destroying as long as they were making the Nazis happy, and most of all they were happy by being murderers and killing as many Jews as they could.

When the Nazis came to our city, they took our souls, our happiness, our laughter, our dreams and our hopes away from us. Right away, they started to murder Jews on the street. They shot them like wild animals and left them lying there. The Jews were treated like dirt. They were beaten to death, laughed at, pushed around by the Nazis, spit on, and the Jews took all the brutality, cruelty, humiliation and much more, only because they did not have another choice. First of all, the Jews did not believe in killing and the second reason was that they could not defend themselves without weapons.

The besoylem (cemeteries) were vandalized, the Jewish miceivys (the stones on the graves) were pulled out and thrown anyplace, the Jewish homes and businesses were demolished, the synagogues were destroyed, Jewish siddurs (prayer books) and talles (prayer shawls) were burned, together with the Torahs, which were also destroyed. The Torahs were the most holy possessions of our faith because everything that happened in our religion since our world existed was written in the Torah. In our Jewish religion, we considered the Torah to be our most precious possession. The Torah always was and still is to this day, our most important belief.

The Nazis gathered together the Orthodox Jews and told them to sing and dance, and they were standing and watching this so-called show that the Jews put on for them by having to obey the Nazis orders. They were laughing and amusing themselves by doing these shameless acts with the Jews. They thought that they had to get the last laugh out of the Jews before they murdered them. After this show, they chased these Jews into the synagogue, together with more Jews, and locked all the windows and doors and they set the synagogue on fire and all the Jews got burned to death. Whoever managed to make their way out of the synagogue, were shot anyway. No matter how anyone looked at this, the fact was that the Jewish people were the Nazis victims. They had no life, no future, no hope, only death to look forward to under the Nazi regime. We were in hell every minute of the day and night. The Nazis caught Jews in the streets and brought them to the marketplace and they shot them. They gave the Jews very little food and in no time, many Jews already suffered of starvation and eventually they died. They gathered the Jews together from around our city and they took all of their belongings away. Whatever the Russians left behind, after they were forced out of our city, the Nazis confiscated and they took all the goods and the Jewish properties away.

They took away the merchandise and liquidated the Jewish businesses. They blocked the Jewish bank accounts and they took all of our savings. I do not think that anyone could or should call this a war. I call it terrorism and hold-ups because the terrorists or the hold-up men attacked innocent people who did not have a chance of defending themselves. That was what the Nazis did, they were hold-up men and gangsters. They caught the Jews, and plain and simple, shot them in cold blood, for no reason except that they were Jews.

The Nazis took everything away from us. The Jews had to surrender all of their jewelry, gold, cars, furs, bicycles and all their possessions. They shande (shamed) us, especially when they cut off the beards and payahs (side burns) of the Orthodox Jewish men. The beards were symbolic to them and they showed that they were a part of the strictly Orthodox Jewish religion. The Nazis made fun of us in the street in front of everyone.

We were not allowed to ride the streetcars, the train, not even a rower (bicycle). They had a curfew set only for Jews. They took our pride, our dignity, our self-respect, our belongings and the final solution was that they took our lives away from us. They treated us as being less than human, worse than any animal. Many of the Ukrainian and Polish Goyim (hoodlums) were just as bad as the Nazis were to us. They were a group of anti-Semites and they were very happy to see what the Nazis were doing to the Jews.

Most of them could not wait long enough to get rid of the Jews. They said that the sooner they will get rid of the Jews, the better it would be for them because they would be able to take all of the Jewish belongings for themselves. Sure enough, they accomplished just what they wanted to. These hoodlums never had anything in their lives that they had to work for and suddenly, thanks to the Nazis, without even lifting a finger of earning it, they became rich with our Jewish sweat and blood. The hoodlums did not care how they got it as long as they got it. They knew exactly where the Jews were living and where they were hiding and they informed the Nazis of it. Right away the SS or the Statspolizei (City Police) came and they took the Jews away. From then on they were never seen again.

A Polish man once told his girlfriend that in the outskirts of our city, near his village, where he had his farm, one day he saw the German Gestapo shoot all the Jews and throw them into the ditches (pits). The girlfriend, right away, told her Jewish friends about it, but they still did not believe that it was true. This was how we got some information of Hitler's actions, because some people worked nearby, and others lived not far from the pits. Some people worked with the underground and they told us what was happening. The people who lived in the villages could see and hear the shots, the screaming and crying of the Jews and they were very upset by it.

# CHAPTER XIX
# THE GHETTO IN OUR CITY WLODZIMIERZ VOLYNSKI

Very shortly after the Nazis came into our city, they made a ghetto. The ghetto was like a prison. A barbed wire fence surrounded the ghetto. The German and Ukrainian guards patrolled the ghetto walls, especially the ghetto gate. They made sure that nobody would be able to escape or nobody would come into the ghetto. Besides patrolling the ghetto they also put up signs on the ghetto fences and they warned the outsiders not to come near the fence. They said that this was an infected area and it was under quarantine.

I think that the reason for it was that they did not want us to have any connections with people on the outside of the ghetto because they did not want them to bring food to the Jews. This way the Nazis would be able to accomplish what they wanted to, to starve us to death. Maybe they thought that we would give them our valuables. I was sure that they had their reasons for doing this and I also think that they did not want anybody to know how the Nazis were treating us. The other reason, probably, was to cut the Jews off from everyone and everything in order that we should not know what was going on in the world. The Nazis thought that by us communicating with people from outside the ghetto, we would get more information about our situation and of their intentions towards us. I did not know exactly what their reason for it was, but I was sure that they knew why they were doing it.

When we had to move into the ghetto, we could take only what we could carry on our backs and the rest of our things we had to leave behind. The Poles and the Ukrainian Goyim (Gentiles) moved into the Jewish homes and they made themselves at home. They acted like our homes belonged to them and they took everything for themselves, including the furniture, all of the household items, and clothing. They took everything that the Jews had accumulated all of their lives by hard work and scraping and putting a penny with a penny together, in order to have a roof over their heads. The anti-Semites took it with the intention of keeping it for themselves. They knew that Hitler's Nazis would see to it that the Jews would never return to their homes and everything eventually would belong to them. That was what they were waiting for. Unfortunately, they did not have to wait too long for it.

I was put, with my family, and all of the other Jews, into the ghetto. The ghetto houses were run down, and none of the houses had any toilets or running water. We could stay in our store because our store fell into the area of the ghetto. They appointed six more people to live with us, in one room. We had to wear armbands with a yellow Star of David in order to be recognized by everyone that we were Jewish. Occasionally, somebody tried to sneak out and mix with the other people in the city.

Even when the Jews were successful in doing this, and even when they took off the armbands with the Star of David, unfortunately, most of the time, they were still recognized by the Polish or Ukrainian police and they got shot anyway. The ghetto only had a few streets. The conditions in the ghetto were terrible. It was very crowded and we had very poor sewage facilities. The water system became contaminated and very shortly after, we had an epidemic in the ghetto.

The Jews started to die and the dead Jews were lying in the streets of the ghetto without anybody paying attention to them. From the beginning, some workers from the city came into the ghetto everyday to take out the trash. They tried to repair the plumbing, to fix the roofs and they tried to do whatever they could to make it a little better and a little easier for us, but no matter what they did, it did not work too well.

Every time the workers came into the ghetto, they always smuggled in some food, clothes, or shoes and they sold it to us for a high price. A lot of times, Polish people came into the ghetto to deliver something. They also smuggled in some food for their Jewish friends. A few nice Gentile people tried to help the Jews and they risked their lives and their families' lives by bringing food into the ghetto. Sometimes a little shiksaleh (Gentile girl) came with her mother and she carried some food for us. She was less noticeable than an adult, because she was a child.

My mother knew a lot of nice Polish people. She also knew some Ukrainian people with whom she was dealing with in business for a lot of years. They liked our family, and they brought us food in exchange for some items that were left from our stores. The conditions in the ghetto were awful. Some Jews got sick from dirt so they caught all kinds of diseases from each other and they died before they were killed. Some Jews died from hunger and some Jews walked around like the living dead. They suffered from starvation and in spite of that, they were forced to work at slave labor. Very soon they lost their faith of surviving and they shrunk up. Their eyes looked like a dead person's eyes and they walked around in the ghetto like they were not in this world anymore and eventually they died. Along with my family of five of us, we had six more people in our room and we were very crowded. There was no place to move around and everyone bumped into each other.

There were at least 20,000 Jews in the first ghetto. We did not have any baths in the houses and women, men and children slept in one room. I remember that we children carried the water from the well in order to be able to wash ourselves. So did everyone else. We filled up a big pot of water and with a sheet we made a curtain in a corner of the room and that was how we washed ourselves.

After ordering all of the Jews into the ghetto, the Nazis told us that this was for our own good and they kept on saying that they will take good care of us. They talked to us like we were brainless and we do not understand anything. The Nazis thought of us as if we were less than nothing and we had to take all of their abuse and humiliation without saying one word because we really did not even have one chance in the world of winning. We had to make peace with our goyrel (destiny) and accept whatever was going to happen to us, even though we knew better that the reason the Nazis made a ghetto was to put the Jews into one area in order to have control over them.

In the beginning, the Nazis used the Jews for all kinds of forced labor and in the end, when they decided that the Jews were of no use to them anymore, they murdered them. We knew it because people from the western part of Poland, while the Russians occupied the eastern part of Poland, ran away from the Nazis and they came to us and told us what was happening in the west. Some Jews still believed what the Nazis were saying to us, that they would take good care of us. The Nazis were right, because they really took good care of us, only it was the other way around. They took care of us by killing us.

We had a communal kitchen in the ghetto, and they divided the food between us. The first Jews who suffered from starvation were the

Orthodox Jews because all of their lives they ate nothing else, but kosher food, so they could not accept another way of eating. In the ghetto, to observe their strict traditions and religious beliefs was impossible.

Our religious way of living, especially the Orthodox way, was to keep kosher, which meant to butcher the animals in our kosher ritual method. Our customs were that we had to eat only kosher food prepared according to the religious law, and to have two sets of dishes, one set for dairy food and one set for meat. We also had to have two sets of pots and pans. Most of the Jews stopped being kosher because they realized that they had only two choices, either eat what they could get or starve from hunger and die. Most of the strictly Orthodox Jews chose the other way and they decided that they would rather starve to death than break their traditions. In no time their bodies got weaker and weaker until they collapsed and died from starvation.

A small group of Orthodox Jews believed that it was more important to stay alive than to worry about our traditional ways of preparing the food and they ate whatever they could get. They decided that it was better to survive and live than to starve and die. They had a saying that "Hunger breaks iron".

We Jews were living in the ghetto and from one day to the other none of us knew what would happen to us. The Nazis had their plans made for us a long time ago, and they were getting ready to do the job that Hitler wanted them to do. Since they now had us all in the ghetto, they started to carry out their murderous acts, and to kill as many Jews as they possibly could. They did not have too many Gestapo in our city and because there were about 20,000 Jews in the first ghetto, the Nazis recruited a lot of Polish and Ukrainian Goyim (Gentiles) to help them by being policemen. They were more than happy to do all the dirty work for the Nazis. They had been anti-Semites all of their lives and now they had a chance to get rid of the Jews so they told themselves, " Why not?"

These Ukrainians and Poles were nobodies before the war, and now, thanks to the Nazis, they felt important. They had enough food, they carried weapons and they could kill as many Jews as they felt like killing. They knew that the Jews had no guns to fight back, and even if they would fight back the Nazis would kill one hundred or two hundred innocent Jews for one Nazi, in order to show the Jews that they would pay a price for putting up a fight.

Life in the ghetto was very depressing, no one was laughing or talking, everyone was preoccupied with their own thoughts. The garbage was all over the ghetto, in spite of the fact that the workers were supposed to come into the ghetto to collect the garbage and the corpses. The bugs and lice ate us alive. In no time we had an epidemic of scarlet fever, dysentery and many other diseases. The Jews were dying like flies and many Jews were lying frozen on the streets.

No matter how sick we were, we had to go to work or we would be shot. The Jews had to report to work every morning. Jews that specialized in some trades or professions had a permit from the Gebitz-Commissar (like a Mayor), and they were assigned to a steady job. Those without a permit were sent to temporary jobs. I was taken to a different job everyday. My mother worked in the communal kitchen in the ghetto and my sister and my two brothers were doing different things in the ghetto, also. Whatever they were told to do by the leader, they did.

Every morning, I was loaded into the army trucks together with a group of Jews and we were taken out of the ghetto to be put to work. An armed Nazi guard watched us all of the time. If for some reason or another, he did not like the way we were working he shot the Jew on the spot. Because I did not have a steady job I was taken to another place and to another job everyday. One job was just as bad as the other job, but I had to go to work everyday in order to try to survive.

The Nazis promised to take good care of us and they did. They interrupted our lives. Right away we had to move to the ghetto leaving everything behind. The minute that the Nazis came to us, we stopped living. We were terrified all the time, but in spite of everything, we kept on hoping that nothing bad would happen to us. Even when we saw death in front of us we still did not want to face it. I guess that we chose to believe what we wanted to believe, even by knowing that they had already taken away our freedom, our homes, our pride, our dignity and soon they would take our lives away from us.

Still, in spite of the Nazis barbaric treatment towards us and all of this brutality, humiliation, starvation and death, we did not want to face the reality and we chose to live in a dream world. We told ourselves that God would help us. The Nazis could not break our spirit or belief, especially the Orthodox Jews. They said that God was right and his mishpit (judgment) was right. The Jews went to their death by saying that this was God's will and he knew what he was doing. Most of the Orthodox Jews felt the same way.

In spite of these bad conditions in the ghetto, like not having enough food, or a clean water supply, and all of the time we were living in great fear, we still did not gave up praying and hoping that somebody will come along and help us. Unfortunately, all of our hoping and praying did not help too much because this somebody never came along to help, and to our regret it was only our wishful thinking.

Some Jews had money and connections with nice Polish and Ukrainian people, so they brought them food to the fence and they threw it to the other side of the fence. In exchange, the Jews paid them with whatever they could. These Gentile people risked their lives by helping the Jews, but it made them feel good. They were religious people and they believed in God. They made a date up for the next time when they would meet again at the fence and the Jews hoped that they would live long enough in order to keep the next date.

Some Jews who did not have connections or money got sick and died of starvation because the food that we got from the communal kitchen was very little, and the Jews were hungry all the time. What the Nazis gave us was enough food for us to starve to death, slowly, but surely. A lot of Jews died from sickness, diseases, filth and hunger. To tell you the truth, if it would not have been for the smugglers who risked their lives to sell us some food, for a high cost, naturally, most of the Jews would have starved to death sooner. In no time at all the Nazis would have succeeded in starving all the Jews in the ghetto, but no matter how the Jews tried to get some food in order to keep alive, it did not work too well. It still was not enough to live on and eventually the Nazis succeeded by starving us, only a little later than they expected to.

The little children were also a big help to us and they smuggled in some food into the ghetto. They dug holes under the walls and they climbed through the ghetto fence. They tried to get some bread, potatoes, carrots, and whatever they could find that was edible. While they were out of the ghetto, they also collected anything they could, like clothes and shoes and they brought it back to the ghetto. Sometimes the SS (Security Service) or the Statspolizei (City Police) spotted them and they shot these children on the spot. This did not stop the other children from doing the same thing because they thought that sooner or later we would all be killed anyway so why be hungry now.

I really think that nobody in the ghetto was afraid of dying. I remember that some Jews used to walk around in the ghetto from door to door to collect potato peels and they told lies that it was for their goat. They were too ashamed to admit that actually it was for them to eat. They cooked the potato peels and ate them, just to try not to starve from hunger.

No matter how bad the situation was, many Jews still did not lose their pride. It was for them a shande (shame) that everyone should know that they were starving from hunger. My mother had a lot of connections with the Polish and Ukrainian people that she was dealing with before the war. She also had some money, so she was able to get enough food for our family and tried to help our neighbors and friends, who we knew before the war.

My mother knew that our friends had no connections with anyone to get them some food and they did not have any money to pay for the food, either. She knew them well enough not to come out and say that she wants to give them some food. She also knew that they would never accept anything that looked like charity because their pride would stand in their way. My mother knew that in order for it to sound right, she had to use the right approach, for them to accept the food. She had to use diplomacy and be very careful with her words.

My mother was a very considerate person and she never said a bad word about anybody or to anybody. She was very careful not to hurt anybody's feelings and she was always very generous with everyone and everything. In order not to embarrass our friends it was necessary to say to them that we had a little too much and it would get spoiled and then she asked them if they could use it, and if yes, they were welcome to it. Believe it or not, some Jews would rather have starved to death than to bend their pride.

Some Jewish people gave up hoping that it would ever get better and they would ever survive. These people did starve and died of hunger or a broken heart or both.

# CHAPTER XX
## JUDENRAT (JEWISH COUNCIL)

When the Nazis came into our city, they immediately dismissed the Polish Mayor and a German Nazi took over his job. In German, he was called Gebitz-Commissar. He had the same functions as the mayor, and besides that he took care of the ghetto the way he thought he should. One morning, the German Gebitz-Commissar (Mayor) came into the ghetto and announced on the loudspeaker that everyone should gather in the center of the ghetto. Then he appointed a few Jews to be so called leaders of the ghetto.

This establishment was called Judenrat. The Judenrat was a Jewish Council and they were responsible for carrying out the Nazis orders. The way the Nazis wanted them to do, the Judenrat had no choice, but to do it. By the Nazis orders, the Judenrat had to register all the Jews in the ghetto by age, physical skills and profession. They also had to register all the Jewish properties. They had the responsibility of organizing groups that would be sent to work. Their other duties were to make up a list of Jews to be deported. Nobody really knew where the Jews were being sent to, but everyone tried to guess and they suspected the worst. Only God knew the truth. Sometimes the Judenrat knew it, also.

The Judenrat had to collect money and other valuables from the Jews for the Nazis, they had to take care of the food distribution so that everyone should get the same amount of it, they had to see to it that everyone was doing their job, but most of all the Judenrat had to be there and wait for the Nazis orders. Whatever their orders would be they would have to carry them out because the Nazis wanted them to.

The Judenrat (Jewish Council) had to do what the Nazis were telling them to do or they would be shot. The Judenrat really believed that by obeying the Nazis orders everyone would survive and be liberated, including themselves. They told the Jews to work hard and everyone would survive. The Jews in the ghetto did not believe the Judenrat and most of the time they blamed everything that happened in the ghetto on them. The Jews did not like anything that the Judenrat did.

They claimed that the Judenrat was showing favoritism to some Jews and they were unfair to the other Jews, like, for instance, the way they sent the Jews to work, the way they divided the food between the Jews, the way they appointed the living quarters, and the way they made up the deportation lists for the Nazis. Whatever the Judenrat was doing was not good enough for the Jews, and most of the time the Jews were right.

It seemed to the Jews like the Judenrat was really showing partiality and they were treating their own families and their own friends much better than the other Jews and they always got special privileges. This was not fair to all the other Jews. They even have an expression that "it is not what you know, but who you know". Sometimes, even when the Judenrat really tried very hard to be fair and they were fair in a lot of ways, the Jews still did not believe them. In some situations a lot of the Judenrat members were decent to the Jews, but it still was not good enough and the Jews still blamed everything on them, in spite of it that the Judenrat also was in danger, just like we were. When the Nazis did not like the way the Judenrat was carrying out their orders, so among the other Jews that the Nazis took out of the ghetto to be shot, there also were the members of the Judenrat.

After they shot the first Judenrat, they appointed a second and a third Judenrat. First, they asked for volunteers, but of course nobody in their right mind would volunteer to carry out the Nazis orders and send our people to their death. Also by not obeying the Nazis orders, they knew very well that their own lives would be in danger and they would for sure be sent to death themselves. That was why no one was willing to take this job. Because they did not have any volunteers, the former chairman of the Jewish community was forced, by the Gebitz-Commissar, to pick some Jews in order to establish another Judenrat.

The new Judenrat knew exactly what their assignment would be and they also knew what the consequences would be for not obeying the Nazis orders. The Judenrat was always in constant fear because they knew that if they were to carry out the Nazis orders, they would not be able to avoid any harm to the Jews. In plain language, it was not possible to do anything right for the Jews. No matter what the Judenrat did or did not do they could never win, because they had to obey the Nazis and carry out their orders, which were always against the Jews and in favor of the Nazis.

# JEWISH POLICE IN THE GHETTO APPOINTED BY THE JUDENRAT

The Judenrat appointed Jewish police to see that the Jews were doing their job. The most corrupt Jews in the ghetto were the Jewish police. They took bribes and pay offs from the Jews in exchange for favors. For example, the Jewish police did not send these Jews to work, they allowed them to smuggle food into the ghetto, they gave them a bigger portion of bread and they had many other privileges, all for a price, of course. The Jewish police helped the smugglers for a bribe, and a lot of times they did their smuggling themselves in order to sell some food to the Jews, because there was always a shortage of food. I think at a time like this and in the situation that the Jews were in, they mostly thought of surviving the Nazis, instead of having morals.

Still and all, it seemed to all of us that a lot of times, the Jewish police showed a lot of brutality towards their own Jewish people. One of their jobs was to help the Nazis gather together the Jews in one place and watch them so they would not run away. The Jewish police did exactly what they were told to do by the Nazis and they watched the Jews very closely instead of looking the other way and give the Jews a chance to get out of the group and be able to hide.

In spite of the fact that the Jewish police knew very well that this group of Jews would be deported in order to be killed, they still did not try to help the Jews. When the Nazis gave an order that all the young men should gather in the center of the ghetto, the Judenrat with the Jewish police saw to it that they did. The Nazis then came with their military trucks and they took them out of town to be shot.

The Judenrat told the rest of the Jews that the young men were working in other ghettos and they were all okay, and soon after they would be finished working there, they would be back here. Everything that the Judenrat told the Jews was a lie, and the Jews did not believe them anyway. Most of the Judenrat members were really disturbed by it because they knew the truth. They knew that the Nazis killed all the young men, and the Judenrat told the Jews in the ghetto a lie.

Occasionally, a Jew came back from the death pits and told us about the mass executions of the Jews. The reason he survived was by just being wounded and pretending to be dead. When the shooting stopped and he did not hear anybody around, he dug himself out of the pits. He was an eyewitness and saw everything that was going on there. After the Nazis got rid of the young people, they gave an order to the Judenrat that all the professional Jews and whoever was an expert in his trade, should gather in the center of the ghetto and the Judenrat, with the Jewish police, saw to it that they did.

The Nazis took them out of the ghetto and they, too, were never seen again. According to an eyewitness, we all knew what happened to them. Polish people who lived near the death pits saw everything that happened to the Jews. The Judenrat leaders also knew from the beginning that by gathering the Jews together for the Nazis, they all would be shot. In a short time, the Nazis killed the young men, the professionals, the trade experts, and very soon after this, the Nazis started to get ready for the next killing.

When the Nazis gave the Judenrat an order to make up a list of women, children, weak, sick and old Jews, the Judenrat had to decide who would be on this list to be deported and be killed. They knew exactly whoever would be on the list that they made up, would be killed by the Nazis. It felt to the Judenrat that they were killing their own people and in reality that was what it was. Every time the Judenrat made up a list for the Nazis, they knew for sure that these Jews were being sent to their death.

It was a very hard and painful decision for the Judenrat to make. If the Judenrat would decide not to make up this list, they knew for sure that the Judenrat members would be shot. On the other hand, if they decided to make up this list they would have it on their conscience. No matter what their decision was, they were always the losers. That was how the Nazis worked. They carried out their murderous acts by using one Jew against another Jew. The Judenrat also was made up of Jewish people and they had the same will to survive like anybody else. They were forced to carry out the Nazi orders or else.

They decided to make up a list of the old, the sick, those who were almost dead and would die soon anyway and those who looked like they gave up and wanted to die. All of these Jews were on the list. The Nazis always wanted something and the Judenrat had to follow their orders in order for them to stay alive, at least for the time being. They knew that they also would be sent to death as soon as the Nazis would decide that they did not need them anymore, and no matter how they tried to carry out the Nazis orders it was never good enough for the Nazis anyway.

Under all of this pressure, some members of the Judenrat had it on their conscience. They started to face the fact that they were sending innocent Jews to their death, so they decided not to follow the Nazis orders anymore. The Judenrat members knew what the consequences would be. It would be death for them, but that was their choice and their decision that they made. Some members of the Judenrat decided to commit suicide themselves before the Nazis killed them.

Other Judenrat members under these circumstances did not have in their mind or on their conscience that what they were doing was wrong. They told themselves that they were only following the Nazis orders. Besides that, their will to survive was so strong that they really did not care about anything or anybody else except themselves. When they had access to the ghetto food supply, to the bakery, to the public kitchen, they took what they wanted, like bread, potatoes, and everything else that they could take. They took for themselves, and for their families, they practically stole the food that had to be divided between so many other Jews.

These Jews were selfish and they thought only of themselves, in order not to be hungry. They tried to survive, no matter what it took. They were never thinking that maybe the other Jew had the same rights as they did, and they should have the same chance of trying to survive by not starving to death. These selfish Jews did not care about others, only about themselves. It really did not matter to the Nazis how hungry, sick or tired we were. We still had to do everything that our leader told us to do.

Every morning, a few of the Judenrat leaders and the Jewish police had a group ready and the Nazis loaded us into trucks and took us out of town to be put to work. All day, we worked with no breaks and very little food or water. Everyone got very tired and weak from such long hours of working. The Nazi guards watched every move we made and the way we were doing our job. If the guard did not like the way we worked, he called us to step out and then we knew right away that it was the end of us.

Some Jews could not keep up with the others. When the Nazi guard spotted them he called them to step out of the line, and he shot them on the spot and left them lying there like nothing happened. After all, he had only killed a Jew. I still remember the incident that happened to me and it still stays in front of my eyes. Once I was working near the train station, moving railroad tracks from one place to another place. The Nazi guard probably did not like the way I was working, but he did not tell me to step out. Instead he came over and started to holler at me and called me all kinds of ugly names. All this time he had his gun pointed at me and I really was very sure that he would shoot me, but he did not. It was like a good angel was watching over me.

He stopped right in front of me, grabbed me by my shoulder and threw me on the railroad track. I remember that I laid there for a while and then I heard him hollering that I should go back to work. The pains were unbelievable and I knew that something happened to my back. With all my strength I forced myself to get up and go back to work. I knew I must work if I wanted to stay alive and not to be shot by the guard.

When I came back to the ghetto I could not move. My back pains were very bad. I started to think that it would be very impossible for me to go to work tomorrow. I knew that I have two choices, either I would try to live with my pain and go to work wherever they sent me or I would give up and not go to work and be shot for it, because when we were not able to work the Judenrat put us on the death list. Right then I decided that no matter how I felt and in spite of all the pain that I had, I must force myself to go to work every day. That was if I wanted to stay alive and maybe then I would have a chance to survive the war.

I worked in different places. I worked in the fields, I dug potatoes and gathered together the corn. I worked in vegetable gardens, and I watered the vegetables, pulled the weeds out, and picked the ripe vegetables. I worked in the factories and I did all kinds of work there, like helping seamstresses by taking the finished pieces of cloth, making bundles and putting them in the right place. I swept and washed floors. Sometimes I could sneak a couple potatoes and some vegetables from the gardens into the ghetto. Other times the working people in the factory gave me some clothes to put on and keep. A lot of times, the people from outside the ghetto felt sorry for me and they tried to help with what they could without being caught by the Nazi guards.

Some nice people, when they passed me, sometimes on purpose, dropped some money and I picked it up. Sometimes they threw bread or other food next to me. They had to be very careful doing it, because if the guard would see what they were doing, they would be shot.

The hardest job was when they took me to dig ditches. I could not understand what the ditches were for, but I had to do what the Nazis told me to do. I asked the other Jews what the ditches would be used for, but nobody knew at first. Nobody could imagine that they would be used for burying all of us. I never knew that I was digging my own and my family's graves.

After coming back to the ghetto from such a hard job, I was so worn out and tired from working all day that I could not think straight. I was exhausted, not only physically, but also emotionally and mentally. My whole body and mind was drained and I really did not care about anything anymore. Most of the time, I felt that I had enough of all the misery. I knew that it would not get any better, only worse and I had nothing good to look forward to. I knew that tomorrow would only be worse than today and usually it was.

In our city, they had a public school and a Hebrew school. All the children in the city could attend public school, but the Hebrew Jewish School was only for the Jewish children who were attending this school in order to learn Hebrew. When the Jewish children were not allowed by the Nazis to go to the Hebrew school or any other school to learn anymore, the Hebrew school building stayed empty. After a while, the Nazis took over the building and they cleaned the building out, their own special way, of course.

The Nazis burned all of the Hebrew books and threw out the Hebrew pictures and Hebrew notebooks. They cleaned out everything. The school building became completely empty. It was as though there had never been a school there and that nothing had ever gone on there. Because of my memories, I knew better. I remembered that this place was once full of life with beautiful, Jewish children and I knew that once this now empty building was filled with wonderful sounds, a lot of activities and laughter, but what once was full of life is now full of death, thanks to the Nazis.

It was a big school building and the Nazis eventually used it for all of the things that they took from the Jews after they murdered them. A lot of Jews worked in the school building. I was also sent to work there. We had to put everything separate, for example, shoes went in one pile, dresses in one pile, skirts in one pile, blouses in one pile, and coats in one pile. In other words, everything had to be separated according to the items.

The work was not hard, but it was a very emotional job because we knew that when they brought a new transport of clothes we were sure that the Jews to whom the clothes belonged to were not alive anymore. Ukrainian and Polish people used to come there to buy clothes and other items like furniture, jewelry, furs, paintings, and many more items that were left by the dead Jews. Everything that was a part of the Jewish life and belongings could be found in the school building.

Even cars and bicycles were sold there. Thousands and thousands of items that were all taken from the Jews were brought to this building to be sold. The people from all over the city would come in to buy things. Everything was sold for practically next to nothing. The Nazis wanted to get rid of all of these things, the sooner the better, because they needed the space for the next transport of the dead Jews belongings.

The people who came into the school building to buy all kinds of items knew very well to whom all of these items once belonged to. Some Polish and Ukrainian people who came to buy really did not care about the Jews to begin with. They bought what they liked. Some people who came in to buy looked at the items and thought about what was happening to the Jews and after a while they walked out without buying anything, as though they felt sorry for us. I thought that they would feel guilty by wearing the Jewish things and knowing that the people who these things belonged to were killed. Their conscience probably would bother them. These people decided that they did not want all of these bargains, instead, they would rather have a clear conscience and peace of mind.

The Nazis came into the school building, not to buy, but to take everything that they wanted. They took the most valuable things, like paintings, furs, gold jewelry, diamonds and all of the treasures that they could find. They took everything without paying a penny, then they sent it all back to Germany. A lot of Nazis never had anything in their life, and now thanks to Hitler, they became rich. This was also the case with the Ukrainian and Polish anti-Semites, those Jew haters who stole all the Jewish belongings for themselves.

Some Polish people came in, not to buy anything, but to tip us off when an oblava or pogrom would take place in the ghetto. They worked like an underground movement. Some worked as waitresses in restaurants where the high-ranking Nazis would come in to eat, they would try to overhear their conversations and then they would inform our Jewish leader about it. Some had a Nazi boyfriend in order to get some information and then they would pass it on to the Jewish leaders of the ghetto. Some Polish girls worked as maids in a high-ranking Nazi home and while they cleaned the Nazis home they collected a lot of information there. Some men worked as butlers at Nazi parties, and they listened to their conversations when the Nazis were drunk and were not too responsible for what they were saying at the time. The butlers understood German so they knew every word that the Nazis were saying. All the information that the underground collected, they informed our Judenrat and the Judenrat told us what was going on.

Believe it or not, some Nazis were forced to become party members against their will. They even hated to think about what Hitler was doing to the Jews, but they could not say anything because their own family would suffer. They really did not approve of what was going on and they were very disturbed by it. They tried in a secretive way to tell us when to watch out. When we knew when an oblava (raid) or pogrom would happen, we had a better chance to survive by going into hiding, but most of the time even when we knew when it would happen, we really did not have a place to hide. In the beginning nobody had a hiding place because almost nobody believed that we would need it. Besides that, we were cooped up in the small ghetto and there were not too many places to hide that the SS and the dogs would not be able to sniff us out.

# CHAPTER XXI
## THE OBLAVAS (ROUND UPS)

## FIRST OBLAVA (ROUND UP)

The Jews who were weak or those who really lost their will to fight in order to live knew very well that the chance for their survival was very slim and mostly hopeless. They gave up and were murdered right away or they just died. Jews, who still had a will to live, struggled to survive any way they could. These Jews, tried to get into a skrytka (hiding place). They hoped that the Nazis would not discover them and they would be spared from death for the time being. The official murdering of the Jews started with the first oblava (raid). Whoever had a skrytka (hiding place) ran into it in order to hide there. The Nazis kept on hollering for the Jews to come out and line up.

Those Jews who obeyed the orders of the Nazis to come out of their houses and their hiding places to line up, were sent to their death. They were taken out of town to the execution pits in order to be shot. I remember when the Nazis came into the ghetto with rifles, guns, and German shepherd dogs and they dragged everyone out of their houses. They told the Jews to line up in the center of the ghetto and then when they thought that they caught all the Jews that they intended to catch, they loaded them into big trucks, took them out of town and they shot them there.

The Nazis had different police units, like SS (Security Service Police), Gestapo (Political Police), Statzpolizei (City Police), Wehrmacht (Secret Police), and Einsatzgruppen (killing squads), which was a special group of police and they called them death squads. This was a special Nazi killing unit whose duty was to make the city Judenrein (free from Jews), to kill Jews on the spot or to transfer them to the execution pits. This group got special privileges from Hitler. They could pick their own method about how it would be best for them to kill the Jews. They came into the ghetto with their German shepherd dogs and they let them loose. Then they gave the dogs orders to jump on the Jews and tear them apart. I saw it with my own eyes and I have lived with these memories all my life. Many times, I think that maybe we were punished by God for some reason.

Besides the Nazis, they had Polish and Ukrainian followers who joined the Nazis hand in hand. There was a group of them who hated the Jews enough that they were willing to do all the horrible deeds and sometimes, they were worse than the SS in torturing the Jews.

They also had a Polish underground movement that worked with the Nazis, like spies, and they could and did kill Jews. Their job was to weed out the Jews from their hiding places and kill them. At the time of the oblava (raid or round up), which lasted about a twenty or thirty minute period of time, the Nazis came in and tried to catch as many Jewish people as possible. Then they rounded them up in one place, and they chased them into the army trucks and took them away to the pits on the outskirts of the city to be killed.

Everyone was running, not knowing where they were running to. It seemed to me that everyone was following each other, my family, me and some of the other Jewish people, maybe about fifty Jews, were running into the same empty house. We were standing in the living room, pressed together like herrings and we did not know what to do. Everyone was very scared and confused.

I was almost near the door, when suddenly the door opened and a young Ukrainian guy in a German uniform came into the house with a German shepherd, which he was holding on a leash very close to his side. I recognized him right away because I went to the Desatiletka School (Russian) with him at the time when the Russians had come to us September 17, 1939 until June 22, 1941. For almost two years they opened the school for the children who wanted to learn Russian. Only those children who had good grades in public school were accepted to the Russian school. Apparently, this Ukrainian guy had good grades in public school, so he was accepted to the Russian school, and he also attended the classes.

I remember it was evening courses and it was in the big public school building. A lot of children got accepted, so the Russians had a lot of classes and all the children were beginners, of course. I was in the same class with this particular Ukrainian guy. I still remember that he was sitting in the front of the middle row and I was sitting on the left side of the row. The classroom had three rows of seats and there were a lot of children in one class, at least thirty-five and one teacher.

This Ukrainian guy was a little slow in learning Russian and the other children used to laugh at him. He felt very embarrassed and I felt very sorry for him. One day I asked him if it would be okay with him if I would help him with his lessons. He agreed to it and he thanked me for being willing to spend my school breaks helping him. On our class breaks, I helped this young man with his lessons as much as I could and he was very thankful for it. I remember that he also liked when I spoke to him in his language, Ukrainian. I learned to speak Ukrainian when I used to come into my mother's store and I spoke to the peasants in Ukrainian. The peasants spoke only the Ukrainian language. Apparently, not too many peasants were interested in learning Polish, so most of them did not know the Polish language.

After the Russians retreated and when the Nazis came into our city in 1941, the Russian school was closed. From this time on, I never saw this Ukrainian guy again. Suddenly, he reappeared in front of me wearing a German uniform and as a collaborator for the Nazis. I never really dreamt that he would join the Nazi party, but he did. He stood and looked at me and I was thinking to myself that now my life lies in his hands. When he saw me in this house with all of the Jewish people, he looked at me as though he saw a ghost, and he looked very surprised. He looked straight at me and I looked straight back at him, but I did not say anything, not even one word.

He looked at all of the Jews in the room and then he stared into my eyes. I do not know what he was thinking, but the minutes really felt like hours to me. Suddenly, with the leash in his hand, he turned the dog around, facing the door, then he walked out and closed the door behind him. I heard him saying in a very loud voice, to the German Gestapo, "Ne mont iz hire", meaning in German, "Nobody is here". We heard the Nazis talking loud and shouting, but not too close to us. They probably walked to another part of the ghetto. Soon we did not hear them at all.

Everyone was stunned. They could not understand or believe what had just happened. After it got quiet, I told the Jews that I knew him from before, by attending the same classes in the Russian school. I thought that he probably remembered that I was nice to him by helping him when he really needed help in school. He saved my life and my family's life and the rest of the Jewish people who were with me. He could have taken all of us out of town to be killed. It looked to me that I got repaid for my kindness after all.

When it got quiet and we did not hear any more shooting or the dogs barking, we knew that the Nazis had left the ghetto and the oblava was over. After the oblava, the Jews who managed to hide survived this time. They started to come out of their hiding places. Of course, everyone was all shook up. In a while, everyone calmed down and then the Jews started to analyze what just happened. I thought in my mind, "Thank God, my family is okay". I think that in a time like this everyone thinks of themselves.

A lot of the families got separated because everyone was running in different directions to look for a hiding place. With the Gestapo and the dogs around us, nobody could think straight. We did not know what to do or where to hide. Everyone was just running without knowing where they were running to, just like my family and I did. Luckily for us we were spared from death, this time.

A lot of people lost some members of their families, mostly older people who could not run and hide fast enough, so they were killed on the spot. Everyone who survived said, "They did not catch us this time, but they will catch us next time and in the end we will all be murdered anyway", and very soon everyone lost their hope of surviving the Nazis.

Some Jews were very hopeless and they really gave up believing that they would ever survive. They did not eat, they did not wash themselves, they did not talk to anyone, and they looked like they did not belong in this world at all. In other words, they did not have any life in them anymore. These Jews were called Musulman.

The Nazis came into the ghetto everyday and we had to line up to be sent to work. The SS looked us over and when they saw someone who looked like a Musulman, they took them out of the line and shot them on the spot. They sent the rest of us to work and they told us to work hard so we would be okay and they would let us live. We knew that it was a lie. They gave us an order to sing Jewish songs and they amused themselves by laughing and making fun of us. When they saw a Jew with a beard, they cut it off right away.

The Nazis made fun of the clothes that the Orthodox Jews were wearing. They made fun of the way we were talking, and they treated us as though we were less than human. I did not believe that all of the people had to be the same. I thought that everyone had a right to be different and by being different it did not mean that they did not have the right to live in this world. In my opinion, the Jews were, are and always will be just as good as anyone else and we still believe in God. I still think that sooner or later the evil people will get repaid for everything that they did to us.

## SECOND OBLAVA (ROUND UP)

One day, while we were working in the cornfields, the Gestapo came and started shooting at us. I stayed in one place like I was frozen. I probably was very miserable knowing that I did not have anything to look forward to except death. Besides everything else, my back pains were very bad and I was in agony all the time. I really suspected that when the SS man threw me on the railroad track it broke my back. No matter how I felt I had to go to work. A lot of times I thought to myself, why do I suffer for nothing. I will not survive anyway.

At the time, while the Gestapo were shooting at us, I really did not care whether or not I would be shot. I still remember how I felt after every shot that was fired. I shook like I was getting an electric shock. The whole scene still stays in front of my eyes. I saw Jews falling to the ground. I do not think that I felt anything. I was just staying in one place and watching the Gestapo running after the Jews with the guns and they kept on shooting at them.

I think that the fear made my mind and my body feel paralyzed and I did not move from the spot. I could only see with my eyes. I really cannot explain how I felt or if I felt anything. The only thing I do remember very clearly is that I stayed in one spot and looked in one direction. I really do not know if at that time I knew what I saw or understood exactly what was going on. Suddenly, somebody grabbed me by the hand. It was our group leader, a Nazi.

The leader of our group was an elderly German man, and he was a Nazi party member. In spite of him being a Nazi, also, for some reason or another he grabbed me by my hand and he ran with me into the barn, then he threw me into a pile of hay and covered me with it. After it quieted down from the shooting, it felt to me like I was waking up from a deep sleep. The first couple of minutes I did not even know where I was and how I got in there. After awhile, I started to hear voices and crying. Finally, my memory came back to me and then I knew what happened. Slowly, I dug myself out of the pile of hay and I came out of the hiding place. I saw that most of the Jews, about fifty people, had been killed, and all I felt was a lot of pain and sadness and I started to cry. The Nazi leader who saved my life ordered whoever was left, to get into the truck and he drove us back to the ghetto.

# THIRD OBLAVA (ROUND UP)

A few days later the Nazis, with the Ukrainian police and German shepherd dogs came into the ghetto in the middle of the day, and they grabbed as many Jews as they could and took them away to the outskirts of the city to be shot. They caught everyone that they could during this time. Nobody knew when the oblava would take place. Luckily for us, there were not too many Jews in the ghetto during daytime, because every morning most of the Jews were sent to work out of the ghetto.

The Nazis had the same procedures and the same routines for everything that they were doing. They were following Hitler's orders step by step. When the first oblava happened in our ghetto, we had no idea of knowing what to do and how to save ourselves from being killed. After the first oblava (raid), every Jew was very aware of the danger every minute of the day. They knew that when they would see the Nazis with Ukrainian police coming into the ghetto, they would have to run and try to hide. Whoever managed to avoid getting caught was spared from being killed, this time.

# CHAPTER XXII
# THE POGROMS IN OUR CITY
# WLODZIMIERZ VOLYNSKI

## FIRST POGROM

Sometime in September 1942, the day began with the same routine. Everyone was sent to work like any other day. Nobody in the ghetto suspected anything and nobody had even the slightest idea of what would happen very soon. We always heard rumors going around, but the Jews took them very lightly and they told themselves that they were only rumors. Nothing serious, even when they saw the Nazis catching the Jews at the time of the oblava (raid), the Jews believed that the Nazis sent them to work someplace else and eventually they would be back.

My mother had a steady job in the communal ghetto kitchen and my two brothers and my sister had some little jobs in the ghetto, also. I was sent to work outside the ghetto every morning to different places and different jobs. This particular morning they sent me to work in the potato fields. We always worked all day until five o'clock PM, and then they brought us back to the ghetto, but on this day they did not bring us back from the field at the usual time and right away my instincts told me that something was wrong. I still remember that the guards stopped at a gas station and they filled up their tanks with gas as if they were getting ready for something.

Nobody in our group noticed anything, but I could not shake off the feeling that I had. It felt to me that something very bad would happen to us very soon because nothing that the Nazis did this day looked like any other routine day. On the contrary, it was altogether different. They brought us back to the ghetto very late. After working all day, I was very exhausted mentally and physically. I remember that when we came back from work and we were near the gates of the ghetto, they did not let us in.

First, a Nazi guard stood at the gate and searched everyone. This never happened before. Usually when they brought us back from work, they always dropped us off at the gate and we walked to our living quarters without anyone searching us. Now I thought to myself that my intuition was right and I started to get scared. I had a very funny feeling about it, but I could not know why I felt this way. My mother and the neighbors were working in the ghetto all day, so they heard news about anything that had been said in the ghetto. They heard all kinds of rumors going around about what might happen.

When I came into the house, I saw that some of the neighbors were sitting around the table and they looked very worried. Now I knew for sure that something was very wrong. I started to ask, "Why is everyone here? Why is the place full of people?" At first, nobody said anything and instead of answering me they tried to avoid saying something to me. I kept on asking the same question over and over again. What was wrong? Finally, they said that they were expecting a pogrom.

Everyone was sitting and waiting and thinking about what they could do to save their own life and the lives of their families. Everyone knew that any minute the Nazis would run in and kill all of us. My mother was sitting near us children and tried to keep us calm.

It was in the middle of the night when we heard the Nazis shouting. We knew that the Nazis were in the ghetto. This was September 1942, when the first pogrom started. I was almost thirteen years old at the time. The Nazis ran into the ghetto with guns and ordered everyone to get out of their houses. They were screaming, "Arous, fafluchte Juden" (cursed Jews). They yelled, "Arous, faschmutzte Juden" (dirty Jews). Our living quarters were one big room and below all the length of the room was a big cellar. When the Nazis started to holler to come out, and if we obeyed and would come out, my mother knew, for sure, that we would go to our death. The idea came to her in seconds that maybe the cellar would be a better place to hide than to sit in the room and wait for the Nazis to come in and take all of us out without us even trying to save our lives.

My mother quickly made the children get into the cellar and we did. The neighbors who came to us, about twenty-five people, ran into the cellar also. We stayed there very still in the dark. Very shortly after, the Gestapo ran into the house, and they found the cellar door. They opened the door and they started shooting into the cellar, but the bullets did not reach us. They started screaming for us to come out, but nobody moved and everyone stayed very quiet. I remember that I thought that my mother was standing next to me, but I was too scared to talk.

Everyone stayed in the end of the cellar against the cellar wall. I had a habit that I always closed my eyes when I was very scared. I stood against the wall with closed eyes. I do not know why, but in my mind I always thought that when I would close my eyes and I would not be able to see anybody, I told myself that nobody would be able to see me either. I stood near the wall, with my eyes closed and I did not move. In a while it really felt to me that I was drifting away to another world, like I was in a trance and I could not think or feel anything anymore. The only thing that I could hear was shooting from far away, even when the shooting was actually very close to us. I was numb and it felt like my body was completely frozen from such fear.

Finally, when it quieted down, I felt like I just woke up and I started to call everyone's name, but there was no answer. Right away, I knew that they had all walked out of the cellar and had left me behind. I did not even know that they had walked out because I was frozen and my eyes were closed. Now I was the only one left. My mother, my two brothers, my sister and all of the other people, had all walked out of the cellar and I did not even know when.

At that time, I felt that my own family betrayed me. I felt that they had to take me with them and we should all be together. I felt that they did not have the right to leave me all by myself. It seemed to me that my whole family deserted me and left me behind, all alone. I have to admit that for a very long time I felt the same way, and sometimes even now, after so many years later, I feel that it really was not fair or right to leave me all alone when I was not even thirteen years old.

When my family was killed by the Nazis, my mother was only thirty years old, my brother was eleven years old, my sister was nine years old, and my youngest brother was seven years old. They did not even have a chance to grow up. My sister and my two brothers were killed before they really started to live. Because of the Nazis inhuman brutality, their lives were taken away from them at such an early age.

The pogrom was in full force and every minute of the day, they caught more and more Jews. After the Nazis caught them, they put the captured Jews into trucks and took them out of town where they had prepared the ditches in advance. These were the ditches that the Jews were digging without even knowing that they were meant for us. I also took a part in digging the ditches when they sent me to work there, without even knowing that all of my family would be buried there and I, myself, was digging their, and probably my own, grave. The pogrom could last a few weeks until the Nazis decided when it should be over.

When the first pogrom was over and the Jews who survived remained in the ghetto, right away they were sent back to work. The SS appointed a group of Jews to bring all the clothing from the dead Jews to the ghetto, in order to search for all of the valuables. After the Jews finished doing this job, the SS also killed them. In a way it seemed to me that the Nazis did not want to leave any living witnesses in order to be able to tell anyone of their brutality because these Jews saw the death pits and they knew where they were located.

The Ukrainian and the Polish anti-Semites took a big part in catching the Jews and helping the Nazis with all of the killing, and after the Jews were dead they threw them into the ditches and covered them with earth. The Nazis tried to cover up the evidence and they probably believed that no one would know the kind of murderers they were, but there was always somebody who saw what was happening to the Jews and they told us.

At the time of the pogrom, the local residents who lived nearby saw what was happening and they heard the shots, screams and cries of the Jewish victims. They could not believe their eyes and ears. No matter how much they disliked the Jews, it was still a shock to them to witness such sadistic cruelty and brutality.

Some people who witnessed these crimes came into the ghetto and told us how it happened. They told us that first the Jews had to undress and they were standing completely nude. Then they had to line up and each Jew was told to move to the edge of the pit. When they reached the edge, they were shot down and pushed into the ditch. Some of them were just wounded, so they pretended to be dead. The SS ordered the local people to bury the bodies by filling up the ditches with earth.

They were residents, who lived not far from the pits, and also living nearby were Polish and Ukrainian goyim who were anti-Semites, and they volunteered for this job. They were happy to do it and many of them took an active part in the murder campaign against the Jews. These nobodies were the lowest elements of human beings without any fairness, decency or compassion to other human beings and like the Nazis they also had the same evil thoughts that the Jews deserved to die, and that was why they must be murdered.

There were also some nice people who witnessed that the Nazis and their collaborators killed innocent Jews and they could not believe it. It was beyond their imagination that this brutality could happen in a civilized world, with people acting like animals without a brain. These brainless people who acted like animals were the Poles and the Ukrainian anti-Semites who helped the Nazis in any way they could to get rid of the Jews because all of their lives they were always jealous of the Jews for being more successful in every way than they ever were. The reason for it was that the Jews were more ambitious to accomplish something in their lives than the Polish and Ukrainian anti-Semites ever tried to be.

A Jewish man came back to the ghetto and told us what happened to him. He said that he was just wounded during the shootings. He was lying in the pit and waited until it got dark. When the shooting died down, he knew that the Nazis had left and nobody was around anymore, so he dug himself out of the pit and started to run away. It was a cold night and he was nude. From the distance he saw a few lit up homes. He kept on running in the direction of the houses until he came to a house. At first he did not know what to do. The only thing that he knew was that he could not stay in the cold too much longer, so he decided whatever would be would be, and he knocked at the door.

A woman opened the door and let him in. She told him to wash up, and she gave him some clothes from her deceased husband to put on. She also gave him some food. He got dressed and ate some food. After he was done eating, she told him to take the rest of the food with him and he did. He thanked her for everything and told her that God will repay her for her decency and kindness and then he left.

This Jewish man was very lucky that he found a nice peasant woman who wanted to help him. If the Polish and Ukrainian anti-Semites who lived near the pits and witnessed all the killing of the Jews, would have seen him they would, for sure, have killed him. A lot of them volunteered to help the Nazis, but some of them remained silent bystanders. They did not like the Jews and they did not like the Nazis, either, so in order to be fair they did not take a part in helping anybody and instead they took care of their own lives.

This same Jewish man who was there and only wounded, who the Nazis thought was dead, also told us that a Gestapo woman in charge said not to waste a bullet on a Jewish child so instead, she stepped on the foot of the child and with her hands she picked up the other foot of the child and tore the child apart. This happened in our city and I think that her name was Madame Priest, if I remember her name correctly.

When they made the first ghetto, there were about 20,000 Jews in the ghetto. We were packed into a small ghetto and the conditions were unbearable. Often, twenty people were living together in one room. We did not have any place in the room even to turn around, but after the first pogrom the Nazis solved the problem of us being overcrowded in the ghetto.

In September 1942, the Nazis murdered 16,000 Jews in our city, including eighty-six members of my family. When the Nazis came to us, I was afraid every minute of the day. I was afraid for my family and for myself that any minute we could and would be killed by the Nazis, and suddenly my fear turned into a reality. I did not have to be afraid for my family of being killed. I did not have a family anymore. My fear turned into anger. I started to get angry about everything and anything and mostly I was angry that my family left me behind, all alone.

I survived the pogrom by staying in the cellar, but I did not feel alive because my family was killed and my family was my life. They were everything to me since my day of birth and suddenly they were taken away from me. My parents taught us children to be a decent, honorable mensch (good person) because that was the way they were. We all believed in God and in the Ten Commandments.

My parents always believed that most of the people had something good in them, that they had some decency, honesty, fairness and goodness in their heart. That was why my parents always gave the people the benefit of the doubt. At this time, no matter what my parents taught me, I was bitter against the whole world. I started to think that my parents were very wrong in their way of thinking, also of believing that God was right and his mishpith (judgment) was right. It did not make any sense to me to lose my whole family and to think that God's mishpith (judgment) was right.

Most of the Jews in our city were religious and many were very religious. The Orthodox Jews prayed everyday, even in the ghetto, and they really believed that God would help them and no harm would come to us. After they saw what happened to the Jews, they felt that God betrayed them and they were angry. Some Jews gave up their beliefs, that God even existed and they stopped praying.

They no longer believed in anything, anymore. They were very disappointed and very confused. They really could not understand or accept that they prayed all their life to God and they felt very relaxed, secure and sure that no matter in what kind of dangerous situation the Jews would be in, they would not have to worry about anything because God would always help them. I guess the strictly religious Jews lived or pretended to live in a dream world and when the real tragedy happened to the Jews and they had to stop dreaming and pretending, they just would not or could not face the reality, and they started to blame God for it. I still kept on asking God, "Why? Why did you let this happen? Why did so many innocent Jews, including my whole family have to be killed? They never did any harm to anybody." In spite of everything that happened I believed and still do believe in God.

I think maybe it had something to do with my upbringing. Maybe I felt and always thought that my parents would want me to believe in God and maybe, by my way of thinking and analyzing the whole situation that happened, I believed that we cannot put the whole blame on God. God only gave man the ability to choose between good and evil. The Nazis chose to be evil and they chose to commit evil acts towards the Jews.

After the first pogrom when I lost my entire family, I stopped being afraid and nothing could touch me, because I really did not care anymore if I would live or be killed. My family, my dreams, my hopes, and everything else was now gone. I thought it was not fair that I was not even thirteen years old and I was left all alone in this world. I thought to myself, what good would it do for me to survive the war. After the first pogrom, everyone tried to get a hiding place because we all knew then, that there would be a second and a third pogrom. We also knew that the Nazis would not rest until all of the Jews would be killed. This was Hitler's goal from the beginning, to murder all the Jews and make Europe and the world, Judenrein (free from Jews).

When the first pogrom was over, we had about four thousand Jews left, by hiding in different places. Under the orders of the Gebitz Commissar, the Judenrat had to make the ghetto smaller and they put more people in a room to live together. The daily life in the ghetto was very depressing and unbearable. Some Jews walked around without knowing what was happening and they acted like they were zombies.

They looked like their mind snapped and in no time they gave up and they died. Some of these Jews were shot on the spot and some were taken out of the ghetto to the pits to be shot. The Nazis thought that the sick and the weak Jews who could not work for them were useless. The Jews who were still able to put in a day's work, were allowed to live for the time being, until the Nazis decided that these Jews lived long enough and it was time to murder them, also.

Our store again fell into the ghetto area. This was on Warszawa Ulica (Street). When the pogrom was over, the Judenrat appointed some Jews to collect all the personal things that the Jews left behind in their houses, before they were taken out and were murdered. Most of the things that they collected after the pogrom, the Jews took for themselves, in order to exchange them for some food. Whatever they did not want for themselves, they took to the warehouse that the Nazis made out of the Hebrew school, which was situated on the next street, not far from our ghetto. Everyone knew that there would soon be a second pogrom. Some Jews still believed that they would be saved by having a good skrytka (hiding place). Some men got together and they dug a bunker in the cellar of our store.

Some Jews tried to make a hiding place for themselves only. Some made a hole like a bunker, some made an opening in the oven where we baked bread. We had to climb through the oven to the end of the wall. The wall slid open and on the other side of the opening, there was a room behind the oven. Some Jews had their hiding places only in the first ghetto. When they had to move to the second ghetto, they lost their hiding places because they had to leave them behind.

Whoever made these hiding places before the first pogrom and their living quarters fell into the second ghetto area, had them already. Whoever did not have a hiding place from before, after the first pogrom most of the Jews, did not want to make a hiding place anymore because they thought that it would be of no use to hide. We knew that we would all be killed anyway, sooner or later. We knew that we would not always be so lucky to be able to escape death and eventually the Nazis would catch up with us and we would all be murdered. It was only through a miracle that some Jews survived, including me.

The Jews were victims of the Nazis persecution and there was nothing they could do to avoid death. The Jews died of starvation, diseases, and having no heat in the winter. The Jews slowly starved to death, were shot to death, froze to death, and were beaten to death. The Nazis saw to it one way or another to get rid of the Jews and slowly, but surely, they got rid of most of the Jews anyway. The main victims of the ghetto were the old and the children and they were shot or died before the others.

Some Jews did not look Jewish and they spoke the Polish language well, so when they managed to escape the ghetto, they could blend in with the Polish people. They had a better chance of surviving, especially when they found somebody nice who wanted to help and save them from being killed by the Nazis. They had to be very careful because when somebody escaped from the ghetto and the SS caught them, they shot at least one hundred Jews for one Jew who tried to escape. They wanted to show the other Jews what would happen when a Jew tried to escape the ghetto.

Even when the Jews really knew what the Nazis would do to the other Jews, every Jew tried to do what they thought was best for themselves in order to save their own life, so no matter what the punishment would be, it still did not stop somebody who tried to escape the ghetto. Some Jews tried and they succeeded, but most of the Jews who tried to escape were caught by the Nazis or by the Polish or Ukrainian police and even when they were already in the city they were recognized as being Jewish and they were killed along with another hundred Jews.

Some Gentiles tried to help Jews who were able to run away by taking them into their homes and hiding them. Others tried to help the Jews escape the ghetto in order to be able to join the underground. All of these Gentiles risked their own lives and their family's lives because if they would be caught they would all be shot.

## THE SECOND POGROM

In November 1942, a few SS men came into the ghetto and they announced on the loudspeaker that everyone in the ghetto should line up in the center of the ghetto. Most of the Jews came out and lined up. Each of the SS men was holding a whip and they kept on walking and looking us over and if they did not like what they saw they whipped whomever they felt like. They did it with a lot of hate and resentment. They were probably angry with us for still being alive.

At the time it did not look like anything out of the ordinary, because we had to line up everyday before they took us to work, but when we saw more SS (Security Service) and Gestapo (Political Police) coming into the ghetto, right away we knew what was going to happen. This was about two months after the first pogrom, when the second pogrom started. It was in the morning. We all knew that we had to run in order to try to save our lives. I ran into our room and together with all of the people who lived there, we all ran into the skrytka (bunker).

The second pogrom started the same way as the first pogrom. The Nazis started to catch whomever they could. Sitting in our bunker we could hear what was going on outside. I heard all the screaming and crying from the captured Jews. Apparently these were the Jews who were gathered in the center of the ghetto and they could not run fast enough to hide so they were the first ones to be caught.

The Gestapo was running around and we heard a lot of shots and a lot of cursing and calling us all kinds of names. It was awful to hear what was going on. In a while it got very quiet. I did not hear any more shooting or any more crying. I thought to myself that the Nazis probably had their trucks loaded with the captured Jews and took them to the death pits to be shot. After they got rid of the first group of Jews, they came back with their empty trucks to catch more Jews.

I still remember that one man who was in the bunker with us had an asthma attack and he started to cough. We could still hear the Nazis above us and they probably tried to hear where the noise of the coughing was coming from. They hollered "Arous" meaning "Get Out."

The Nazis did not come into the cellar. They were probably afraid because they did not know what to expect in the cellar. Instead, they shot into it. They walked around in the house and thought that maybe they would hear some noises of the hidden Jews, so they would flush them out and kill them. They punched holes in the walls, in the ceiling, in the floors, and they were searching all over. Whomever they could find, they shot them on the spot or they loaded them into the trucks, to be taken to the death pits.

After a while the Gestapo walked out and we could hear every step they took because our room was right on top of our bunker. If they had come into the cellar they would have seen the bunker. They could still hear from a distance the noise of the coughing. Even when the man was trying his best to cover his face, especially his mouth by almost choking to death, it still did not help too much. We thought that the Gestapo left, but apparently they came back or other Nazis came in to search for Jews. Maybe they, too, heard the coughing. Everyone in the bunker was angry with the poor man, even though it was not his fault that he had asthma.

The Gestapo kept on running around from one end of the room to the other end, but they could not find an opening to the bunker because the bunker was underneath the cellar. The Nazis were very determined to find us and they really tried their best, but thank God their best was not good enough for them, so after searching the room, attic and shooting into the cellar among all the other things that they did, like throwing things around and hollering, they finally gave up and left.

I heard them cursing and calling us all kinds of names. This was one of the Nazis ways, to curse the Jews and to call the Jews the most ugly names that they could think of. After a few hours we did not hear anything. The man with asthma kept on coughing and he could not breathe. I opened the door and I walked out of the bunker into the cellar. Finally, the poor man with the asthma started to catch his breath. I stayed near the cellar door for a while and when I did not hear anything I thought that the Nazis had left. I came out of the cellar into the living space of the store. Very slowly I walked over to the front door. The door was wide open. I stayed behind the door for a while and listened.

At this time everything looked and felt very strange to me. I did not see a living soul in the ghetto and I became very sad. It felt and it looked like no one was alive anymore.

I still remember that in my mind, I really thought that the whole world had ended and we were the only people left. It felt to me that I was almost sorry why I was left in this world and nobody else. I felt very empty and confused and I started to imagine all kinds of things, like I could still hear the shooting and the Gestapo screaming and cursing. I think subconsciously these awful things stuck in my mind. At the time, it felt to me like somebody was leading me and telling me what to do next, step-by-step. I was only a child and suddenly I was taking the responsibility of leading others without even knowing what I was doing and everyone in our group was obeying me.

My mind also told me to be very careful in order not to get caught so I started to be even more careful. Very slowly I put my head out of the door, but I could not see anyone outside. I really thought that no one was left in the ghetto anymore. I ran back to the cellar and I told the others to come up. Everyone came up, then we walked out of the house and we stayed near the door. I saw dead Jews lying on the sidewalk that the Gestapo killed. These Jews had probably tried to run away and they could not make it. The Jews, who were hidden, and the SS did not discover them, came out of their hiding places, and little by little more Jews started to come out. Nobody said anything. Everyone was stunned. Most of the Jews did not show any emotions at all.

For maybe a week or more, I really do not remember exactly how long it was, we did not see any Nazis coming into the ghetto. After the second pogrom and the extermination of the Jews, only about one thousand Jews were left in the ghetto. This was out of 20,000 Jews who were originally in the ghetto in the beginning when the ghetto was made. The Nazis did their job and carried out Hitler's orders very well. They managed in a very short time to get rid of 19,000 Jews, just from our ghetto only.

Very shortly after the pogrom, whoever survived was sent to work. Everyone knew that there was one chance in a million to come out of it alive, and live through Hitler, but some Jews had a strong will to live and they told themselves that they will survive the Nazis. Everyday of the week, no matter how sick I felt, I was still sent to work and I had to go. After a days work I came back to the ghetto with a headache, a backache and with bleeding hands. My whole body was in pain and aches and I felt more dead than alive.

I came from such a hard day of work to a filthy room with no food, no water, no nothing. I thought to myself that even the rats live better than the Jews. After the second pogrom we stayed in this ghetto for a while. Nobody complained that it was too crowded. There was practically nobody in the ghetto anymore to complain. Before the second pogrom, in this ghetto we had four thousand Jews and now we had only one thousand Jews left in the ghetto. Some Jews were envious at the Jews who were killed. They said that they were the lucky ones because there was no more suffering for them and now they could rest in peace. Some of the Jews still had a will to live in spite of all of these happenings and the situation that they were in. I personally, really did not feel anything one way or another and I really did not care which way it would go. Come to think of it, I was never very determined to survive, and I really did not even try or care enough. Maybe deep down in my heart I did not want to survive, but I would not try intentionally to get killed either. If I did that it would be like I was committing suicide and in the Jewish religion this would be considered a sin.

I felt lost without my family and many times I even thought that I would be better off to be with my dead family. A lot of times, I was very angry at my family, about why they walked out of the cellar and left me all by myself. There was nothing I could do then and there was nothing I could do now. No matter how many times I was very close to being killed by the Nazis, something always happened and I was always spared from death. I think that this was my mazel (luck). It seemed to me that somebody was watching over me and they wanted me to survive and no matter how I really did not try to stay alive it looked like in spite of my will or my desire, I had to live and go on suffering.

After the second pogrom when there were only one thousand Jews left in the ghetto, the Gebitz Commissar (Mayor) decided that we did not need all of the space, so under his orders the Judenrat transferred us to a smaller ghetto in a different location and in another part of the city. It was in the downtown area. I did not have too many things to take to the other ghetto because when the war started in 1939 and when the bombs were thrown on our city, our house burned down together with my, and all of my family's belongings.

The life in the ghetto was very depressing and everyone was worn out from the oblavas, pogroms, and all of our other happenings. The Jews really had enough of the misery that the Nazis inflicted on us. Everyone made peace with their goyrel or shykzal (destiny) and they said whatever will be, will be. The Jews did not have any strength anymore to take all of this tsures (troubles) and they lost their desire to fight for their survival. Most of the Jews said "enough is enough".

I do not remember how long we stayed in the smaller ghetto, but I think that it was more than a year. It was the same daily routine to go to work everyday, and live with all of the fears and uncertainties by not knowing what was waiting for us the next day or even the next minute.

# THE THIRD AND FINAL POGROM
# JUDENREIN (FREE FROM JEWS)

One day we received some news that we could expect a pogrom very soon. This would be the third and final pogrom in the ghetto. The Nazis called this pogrom Judenrein, which means free from Jews. The reason that we knew about this pogrom in advance was because the Judenrat told us about it. The way the Judenrat knew about it before it happened was because they got a tip from one of their connections. We knew that we were in trouble and the Judenrat warned us to be on the watch. We already knew what we could expect very soon, but there was nothing that we could do to help ourselves in order to be spared from death. There was no place to hide or run to. We asked ourselves, "What can we do about it?" We really could not do anything. We just did not have any way out, in order to save our lives. Everyone, including me, faced the reality that we will all be killed very soon. I remember that everyone in the house where I lived with the other people was dressed and waiting. Nobody said a word. Everyone was very calm, like nothing was happening. I think that everyone accepted the fact about what was going to happen and we all knew that it was the end of our lives. I still remember it got darker outside and it was almost evening time when the pogrom started.

The Nazis surrounded the ghetto and no one was able to run out. They started to shoot into the ghetto, and everyone started to run in different directions not knowing what we were doing or where we were running. Right after the shooting, the Nazis came into the ghetto with the German shepherd dogs and they started to grab anybody that they could catch and threw them into the trucks in order to take them out of the city to the death pits.

I still remember everything like it just happened. I kept on running and I saw that a Nazi ran after me and he was trying to catch me. While I was running, I noticed that I was almost near the ghetto fence. I really do not remember how I ran into a house. It was a place where the Nazis were storing furniture. By this time it was dark and I could not even see where I was or anything around me. I remember that by running around in the rooms of the house, and not seeing where I was I ran into a wall and it knocked me down. Without even thinking about what I was doing I kept on pushing myself towards the wall. I really did not know when and how I climbed behind a headboard that was leaning against the wall. While I was sitting there, right away I touched something and when I picked it up and in spite of not being able to see what it was, I knew right away that it was tefillin (phylacteries). Tefillin is something that religious Jewish men put on their forehead when they prayed. I remember thinking to myself that now I was going to be saved and nothing could or would happen to me. I even started to feel less afraid.

The same Nazi who chased me and saw me running into the house ran after me, and started to holler for me to come out. He started to throw things all over the place and of course, him not knowing that I was under the headboard, kept on throwing chairs in different directions, including where I was sitting. I could see him through a little hole that was in the headboard. He knew that I was there someplace and he was determined to find me. He really tried his best and kept on running from one place to another and kept on throwing things all around. He was furious that he could not find me. Eventually, after a while he got angry for not being able to find me and walked out. I do not remember how long I sat there. I kept on listening and wondering if the Nazis were still in the ghetto or not. When I did not hear anything anymore, I came out of my hiding place.

For the first time in a long time, I started to get scared again. After my family was killed I was not scared of getting killed because I really did not care if I would live or die. When I was in the ghetto with the other Jews, I was not scared either, because I was with other people. Now, suddenly my fear came back and I started to get scared all over again, and I almost became panicky. Right then, I knew that I have to snap out of this way of thinking very quickly because every minute was important and every minute counted. I also knew that if I would lose control over myself, I would be caught and killed, and all of the misery that I had gone through because of the Nazis would be for nothing. I started to tell myself that everything will be okay, like I always did when I was in trouble. The ghetto looked like a cemetery. I did not see one living soul around.

I remember that it was pitch black and I could hardly see where I was going, but I knew the ghetto very well, so I found my way and I went in the direction where I wanted to go. Quietly, I started to walk towards the ghetto gate. I was trying to pass the office of the Judenrat, which was also the Nazis Headquarters that was located right before the gate.

As I kept very close to the building walls, I heard the Nazis singing and celebrating their victory. It was a great accomplishment for them. They achieved Hitler's goal to get rid of the Jews. They thought that they carried out their assignment very well and they were right. They even got rid of the Judenrat together with the rest of the Jews because the Judenrat was nothing special to the Nazis, either. After all, they were also Jews.

The Nazis felt good, of course, because they knew that they did a good job. I stayed for a while against the wall not far from the gate and when I thought it was the right time I started to walk towards the gate. The gate was wide open and unguarded, and finally I passed through the gate and I found myself out of the ghetto in the streets of the city.

The third pogrom took place on December 15, 1943. This was the final liquidation of the ghetto and this was called Judenrein (free from Jews). A city that was once a religious and cultural Jewish center was now completely without Jews. Wlodzimierz Volynski, before the Nazi occupation and before Hitler's regime came to power, had been the home of my family and their families for generations. They lived there far back before the Holocaust, but now for the first time our city was going to be a city without Jews.

All of the 36,000 Jewish people from our city and the vicinity were wiped out, off the face of the earth at the hands of the Nazis, like they never existed. I had lived through, and experienced the tragedy of three oblavas (raids, round ups), three pogroms and Judenrein (free from Jews). When I thought about it, most of the time I wondered how I could come out of it alive, in spite of all these dangers that I faced every minute of the day under the Nazis regime. Most of the time I thought that it was a miracle.

After Judenrein, the Nazis had the city under strict guard. I was all shook up and really scared that I would be caught by a Nazi and be killed. After all the misery and suffering that I went through with the Nazis and all of these unbearable conditions in the ghetto, I hoped that maybe now I would have a chance on the outside to survive. Now, I really did not want to be shot by the Nazis or by anybody else.

Once again, I was totally alone. Even when I did not have my family anymore, I was still with other people, until now. I kept on thinking and telling myself that I would be okay. I had a habit that when I was in trouble I always told myself in my mind over and over again that I would be okay and very soon I started to believe it and only then I calmed down.

# CHAPTER XXIII
## MY HIDING PLACES

## MY FIRST HIDING PLACE

I knew our city very well. I had a lot of girlfriends who lived all over the city and I visited them quite often. Besides that, I used to go with my mother to deliver the merchandise to her wholesale customers who had their stores in different parts of the city, but knowing the city did not help the situation that I was now in. I knew that I could not wander around all night because I would be spotted in no time by the SS or by the Polish or Ukrainian police and for sure I would be shot. I really did not know where to go or what to do now. I was thinking to myself that I was lucky until now, but my luck can and probably will run out and eventually I would be caught by a Nazi and be killed. I really tried very hard to stay calm and just think.

I kept on walking the streets, not knowing where I was going to. Luckily for me, it was a very dark night and there were not too many people on the street. I passed quite a few SS soldiers, but they did not stop me. Suddenly, something came to my mind and I started to remember that my mother once, and only once, said to me and my sister and my two brothers, that if something will happen to her we should know that she bought a hiding place for us and she told us the name and address of the people to go to and they would hide us. She said that she paid them a lot of money and gave them jewelry and clothes and in case we will need help from them, they have to and they will help us. Of course, at the time when she told us this I did not even listen or pay special attention to what she was saying. I probably did not understand everything that she was telling us to begin with, and another thing, she said it to us only once and I never thought of it since that time. The fact was that I forgot right away what she said to us. This conversation took place right in the beginning of the Nazi occupation.

My mother knew these people for a long time. They were very good Polish people and they acted very nice and respectful towards my mother, so my mother considered them of being our friends. Of course, to know somebody and to deal with somebody was two very different things. I thought and I felt that my mother judged everyone's goodness and loyalty of being a friend by the way she was.

In her life there never were two ways about it, there was only one way, either you were a sincere friend or you were not a friend at all. I have to mention that this philosophy of living, doing, and acting I learned from my mother, and all my life I was the same way with everyone. I will do everything for a real friend, but only so called friends, I will stay as far away from them as possible. For some reason or another my mother liked this family very much and she had complete confidence in them without any doubts. She was sure that they would keep their promise and help us if the time came, and we would need their help.

They were Polish people and my mother trusted them. My mother could have picked other Polish people to make this deal, but she decided that they were the best. A lot of Jews gave their life savings to Polish people, so-called friends, whom they knew for a long time, and they made an agreement that if they will need a hiding place they were paid to help them. Some of the Polish people kept their promise, but most of them, after taking mostly everything from the Jews, they did not want to know the Jews anymore. Our Polish family, whom my mother trusted the most, were always nice to us, so my mother decided to make an agreement with them to hide us, in exchange that my mother will and did give them all of her valuables.

After the Nazis made the first ghetto, they used to bring us food and my mother paid them for it. At this time, while I was wandering the streets, the only thing that I started to concentrate on was what my mother told us children to do. I started to feel much better and calmer. I began to feel happier that finally I have a place to go to and I was going to my mother's friends, who would hide me.

I was almost sure that when I would reach their house they would be happy to see me alive. I started to think that now I have someone to depend on and someone who will take care of me and protect me. After all, they were paid for it that in case we all will need a hiding place we will have it by them, in the bunker that they prepared for us. That was what they said to my mother. Apparently, my mother thought that everything was being taken care of and she never talked about it to us, again.

I started to walk towards their home. They lived on the other side of the city. I was stopped by the German patrol because there was a curfew for everyone. People could be on the street until nine o'clock PM. After nine o'clock PM nobody was allowed to be on the streets anymore. Of course, I did not know about this curfew and I did not know what time it was to begin with. When the German patrol stopped me after nine o'clock PM, I explained that I just finished my work and I had to do some extra cleaning. Luckily for me, I spoke good Polish and he took me for a Polish girl. I looked tired and dirty, so after a while he let me go. I was sure that he did not understand one Polish word that I said to him, because the Germans did not know Polish. The German patrol also did not know that I was a Jew and that I just came out of the pogrom alive, in spite of the ghetto being Judenrein (free from Jews).

Finally, I reached the Polish family's house. The husband opened the door and let me in. He was happy to see me, and he started to ask me all kinds of questions about my family. When I told him what happened to them, he became very sad to hear it, and he kept on saying to me that he was very sorry. I felt that he was sincere, but right away I started to feel that his wife was not too happy to see me alive. I had a very bad feeling that if she would have come to the door and she would have seen me, she would not have even let me in. In spite of how she felt, she kept me hidden for the time being.

I went into the bunker that they prepared for all of us, and all of the time I was lying there, I felt a lot of tension from her when she brought me some food. It did not matter to her that she took everything away from my mother and promised her that if and when the time would come and we would need them to hide us, they would do just that.

I think that maybe at the time, they were quite sincere and honest about it, especially her husband, but the times changed and nobody knew how they would really act under pressure and in difficult situations and circumstances that they could be in. I thought that no matter how much pressure or what kind of circumstances they were facing, when they made an agreement they had an obligation to stick to it. I think maybe the reason that they were so nice from the beginning was that they wanted to take everything away from my mother and after that, to wash their hands from the whole deal.

It really did not take too long for me to find out that I was right all along, and the friends that they pretended to be to my mother were not friends at all. They have an expression that, "with friends like this we did not need any enemies." They knew from the beginning that there was a risk involved before they took everything from my mother by pretending to being a friend, and they also knew that they did not have any intention of living up to my mother's expectation. It was a shande (shame) that my mother trusted them.

I stayed in the bunker, in their house, for a few weeks. Then the wife told me that her neighbors were getting suspicious. I was almost positive that it was a lie because her neighbors never saw me. I never left the bunker and I was sure that she was only looking for an excuse in order to get rid of me. After all, she had everything already, so why and for what reason did she need me. Why should she have all the responsibilities of feeding me and worry about certain things when she really had a chance to get rid of me. She took everything from my mother, and did not want to give anything back in return.

I knew that she was planning to get rid of me, and I felt that the time would come very soon. From the beginning, I did not like the way she was acting towards me. I sensed and felt that she was preparing me for something, and I was almost positive that I knew what that something would be. The first week of being there I knew that she was not going to let me stay with her.

One day, when she came into the bunker to bring me something to eat, she started a conversation with me. She told me that she was getting scared to hide a Jew because the Nazis were really strict about it, and when they found out that somebody was hiding Jews they killed their families. She kept on saying that in case her neighbors will report her, she would be shot. I think she had to think about this before she made the agreement.

Apparently, she did not have any intentions to stick to the agreement that she made. She knew exactly that she would have to face some risk, but according to me she never thought of keeping her promise. She only thought of getting all the diamonds, the gold, the money, and generally everything from my mother and forget about her promise. What a shande (shame) that my mother thought of her as being a real friend.

Apparently, she was never my mother's friend, she only pretended to be one, only for her selfish reasons. Finally, the day came when she told me that I have to leave. Her husband was not too happy with her doings, but apparently he did not have an opinion in this matter according to her. To me, it looked like she was the only one making all of the family decisions, and whatever she decided her husband had to agree with her.

After not even two weeks of me being there, in her hiding place, she threw me out. I left without knowing where I was going. I was thrown out in the middle of the night and she did not even give one thing back to me that my mother gave her. She did not even have the decency to give me a piece of bread to take with me. She practically pushed me out of her house and out on the street, just to get rid of me.

## MY SECOND HIDING PLACE

It was the end of December 1943 when I was thrown out into the street without knowing what to do next or where to go. I remember at the time I felt like sitting down in the snow and falling asleep. If I would sit in the freezing cold in the snow I would never wake up, and instead I would freeze to death. I knew then that I had to decide if I wanted to try to live a little longer or if I wanted to end my struggling right then.

I really thought that I had more than enough of my share of misery and at that time I could not have cared less if I lived or died. It was a very cold winter night with below zero degree temperatures, but at that time I could not feel the cold. The only thing that I really felt was a lot of anger and resentment towards the woman. I thought to myself, how can people be so cruel, selfish, and heartless, like she was. While I was furious at her, I started walking without even knowing what I was doing or where I was going.

I remember it was snowing and the wind blew the snow in my face. When I calmed down a little I started to realize that it was very cold, but there was nothing that I could do about it. I started to walk a little faster. I knew that in this freezing cold weather, if I would stop walking, I was very sure that I would freeze to death. I knew that I must keep on walking if I still wanted to try to survive. I started to think of my mother and how she tried to keep warm in the store in wintertime, so right away I started to do the same.

I remember that I kept on blowing into my hands and kept on knocking my feet together, but it did not help too much. I did not wear any warm clothes or good shoes so no matter how I tried not to give up, I really thought that I would freeze to death and this would be the end of my suffering, and finally my life struggle would be over.

Suddenly, my mind and my thoughts turned to other things. Instead of just freezing, I started to think of starving and I became very hungry and thirsty. I still remember that I bent down, got a little snow and I put it in my mouth. My mind jumped from one thought to another as if I did not have any control over my actions or my thoughts anymore. I got very confused, and scared, and I began to feel sorry for myself and I started to cry.

I kept on crying and talking to myself very loud. I was saying that I was hungry and I was cold, I did not know where I was going, and I was lost and all alone. What should I do now? In a while I was starting to tell myself, "You'll be okay, everything will be okay," and right away I felt much better.

It felt like somebody or something was controlling my mind and did not want me to give up. Instead it gave me strength, hope and courage to go on. Come to think of it, this happened to me a lot of times when I was still in the ghetto under the Nazis and when I got out of the ghetto. A lot of times I felt that somebody was watching over me and a lot of times I was spared from death. I really believed then and I still believe even now that somebody gave me a will to go on. No matter what kind of terrible situation I was in under the Nazis, I always managed to come out of it alive.

I kept on walking and thinking of all the things that had happened to me, good things and bad things. It felt like my whole life was flashing in front of me. I probably got so carried away thinking of my past that I really forgot about the present situation that I was in. I did not know how long I was deep in my thoughts of my past, but I snapped out of it and I started to think of the present. I started to think about how cold, tired, and hungry I was and on top of everything I did not know where I was, or where I was going. All of these things made me very scared and confused.

After so many hours of walking in the freezing cold weather, I was very exhausted and I really could not drag my feet anymore. I wanted to sit down in the snow. I felt that I had enough and right then I stopped walking with the intention of sitting down in the snow and freezing to death. Suddenly, I started to look around to see where I was and where I was going. I found myself out of the city near a village. I knew the outskirts of the city very well because my parents had a datshe (vacation place) for the summer in one of the villages and it was about seven miles from our city.

When I saw from a distance, little lit up houses, I knew I was close to a village and right away I felt much better, like I was going to join the world again. I started to feel more hopeful and not as lonely anymore. As I came closer, I saw people in the houses. I do remember that when I passed the first house, the dogs started to bark, but I really felt that no matter what will happen, I just could not walk anymore. I did not care anymore about what would happen to me. I just sat down near the wall of the house and instantly, I fell asleep.

I think that when the lady of the house heard the dog barking, she came out to see why the dog was barking without a stop. She probably looked around and saw me sleeping there. Suddenly, I heard voices near me. When I opened my eyes, I saw the lady leaning over me and she started to smile, and then she said to me, "Don't be afraid. Don't be afraid." She took me by my hand and walked with me into the house. I still remember that when we came into the kitchen, she told me to sit down on a sofa that was near the kitchen window. The first few minutes I thought it was a dream. Eventually, I became wide-awake and I started to feel very strange, scared and I got very confused.

The Polish lady kept on holding my hand and said to me, "You don't have to be afraid here." Then she asked me, "Where are your parents?" I did not say anything, then she asked me again, "Where are your parents?" Finally, I told her that the Nazis killed my family. My whole family was dead and I was the only one left alive.

She looked at me and started to cry and then she hugged me and kissed me. After a while, when she calmed down a little bit, she said to me, "You look like my daughter who the Ukrainians killed because she looked Jewish. The Ukrainians thought that she was Jewish." While she was talking about her daughter she got very sad and she stopped talking for a while. Then the Polish lady made a statement and she said to me, "I will hide you and see to it that you should survive." All the time while she was talking to me she kept on hugging me and we were both crying.

The Ukrainians were as bad or even worse than the Nazis. They were determined to show the Nazis that they were very dedicated to them and they tried in the worst way to do a good job of catching and killing as many Jews as they possibly could. They knew all the places where the Jews were hiding and gathering together, but sometimes some good Ukrainians and Polish people risked their own lives to help the Jews. Everyone did it for a different reason.

Some were personal friends of the Jews, some felt sorry for the Jews, some were religious and they believed if they would help Jewish people survive, they would do what God wanted them to do. Some people were plain, good natured, decent human beings and they felt very strongly that it was their obligation to help another human being when they were in trouble, and it did not matter to them what race, nationality, or religion they were. According to these nice people, everyone deserved to live in this world. Some people thanked God that they were able to help the Jews.

Some people helped the Jews without even thinking of the risk that they were putting themselves and their families through. They still thought that they were doing their obligation in order to help human beings. These kinds of people were very noble and they had feelings and consideration for others. Some good people thought that it was a must to help the Jews because the Jews were innocent victims of the persecution.

This Polish woman was one of these people who thought of helping a Jew without any other thoughts in her mind except being a sincere, honest, decent and loyal person. She felt that one human being should help another human being because this was the right way of doing, and living in the world.

In spite of me not giving her anything because I did not have anything to give her, she took me in. The first Polish woman took everything from my family and then threw me out in the street to die, like the Nazis did to us. This kind of a selfish, egotistic woman did not care about doing anything for us, only doing everything for herself. She cared only to lie, cheat and grab whatever she could from the Jews.

The second Polish woman took me in and I stayed with her and her two daughters for almost three months. They treated me like I belonged in their family. Deep in my mind I had different kinds of thoughts. My conscience always bothered me and I always felt that it was not fair of me to let them jeopardize their own lives in order to save me. I always felt guilty and selfish enough for letting them do it just because I wanted to have a hiding place with them and they wanted to help me.

This was not a business agreement. It was not like the first Polish woman who made an agreement with my mother and she was paid for hiding all of us, but even when I was the only one left alive and I needed her help, she did not live up to her agreement. This nice Polish lady, got absolutely nothing from me, but she helped me and did it only because of the genuine goodness of her heart, without any pay or any obligation towards me. I always hoped that nothing bad would happen to them because of me.

In spite of the fact that I wanted to survive and had a hiding place with them, I still could not help worrying about their well-being. I guess that I was more concerned and worried about their lives than my own. Her daughters had a lot of parties in the house and they invited the whole village of peasants, including the German patrol. The Nazis had their headquarters in this village. I was always scared that eventually someone would discover me. At the time of the parties, I hid in the spare room, like a storage room, where no one came in, but I was always afraid that someone would open the door and see me there. If this would happen they would, for sure, report them to the Nazis. I thought to myself that it really could happen, and the Polish woman with her daughters would be shot for hiding a Jew.

She knew about my bad experience with the first hiding place, I told her how that woman took everything and threw me out without any human pity or having any conscience. This lady heard what I went through and she said to me, "Do not think of it anymore, now you are with us and you will be okay". I was always worried about them much more than about myself. I asked her a few times, "Why are you doing this for a stranger and a Jew without getting anything out of it?" and she said to me by looking straight in my eyes, "I don't see you as being a Jew,

I only see you as a human being who needs my help." I remember that it was a very emotional moment for both of us and we hugged and kissed and we were both crying.

After a while it become very dangerous. I suspected that their neighbor knew about me. I always slept in the kitchen on the sofa and once I probably forgot to cover the window, so in my mind I started to imagine certain things and I told myself that the neighbor looked into the window and saw me there. Since then I became very worried that eventually I would be discovered and they all would be shot because of me. I knew that they were too good and they did not deserve to be killed. I just could not let it happen.

One day, I had a talk with her and I told her that I really cannot jeopardize their lives for me and I must leave. She felt very bad and we were both crying. She knew that I was going to leave because I wanted to leave once before and she talked me out of it. She kept on saying that I should stay with them and the war will soon be over and then I would go back to my hometown. I thought the reason that I let her talk me out of leaving before was that I was not completely sure that I really wanted to leave.

This time, I did not want to change my mind and let her talk me out of it like the first time. This time, I made my mind up, that I did not want them to be in danger because of me anymore and I knew that she would never throw me out. On the contrary, she liked me and she was very worried about me. She kept on asking me, "Where will you go?" and I said to her that I would try to join the partisans in the forest. I told her that she should not worry about me and I would be okay. I thanked her for everything that she did for me and I told her that I would never forget her. After almost three months of being there, I decided to leave of my own free will. It was sometime at the end of March 1944.

Once again, I had to start my journey all over, and once again I did not know where I was going, and what I could expect in the future days ahead of me. In spite of it, I decided that no matter what would happen to me, I still felt that I would be doing the right thing by leaving her and her daughters, in order not to jeopardize their lives for me.

Finally, the day came and I said goodbye to her daughters, and everyone was crying. I guess that we got used to each other and I really knew that I would miss them a lot, but I also knew that I must leave, even if it was only for my peace of mind. The Polish lady took me as far as she could, close to the woods, then she gave me a bag with food and some warm socks and a shawl. She kissed me and said to me, "Go with God."

I still remember that I kept on walking and crying and I kept on looking back until I did not see her wagon anymore. I missed her already, she was like a mother to me, and she really worried about me, and I worried about them also, but I felt good about my decision to spare them from the danger of being killed. That was my only reason for leaving them.

# CHAPTER XXIV
## THE RUSSIAN PARTISANS
## AND MY LIFE IN THE FOREST

The village where I was hidden was just about six or seven miles on the outskirts of our city. I knew that not far from our city, we had deep woods. These woods were about one hundred kilometers long. I overheard the Jews in the ghetto talking about the forest. The forest was in the vicinity of the Polesie district in the eastern part of Poland where I lived in the city, Wlodzimierz Volynski.

Everyone in the ghetto knew about the forest. It was a very thick forest. Some Jews who managed to sneak out of the ghetto ran to the forest to hide. Some Jews managed to escape the ghetto and some Jews were shot by the ghetto guards, but everyone knew that if they were willing to take a chance to sneak out of the ghetto without being caught then they might be able to make it to the forest and maybe they would have a better chance of surviving. We heard rumors that they had different groups of partisans in the forest like the Russian, Ukrainian and Polish partisans.

When I got to the forest, I remember that I felt very scared and lonely. Shortly after, while I was walking, I saw a few Jews also wandering in the woods. I also saw Russian soldiers who were on the move for about two years already, since the Nazis took over the eastern part of Poland. The Russian soldiers kept on moving from one area of the forest, to another area, and from one place to another place. We all joined up together and kept on walking, the Jews and the Russians. Soon we were sixteen Jews, all single people who had no one. We had all lost our families.

I did not know anyone in the group, but all of the people were from the general area of Volyn. The longer we walked, the more we saw Soviet soldiers. They seemed to be lost also and they told us that somewhere they heard that the Nazis surrounded at least 10,000 Soviet soldiers in the forest and there was no way out for them. They could not get out of the forest without fighting the Nazis, but they were afraid of fighting because they would lose a lot of soldiers and they probably were right. The Russian soldiers decided to hide out in the forest and see what would happen. Now, we all were looking for the Russian base in order to team up with the Russian partisans.

We had to be on the watch constantly, because even in the forest nobody knew who could be hiding under a tree or a bush. There was a war going on and we were caught right in the middle. People were killing each other for no special reason at all. We also had other dangers, such as watching for snakes, different kinds of animals that were not afraid of people, and Nazis who may be hiding there in order to catch some Jews and murder them. I think that besides fear, we all became very paranoid and every little sound triggered us off and we became extra careful and scared. Sometimes we were even scared of our own shadow.

The reality of it was that even though there was no ghetto in our city anymore, the war was still going on and the Nazis were still all over our city and the surroundings, including near the forest where I was. If they would see us, they would kill us on the spot. It really would not matter to them where they were catching the Jew and where they were killing them, in the ghetto or outside the ghetto, as long as the Jews were dead. I was constantly in fear from the minute that the Nazis came to us and even now. I remember a period of my life in the ghetto when I really did not fear for anything or anybody, because I really did not care enough about what would happen to me. This was after the Nazis killed my family. I did not care if they would kill me, too, but as time went on for some reason or another I wanted to stay alive.

In a way I was glad that I was with the Russian soldiers. We joined up with them while we were walking together in the forest. Of course, they were armed and I felt much safer with them. We really did not see any Nazis around, but the fear was in us and with us all of the time. While we were walking deeper into the forest, we got really hungry and thirsty. Nobody had any food with them. I had some food that the Polish lady gave me when I left her, but I ate it in a couple of hours.

I hoped that the Russian soldiers would do something in order to get some food for us and for themselves. We kept on looking for farmhouses. Eventually, from time to time, we saw some houses, so we stopped to ask for some food. Some peasants gave us food and some would have killed us if we had not been with the Russian soldiers. As soon as the peasants saw the soldiers with their guns, they got scared of them and gave us some food.

It was a good thing that we stuck with them and their guns. We kept on walking deeper and deeper into the forest, and we had to walk through the swamps and thick woods. Actually, nobody knew where we were going. The Jews thought that the Russian soldiers knew the woods because they were already hiding out there for almost two years, but they really knew less than we did. The only thing that they were interested in was to find the Russian partisans and join up with them.

The woods were called "puszcza" in Polish. We met different groups of partisans in the forest. From the beginning of the war, the people who ran to the forest and formed their own groups were more or less on their own. They were wandering in the forest and they did whatever they wanted to do. They were not organized, and they did not have any leader to control them. There were some Polish groups that killed every Jew they met and after killing them they took all of their belongings away. These Polish anti-Semites hated the Jews all of their lives, and they were very happy to have a chance to get rid of the Jews.

There were groups of escaped prisoners, and there were groups of bandits who had a goal of robbing and killing the Jews who escaped the ghetto. There were Ukrainian anti-Semites, and other groups who also did not want the Jews around and as soon as they saw a Jew they killed them on the spot. Some groups that worked with the underground were nice and they felt sorry for the Jewish refugees. They did not harm the Jews and they even tried to help them by giving them food and some courage to go on.

Finally, we found the partisan camps with the Russian partisans. The Russian soldiers who we met and sticked together in the forest were very happy that they found the place. Right away, the partisans accepted them and they joined the partisan unit. We, sixteen Jews, decided to stay close to the Russian partisans, and we started to set up a place not too far from them. In a way we felt more secure with them close to us.

The reason that there were so many Russian partisans in the forest was, that when the Nazis pushed the Russian army out from the eastern part of Poland in 1941, it was a very big surprise to the Russians because they did not have the slightest idea that the Nazis would attack them. After all, they had made a non-aggression pact between each other and they were very sure that the Nazis were the Russians friends. The Russians told themselves that the Nazis liked them. What a laugh that was, to even think that Hitler could like anybody else, except himself.

When the Nazis attacked the Russians, a lot of Russian soldiers ran back to Russia and a lot of the Russian soldiers ran to the forest. The German army cut off some Russian troops and they got surrounded. The Russian soldiers knew that they were stuck in the forest with no way out so they decided to make the best of it. They got organized very quickly. They set up headquarters, they picked their leaders, and they started to function like partisans, almost like a disciplined army.

Everyone had to obey the orders of the leader, and with such strong discipline, the Russian partisans became a very good and successful movement. Instead of fighting on the front, they were fighting behind the front, and it worked out very well for them. These groups of partisans did much damage to the Nazis.

The Russian partisans were not too friendly to us. They did not want the Jews near them, even though we were just close to them, but never near them. They had anti-Semitic attitudes towards the Jews, like the Polish and the Ukrainians. They did not tolerate the Jewish people and they considered us as being a nuisance to them. The Russian partisans said that the Jews were charity cases and we were burdens to them. They said that we were in their way and they really did not want any civilians near them, even when we had our own place farther away from them. We really tried not to be too far away, though, no matter how they felt about us. We did not care if they wanted us or not, so when they moved, we moved also, not near them, but close to them.

Besides not wanting us near them, they did not trust anyone whom they did not know. Sometimes they had a good reason not to trust strangers, because they had a bad experience with strangers. A lot of times the Nazis sent spies into the forest who were posing as peasants and they came into the forest to spy on the partisans. Most of the time, the spies looked and acted very innocent.

The Russian partisans thought that these peasants really ran away from the Nazis and they needed some help, so the Russian partisans let them stay with them. In the meantime, the spies got acquainted with the whole set up of the partisan camp. They collected and stored in their mind all of the important information in order to be able to let the Nazis know everything. When the spies thought that they got all of the information they needed, like where the Russian partisans had their bases, and what their missions were and when they planned to attack, suddenly, these peasants disappeared into thin air. The spies reported everything to the Nazis.

The Russian commander, the leader, had the power and he had his ways of punishment and dealing with traitors, and all of the obstacles that were standing in his way. The way he decided to deal with them was that most of the time when they spotted a traitor, they shot him on the spot and the same punishment was for the partisans who did not obey the leaders orders.

When the leader assigned his partisans to do certain jobs, such as getting food or carrying out the sabotage missions, no one would dare to refuse an order from the leader. When he told someone to do something, it was done without any questions, and they knew they had better do it or else. Even if this was not a regular army, the Russian partisans functioned the same as if it was a regular army.

The Russian partisans looked at fighting the Nazis in a military way, because it was a war and of course the Russians wanted to win the war. They knew that the Jews were there only for one reason, and that reason was to run away from the Nazis in order not to get murdered by them. They also knew that the Jews were there, not to fight the war, only to survive the war. The Russian partisans did not want anybody, especially Jews, to distract them from their goals and their plans of defeating the Nazis.

The situation was very tense in the woods because every minute of the day or night we could be discovered and attacked. Everyone was very scared of their own shadow. The Russian partisans usually slept during the day and when it got dark they went on their missions that they were appointed to. Their missions always were very risky and every time they left the base, they did not know if they will come back alive or if it would be the last time for them, but they were soldiers and they were trained for it. It was their duty to do what their leader ordered them to do no matter how it would turn out. Russian partisans trusted their leader. They picked him and they trusted his judgment, even at times when he seemed to be very strict and demanding, but in spite of it, they all respected him and they had confidence in his decisions.

The Russians never undressed to go to sleep. They even went to sleep with their boots on and their guns were held by their side. While some Russian partisans slept, the others watched the base and vice versa. Most of the time they slept daytime.

The Jews never undressed either, but they slept during the night. While the Russians slept, the Jews were keeping an eye on the surroundings. They listened in order to hear if anything sounded different than usual. By living in the forest we got to know practically every sound. Our eyes and ears got so used to it, that we could sense right away if something was different.

We were always ready to run in case we were in danger. We ran from one place to another place or from one area of the forest to another area of the forest. We moved very quickly and wherever the Russian partisans settled, we were right behind them. Not that they needed us or wanted us around them, but we felt safer not to be too far from them.

Life in the forest was very hard and we were always hungry, dirty, and constantly on watch without a peaceful minute. We had to fight for our survival. The forest was full of swamps and thick trees, and with all kinds of insects that ate us alive. There were also a lot of wild animals and big birds. Besides all of these things, every minute of the day, we feared that we would be discovered. Usually the Nazis did not come into a place that they did not know. We knew that the Nazis would not take as much of a chance to come into the forest, but the collaborators would come in to spy anytime of the day or night. The Ukrainian and Polish underground, also, knew the woods much better than the Russians or the Jews and a lot of times they shot up the Russian bases and the Russians had some casualties. The Nazis knew that eventually, no matter what, and how long it would take, the Russian partisans had to come out of the forest to get some food in order to survive, so the Nazis thought of ways to make it harder for the Russian partisans.

The Nazis burned all the villages and farmhouses close to the forest in order for the Russian partisans to have to go farther out of the forest for their food supply. In spite of all the efforts by the Nazis, the Russians found a way to get food and carry out their sabotage missions without too many difficulties. Sometimes the Nazis were able to catch some Russian partisans and they shot them on the spot, but most of the time the Russian partisans were very successful in their missions. They killed plenty of Nazis and destroyed their bases because the Russian partisans were much better fighters than the Nazis.

When the Russians were fighting, they did not have any fear of dying and they were much braver than the Nazis. The Nazis were not fighters, instead they were cowards. They were just murderers and killers. They could only kill unarmed people like the Jews who did not have a chance of fighting back with only their bare hands against the armed Nazis.

In spite of all the danger, we had to get some food. We knew a shortcut to go from the forest to the village and the only safe way was by not going with the road, but only with the forest. In the evening when it got dark, we came out of the forest and we walked to the potato and cornfields and everyone took as much as they could carry on their backs. Sometimes we came across different things, like carrots, sunflowers, sweet potatoes and radishes. This was a treat for us. We Jews never went into the village like the Russian partisans. We only got as far as the fields, but the Russian partisans went into the villages to the farmers and got some food from them.

When we came back, we wanted to cook some food, but we did not have any water. Every time we moved to another place, we had to dig for water. Most of the time, the Russian partisans dug for water and we also used it. Sometimes we had to stay out of their way because when something went wrong for them they picked on the couple of Jews. We really did not know how they would act towards us, after all, they had guns and we never knew how, when, and on whom they would use them.

The Russian partisans started to dig a hole for water, and we watched them in order to see the way they were doing it, then we did it, too. The hole that we dug filled up with water right away. We then made a fire and we filled up a big pot with water, then we put in the potatoes, corn and whatever else we had, and it started to cook. When it was done, everyone ate and had to like it because it was better than nothing. We had to cook our food in the evening, only when the forest was very foggy and in this way the Nazis would not be able to see the smoke or the fire from the distance. The Russians cooked their food in the evening, also. They thought that it was much safer and we all had a better chance not to be discovered.

When the Russian partisans went to the village for food, they never knew what to expect because the village was full of Nazis. Sometimes, the peasants wanted to get rid of the partisans so they told the Nazis that the Russian partisans came into the village looking for food almost every day. The Russian partisans did not know that the Nazis were waiting for them and when the partisans came the Nazis caught them and shot them on the spot.

When the Russian partisans went to get food and they were supposed to come back from the village at a certain time, more or less, and when it took longer than it should take and they did not come back to the forest, everyone in the camp including the leader, already knew that they, for sure, were killed.

The leader right away suspected that somebody had informed the Nazis that the partisans were coming to the village every so often to get food. We all knew that the Russian partisans would not rest until they would take revenge and strike back, so their next mission was that they burned down the whole village as a punishment to the traitors. This was a lesson for the peasants. The peasants from the other villages were already too scared to go against the partisans and tell the Nazis about them.

After their lesson, when the partisans came, the peasants gave them as much food as they needed and wanted. Sometimes, they even bought some food from farmers from the other villages just to have something for them when they came, because they were scared to say that they did not have anything for them. The partisans had to depend on the support of the local peasant population in order to get food for themselves. The Russian partisans sometimes paid them with some money, but not enough for what they took from the peasants. Over all, they paid them more than the Nazis did because the Nazis did not pay them at all. The Nazis came to the peasants' homes and they took whatever they wanted, without giving them one penny.

The partisans walked into the village, and told the peasants that they came for food. When the peasants saw armed soldiers, they gave them what they had, so the Russian partisans had bread, butter, bacon, eggs, milk and a lot more. Sometimes the leader, only when he was in a good mood and he started to feel sorry for the few Jewish refugees, gave us some food, clothes and other things that we needed and they could not use. Sometimes he gave us something good to eat, things that the partisans had too much of, so they shared with us.

He told us that they could get as much food as they wanted to and he told us why the peasants were afraid of them now. We were very thankful for anything we got to eat besides corn and potatoes because we only had the opportunity to steal what was in the fields and mostly the fields had only corn and potatoes. This was much better than nothing. Actually, nobody complained too much because we had it much worse in the ghetto. We could not go into the villages because if the peasants would see us they would probably kill us or report us to the Nazis that they saw us. The peasants were afraid of the Russian partisans because they were armed and the peasants knew if they would not give them what they were asking for, their lives would be in danger and their houses would get burned.

The Russian partisans were fighting for their survival, and they did not let anybody or anything stand in their way. They knew that they were fighting a war and they also knew that there were two ways about it, to kill the enemy or be killed by them. At the time, while we were still in the ghetto, some Jews sometimes managed to sneak out of the ghetto. The Jews were also determined to live and they tried very hard to survive the Nazis, but even when they managed to get out of the ghetto, the Jews were still recognized by the police and they got shot anyway. In spite of all of the obstacles, the Jews still tried very hard to come out of the war alive, no matter what it took.

I was very happy that I did not see the Nazis and their murderous faces anymore. I could not forget, not even for a minute what they did to my life and to the life of my family and the rest of the Jews. I was also happy that I joined up with the partisans, and we few Jews, felt that somebody, sort of, was taking care of us. No matter how it was, we were in the forest together right near them and we did not feel all alone.

The forest had blueberries, strawberries, wild berries, blackberries, mushrooms and bushes of wild cherries. We ate whatever we could find, anything that we thought was edible. We always got stomachaches, but no one cared because we were very hungry all of the time.

The Russian partisans were like terrorists, like a guerilla movement. They did a lot of damage to the Nazis. They had organized groups with different ammunition and they carried out the leaders orders very well.

They blew up the railway station, the railway tracks, the Nazi bases and their barracks. The partisans killed Nazi guards, blew up their police stations, sabotaged the railroads, blew up bridges, blew up the water tower, and did as much damage as they could do. The Nazis knew that the Russian partisans were in the forest, so the Nazis decided to patrol the end of the forest.

After that, it was very hard for the Russian partisans and for us to get into the village by the road because of the Nazi patrols. Most of the time we were hungry because we could not get any food. We could go to the village through the forest, but it was a very hard and difficult walk. The forest was full of swamps and the mosquitoes were very bad. Besides that there were a lot of snakes, animals, and wild birds and we had to be on the watch every minute of the day. In spite of everything, there were no two ways about it, only one. If we wanted to get some food, the forest was the only way to get to the village without jeopardizing our lives.

We knew the forest very well, by this time. In order to be safe we went through the forest to the village most of the time, instead of by way of the road. In some parts of the forest, the woods were so thick that if we were to stand near one tree we could not see who was standing at the next tree. The Russian partisans also had to go through the forest to the village to get some food, so they decided to burn down the villages around the forest with the German headquarters and all the tents that the Germans set up in the villages. The fire spread very fast from one house to another. The houses in the villages had a straw roof and they caught fire very quickly. In no time, the villages were burned to the ground and they got rid of the German headquarters. The peasants had kept their food supply in their bunker so the Russian partisans were able to get their food.

We, the sixteen Jewish people, were only allowed to take whatever was in the field and whatever was left in the garden. The Russian partisans did not let the Jews get into the bunkers, they said that someone could hide there and we would be shot by them. We took whatever we could, from the fields, just to have something to eat.

It was not enough that we had dovolno (plenty) of tsures (trouble) and we were dirty and cut off from the world without knowing what will happen to us, but on top of our troubles, we had more troubles. The high-ranking Russian leader, who gave orders to the partisans, was very nice, intelligent and also polite, but he resented that the Jews were following them.

One day he came over to us and started to tell us that we really did not belong near them. He told us that they were partisans and they were part of the Russian army and we were only private citizens, and especially Jews. I mentioned this before, that the Russians had a lot of reasons to dislike strangers, because they really did not trust them. They felt that they should not have any civilians around them. The leader knew that we were only hiding out there in order to survive. I think that everything he said made a lot of sense, but the reality of it was that we really did not bother them. We set up our place farther away from them and we were not in their way at all. They could only see us and we could see them.

Apparently, just the thought of knowing that we were close by was too much for them, but we felt much safer knowing that they were here and we were not alone. We watched every move they made and when we saw that they were getting ready to move, we got ready also. In spite of all of the speeches from the leader we followed them anyway.

We all knew that the Russian partisans really hated to have us around, but we thought and hoped that they would not shoot us just to get rid of us. At least that was what we told ourselves. They even tried to sneak away from us, but they did not succeed because we watched them all the time. I remember that one time the partisans and we started to move from one place to another place. At the time the forest was covered with a heavy fog and we could not see what was going on even right in front of us. I heard the Russian leader give an order to have our eyes and ears open and to watch and listen for anything that looks or sounds different and everyone tried to do what he told us to do. Luckily, for us we made it. The partisans started to set up their base, and we did the same.

It was a very harsh life in the forest, but we hoped and prayed that someday and somehow we would survive the war. We all tried our very best, including me. I kept on hoping that maybe the war would come to an end soon and I would come out of it alive, and maybe somebody from my family had survived and I would find them alive, also. I was thinking that every one of us had the same thoughts in their mind and everyone kept on hoping for a miracle.

In spite of the fact that the high-ranking Russian leader did not want us around, we still stayed very close to them. The Russian people, especially the men, had a reputation of drinking a lot of alcohol, mostly straight vodka. I still remember this incident. One night the leader got drunk and when we were all asleep he came to the area where we set up our station and took apart our tents that we put up. Then he made a fire in the middle of the night and burned all of our few possessions. Some of the people had blankets, shoes and other items. I did not have too much, but whatever I had got burned, together with the others belongings. The leader kept on screaming at us, but nothing that he said made any sense. He was too drunk to know what he was saying or what he was doing.

The next day, after he sobered up, he came over and apologized, but by then it was too late. Nobody had any of their few belongings anymore because of him everything got burned. He had a close friend who tried to stop him, but he could not. It did not help because the leader did not listen to anybody. When he was drunk he was out of control. He was not a happy drunk.

Of course, the leader was under a lot of pressure and he had a lot of responsibilities. I was sure that it was not so easy to be a leader under these conditions and circumstances. I think that was why he drank more than he should. Maybe he was scared about the outcome of the war, or maybe he missed his family, or maybe he was worried that he would not be lucky enough to come out of the war alive. Maybe he was so miserable and frustrated enough, that he decided to pick on people who never did any harm to him. We stayed out of his way all the time. I think that maybe, all of these maybes were not good enough or fair enough to pick on us, and be mean to us, for no good reason at all. I also think that maybe we had more than enough of our share of misery that the Nazis inflicted on us, and we did not need any more misery from him. We really could not be surprised by his actions towards us because this was our mazel (luck) and everyone blamed us for everything all of our lives, so why not him, too.

I only had one skirt and blouse that I was wearing. I remember I had a big silk shawl and I made a dress out of it. I folded the shawl into two, then I sewed by hand two seams and I cut out a neckline. When I washed the skirt and the blouse that I wore, I put on my dress. For some reason or another, to my surprise, the Russian leader took a liking to me and he tried to talk to me, but I did not want to talk to him, so when I saw him coming, I ran away and hid under a tree. He saw me running away, but he was not so drunk to make a fuss over it. He behaved more civilized when he was not drinking and he even stayed and talked to the Jews in a nice way. Apparently, he pretended that he did not see me running away from him.

When he left our group I came back to the Jews, only to hear their complaints against me. I had the most miserable time. The Jews were mad at me because I ran away from the leader. They said that he only wanted me to be nice and talk to him. When he was good and drunk, he hollered that he would bring me a ton of butter and a ton of bacon (wegone masla, and wegone salah in Russian). He hollered, "Sonka, Ja tibia lublui", which means "Sonia, I love you." In the middle of the night he hollered so loud that he woke everyone up, including most of the partisans.

His friend was from the same city that he was from, and they had known each other all their lives. His friend once told me that the leader, Misha, that was his name, was a lawyer before the war, he was married and had two children, whom he missed a lot. His friend also said that the reason he was drinking so much was to forget that there was a war going on and he would feel better to have somebody to talk to. I thought to myself that I really did not care how he would feel. I just wanted to be left alone and I was thinking that I would also feel much better to have my family with me to talk to.

The reality was that I just did not want to be involved and to hear about someone's troubles. I really did not need to get more depressed than I already was and more confused with the whole situation that I was in. I had enough to worry about my own troubles. Most of the time I remember that I used to sit under a tree for hours and hours all by myself because I really tried to stay away from everyone and be alone with my misery. There was and still is a saying that "misery likes company", but this was not the case with me in the forest. I really did not want anybody around me at the time, and I felt that I just wanted to be alone with my thoughts.

The Jews said that it was all my fault and that I should be nice to the partisan leader, Misha. He did not ask for anything else, but to be nice to him and to talk to him, but I still did not want to talk to him or look at him. Even when I heard someone else talking, it irritated me an awful lot. I still remember that I felt very nervous all the time.

I really did not know for sure why I was so stubborn and acted the way I did. Maybe it had something to do with my upbringing. The strict Orthodox Jewish women did not socialize with men until they got married. Then, they had one man in their life, and this was their husband. Maybe this was the reason that I did not want to talk to him, or maybe I was not used to seeing someone drunk.

Every time the leader was drunk and I could not run away from him fast enough, because from the beginning I was not too careful to look out for him, he grabbed me by the arm and put his gun to my brains, and then he said to me that he was going to shoot me. He did this almost everyday when he was drunk and he caught me by sneaking up on me. Sometimes, when he was not too drunk, he came over to talk to us and he really was very nice to everyone.

I remember that I was sitting in fear and I could not even concentrate on what he was talking about. I really was scared of him because every time he put the gun to my brains I thought, "This will be the end of me". I did not care about getting shot, but to know exactly how and when it would happen, did not give me a good feeling. One day, when I ran away from him, I spotted a skrytka (bunker). I thought to myself that this would be a good hiding place for me and maybe it will save my life.

When I came back to the Jews, I told them about it and I told them where it was. I did not know how or who dug this big hole in the middle of the forest. Maybe somebody was hiding there, also, or maybe some of the animals made this hole for themselves.

It looked like a bunker and it was not far from the place where we were in hiding, so when Misha started to call my name, I knew that he was already good and drunk and I had to run away. This time I ran straight to the bunker. I sat in the bunker and the insects and mosquitoes ate me alive. It was awful, and I could see the mosquitos' bellies filling up with my blood, but I decided to stay there by myself, away from him, just to have some peace and quiet. I knew that the way I felt, I really could not take all of this pressure anymore among all of the other things. I felt that my nerves would not take too much more and eventually I would crack up. I knew that I could not go on this way day after day, without one peaceful moment.

It really looked and felt very impossible for me not to lose my mind so by staying in the bunker it helped me a lot to calm down and collect my thoughts. It also gave me plenty of time to think, listen and observe everything that was going on around me. I sat in the big hole and I was able to look out. It seemed to me that I saw everything for the first time, in spite of the fact that I had been in the forest almost three months already.

I always loved nature, and everything that I saw in the forest fascinated me. I could hear noises of the birds and the sounds of the wild animals from a distance. I still remember that it was my first time being in the bunker all alone, when it started to rain very hard, like a windstorm. The trees bent almost to the ground. I was staying in front of the bunker near the entrance shaking like a leaf from fear, but I watched and observed everything. In no time I got so carried away by the surroundings that I felt like I was in a deep trance and I did not feel any fear anymore. With this first experience of being a part of the storm in the forest, I felt like I was hypnotized and I was in another world. I kept on watching and observing what was going on. It was very interesting and exciting and very different from our storms in the city. The storm finally let up and I came back to normal.

At the time of the storm, I thought to myself that when I was getting scared I could start pretending that I was not scared. Soon my personality and my mind started to work very different than it would work normally. It always felt to me that sub-consciously I was hypnotizing myself. Believe it or not, and even until this day I can talk myself into some things and I can talk myself out of some things. It seems to me that I can control my mind the way I want to. When the rain let up and the sun came out, it looked and it felt very peaceful again.

I sat in the bunker and I felt very much alone, but I was afraid to come out because I started to think about my situation that I was in. I did not know what could and would happen when the leader, Misha, would see me. The Jews were angry with me, but they still brought me some food while I was in the bunker. One day when the Jews brought me something to eat and everyone was sitting in the bunker talking, I remember that I was crying and I felt very miserable, lonely and lost. Everything seemed to me like it was a very hopeless situation and I kept on saying that it was no use fighting it. At this time, I felt very depressed and on top of it the Jews still kept on blaming me for everything. They kept on saying that it was all my fault. They never, not even once, tried to say a nice or an encouraging word to me.

Suddenly, out of nowhere, the Russian leader, Misha, showed up. He came into the bunker and he started hollering at the Jews. He accused them of teaching me that I should not talk to him. He also said that the Jews do not want me to be nice to him and he started a fistfight with everyone. He then took out his gun and he said, "I'm going to shoot all of you". He was not drunk then, it was daytime. I ran over to him and I pleaded with him not to do it, and I kept on saying that I would be nice to him. After he calmed down, he let all of them go, and then he dragged me out of the bunker and asked me if I will run away from him again. I said, "No." He told me to go back to the Jews and I did. I think that when I did not want to talk or look at him, it hurt his pride.

After this incident, I thought that the Jews felt that they had enough of this harassment, like burning all of their things and being accused by the leader Misha of instigating me and telling me that I should not be nice to him when it really was the other way around. The Jews kept on telling me to be nice to him. In his mind, he told himself that it was all the Jews fault and he blamed the Jews for my actions, and the Jews kept on blaming me for being so stubborn.

As soon as they came back, they started to get their things together in order to move away from this place to another place in the forest. Without me saying one word to them, I also got my things together. They kept on giving me dirty looks, as though they really hated me. I knew that they were still all shook up and probably still scared from what happened in the bunker and of course, they blamed me for it.

I knew that they were angry with me, but I did not think that they would want to leave me behind, all alone. I started to think to myself that if the leader would not have let me go back to the Jews right away, they would have moved away to another place and I would have been left all alone. Just the thought made me even angrier and I started to hate them. I kept on walking behind them. As soon as they saw me following them, they said to me that they do not want me around, and they did not want me to go with them, they kept on hollering at me, that it was all my fault and they could and would be shot because of me.

They kicked me back and they blamed me for all of their troubles and misery that they said I put them through. I really thought that no matter how the Nazis treated us, the Jews could still behave in a more civilized way and they could still act with dignity and at least have respect for each other. I remember that I was crying and I kept on running after them, but they kept on pushing me, kicking me and hitting me. They really acted like the Nazis acted towards the Jews. In spite of their behavior towards me, it did not help them because I kept on running after them, anyway.

When the Jews settled in a new place, I tried to stay away from them as much as I could. I could not even look at them because of the way they behaved and treated me. They acted like wild animals. After this incident in the bunker, it was very quiet. We did not see or hear from the Russian leader, Misha, and everyone started to calm down. The Jews started to be much nicer to me. I thought that they felt guilty for the way they behaved towards me. In the beginning, I was very angry with them and when they talked to me, I answered them as shortly as I could. Little by little my anger faded and I started to get a little friendlier towards them, but never too friendly. I just could not forget the way they behaved and treated me. I guess they thought that I was jeopardizing their lives by being so stubborn.

Most of the time I was on my own. I picked blueberries, strawberries, and whatever I could find in the woods. I tried to be occupied, in order just not to be too close to the other Jews. I still felt hurt and angry at them about how they had acted towards me and I remembered how they wanted to force me to do something that I really felt very strongly against. When I did not want to talk to the leader, I thought that this was my prerogative. Even when my life was in danger, and when the leader, Misha, put the gun to my brains, I still stood by my principles and this was my choice, also. In spite of it that we moved to another place, I was still very self -conscious and still very scared that he could find us and would start the same troubles again.

A few weeks passed and we did not see the leader, Misha, coming around. Suddenly, in the middle of the night, we heard a lot of commotion. Everyone woke up and we ran to the Russians to find out what was going on. We heard them talking about how the Russian leader, Misha, and his friend went to the village. His friend came back alone and told everyone that the Germans caught Misha and they shot him on the spot, but he had managed to escape. Finally, we had peace and quiet from Misha.

Needless to say, after so many months of being harassed and threatened, I really had to admit that I felt relieved and free of all of the pressure and danger that Misha put me through. I felt that I was free from all the fear of being shot by him. Between him and the Jews on my back constantly for almost four months and all of the misery that they inflicted on me I could not be so noble to feel sorry that he was killed. Misha's friend also told us that he saw the Nazi bases in the village were empty and most of the Nazis were gone. He also mentioned that he asked one of the peasants what was going on and the peasant told him that he heard that the Nazis had lost the war and the Russians won, and finally the war was over. The peasant also told him that when the Nazis felt that they were losing the war, they tried to dispose of the bodies that they had killed at the time when they still had their bases in the villages. The Nazis poured gasoline over the bodies and burned them. They thought that by hiding the evidence nobody would know what kind of murderers they were.

# PART THREE

# CHAPTER XXV
# THE END OF THE WAR AND THE LIBERATION

## THE SEARCH FOR MY FAMILY

It was July 1944 when we got the news that the Nazis retreated and the war ended. Everyone was very excited. We heard that the Soviet troops entered the eastern part of Poland for the second time. We packed up and watched what the Russian partisans did. They celebrated for a while and then they got everything together and started their march out of the forest. The partisans tried to be careful, just in case the rumors were not true, and the Nazis really were only planning to get the Russian partisans in the open in order to shoot all of them. The Russian partisans thought that it was better to be careful than sorry, so they decided that instead of walking with the road we all kept on walking with the forest in order not to be spotted by anybody.

We kept on walking and everyone tried to be very quiet and careful. Nobody said anything. Instead, everyone probably was thinking, including me, if it was true or not, if we were really free, and if the war was really over.

Now, since Misha was killed, Misha's friend was in charge of the Russian partisans and from time to time he gave an order to tell us in which direction we should go. Of course, everyone in the group obeyed his orders. I think that he was a very good leader and the partisans really liked him. I think that they had more confidence in him because he was never drunk, not like Misha.

The sixteen Jewish people followed the Russian partisans every step of the way. Now the Russian partisans did not mind it at all that we were near them because now they were more relaxed than when they had to go to carry out dangerous missions without even knowing if they would come out of it alive. Now they felt more responsible towards us and they treated us much nicer.

They really watched us so that we should not fall behind. We walked into the forest swamps, deeper and deeper. We heard shooting from farther away. We also heard the Nazis Luftwaffe airplanes flying. They were probably on their way back to Germany. It made us feel good to know that finally, we were getting rid of the Nazis and the war was over. It seemed this way to us, but the reality was that nobody felt completely safe or sure that it really happened and that the war ended. I personally had a doubt in my mind that maybe it was not really true, or maybe I just could not believe it, that we got rid of the Nazis and I had lived through the war.

Finally, we got out of the forest. We passed some burning villages and small towns. Most of the houses were destroyed from the bombs and the fires that the Nazis and the Russian partisans had made. The road was filled with abandoned Nazi military vehicles, tanks, jeeps, cannons, army trucks, but no Nazi soldiers, anywhere. It looked like it was really true, that we were free, and the war was really over. Everyone started to feel more positive that it was not just a rumor, but it was a reality that we got rid of the Nazis for good.

We also saw all of the German bases empty. No more Nazis. We kept on walking and on the way we met some Ukrainian and Polish people. They looked at us in a wondering and surprising way and they probably thought, "How come you are still alive?" They expected Poland to be without Jews and without Communists, because they hated Communists as much as they hated the Jews.

While we kept on walking, some Polish people stopped and they said to us, "What a shame that you are still alive and the Nazis did not kill you." We did not pay too much attention to what they said or thought of us. We always knew that they were anti-Semites, Jew haters, and we always thought of them as being nothing else, but trash.

When the war changed in favor of the Russians, and the Nazis retreated, the Russians once again occupied the eastern part of Poland, including Wlodzimierz Volynski. This was the second time that the Russians occupied this area. The first time was on September 17, 1939 and then again in July 1944 when they won the war against the Nazis, and the eastern part of Poland was liberated by the Russians. The last German forces were finally pushed out from Poland in early 1945.

I hid in the woods with the Russian partisans for four months from the end of March 1944 to almost the end of July 1944. Myself and fifteen other Jews, with, more or less, 10,000 Russian partisans who were hiding in the Polesie district in the eastern part of Poland in the forest near the town of Michaliczky, all walked out of the woods together.

Everyone was still very unsure if the war was really over and everyone was asking each other, "Is the war really over? Are we really free?" but nobody knew the right answer for sure, until finally, from a distance we could see the road. We kept on walking towards this direction and when we came to a highway and we saw trucks full of Russian soldiers, singing Russian songs and laughing, they were very happy to see all of us alive, especially the Russian partisans. We knew for sure then, that the war was really over for us. It was on July 20, 1944.

The Russian soldiers were hollering, "We won the war, we won. Death to the Nazis." Everyone got excited and they started hugging, and kissing each other, and everyone was crying. The first few minutes, I felt almost happy that I was finally alive and free, but the happiness did not last too long. I started to think about my family and I realized that I was really free. Free from everything and free from everyone whom I ever had and loved, and who I always will. This was the bitter end of the war. The awful war that the Nazis had inflicted on me by murdering my whole family and six million Jews for no reason at all.

Now, once again, I was all alone and I had to make all the decisions by myself without even knowing how to begin. The only thing that I really knew was that I did not have anything from my past life, and what was left of it for me, was only the awful memories. I also knew that on the day of the liberation my life was starting from the beginning.

When I started to ask myself, "Where can I go from here, and what can I do from now on?" the answer to my questions was that I really did not know. What I knew was that I was homeless, penniless, all alone, and I had to face my future all by myself without any of my family left to depend on. As young as I was then, not even fifteen years old, I knew that I had a very difficult road ahead of me. I tried to tell myself that everything would be okay.

I felt all worn out and drained physically, mentally and emotionally. My thoughts and my feelings were very mixed, and I was very confused with my whole situation. It seemed to me very impossible to begin my life. The reality of it was that my past was completely erased, as though

I never existed and I had to start my life from the beginning, like I was just born without anybody and without anything. I really did not know at the time if I even wanted to try. I felt very tired and hopeless and nothing really made any sense to me. Even though the war was over, I had to start fighting another war only to stay alive.

I kept on asking myself, for what reason did I want to stay alive, and for what reason did I want to fight another war? I was very uncertain and my mind was really not too steady. One minute I was happy that I was alive and the next minute I was sorry that I had lived through the war. One minute I had hopes that everything would work out for me, and the next minute everything seemed to be hopeless. One minute I was telling myself that everything would be okay and the next minute I was asking myself, how could it be okay? Deep in my heart I felt that it would never be okay.

I thought that it was impossible for me, being all alone, to start to rebuild my life and take care of myself, by myself, and to do all of these things only for one reason, just to exist in the world. I remember since my mother, sister, my two brothers and the rest of my family got killed, murdered by the Nazis, I really did not care anymore if I would live or die, and I really did not care about anything that could or would happen to me. I did not push myself to get murdered, but I never tried to prevent it, either. It was just my good mazel (luck) or my bad mazel (luck) to live through the war without really feeling alive.

I kept on walking and the Russian trucks with soldiers picked me up. I wanted to go to Ludmir, my city of Wlodzimierz, Volynski, but the Russian soldiers said that we could not go in there yet, because the mines were still there and they did not let anyone into the city. Instead, I went to Lutsk because it was the closest town to my city. After a few days when the mines were already cleared, I was on my way to my city. I hitchhiked and the Russian trucks with their soldiers gave me a ride. Coming back to my city, it looked like nothing ever happened and nothing changed. The same houses, the same buildings, the same streets and the same Gentiles, but to me it did not look the same, and it did not feel the same, and it did not sound the same because it was not the same city that I knew before the war. To me, my hometown looked and felt like a besoylem (graveyard). Not even one thing was the same.

I did not see any Jews anymore, I did not hear anyone speaking

Yiddish, I did not see any Jewish children playing. I did not hear any praying or singing voices from the synagogue. I thought to myself, "What happened to the city that I used to know?" I kept on asking myself the same question over and over again. "Was it really true that the Nazis wiped out our entire Jewish population, and was it really true that nobody was left of my family, my neighbors and our friends in the whole city?" It really sounded unbelievable to me, but unfortunately this was the bitter truth.

The city where I was born and raised, and lived in until the war, and every house in our neighborhood reminded me of the Jewish people who used to live there, did not exist anymore. The Nazi murderers took their lives away from them. Now the Poles and the Ukrainian anti-Semites took over and they lived in our Jewish homes. They took our belongings and everything that we had owned. They took over our businesses with all the goods that were left in them. They really took over our lives and everything in it, and they acted as if it was theirs and belonged to them.

My parents saved and put together a penny with a penny to leave something for their children and they did not dream that such an awful tragedy would occur. Now the Poles and the Ukrainians and whoever else wanted to benefit from our tragedy, did. On top of it, after the war, we were not allowed or welcome on the land where we were born and lived until the war, as a Polish citizen.

The fact was that because of the Jewish misfortune the anti-Semites were fortunate to have everything that they ever wanted without the slightest effort of having to work for it. Everything came to them very easily. Thanks to the Nazis, they got rich with the Jews sweat and blood and with everything that they took, after the Jews were murdered. It was very hard for me to see all of these things without getting emotional, but there was nothing that I could do except to feel all the pain and sorrow.

I kept on walking and I saw that all the stores that once belonged to the Jews were now occupied by the Poles who had changed the names on the signs to their names. At the time, when I came back to my city, they had the bazaar day. The bazaar, which used to be twice a week and was always very busy and lively, was now very depressing with no life in it at all. It looked and it felt like a besoylem (cemetery or graveyard). I think that when the Jews were there, everything was and felt alive. Now, since there were no more Jews, everything in our city died with them because the Jews had a special talent for business and for making everything look and sound lively. This was our way of living and doing things in order to feel alive.

I came to the street where we had the biggest synagogue. It was a beautiful synagogue, but now everything in it was burned and the Venetian glass windows were broken. Only a skeleton was left of it. All the other synagogues were demolished, also. Suddenly, it came to my mind to go to the besoylem (cemetery) to see my father's and my grandfather's keiver (grave- berier). They died before the war. The cemetery, as I remember, was fenced in by a brick wall around it, and in the front it had a big double iron gate.

When I came closer, I did not see the gate in the front of the cemetery. I only saw an empty lot with a lot of pieces of stones. I really could not understand what happened to the miceivys (headstones). I walked out of the lot and the first Polish man who I saw, I stopped and asked him what happened to the headstones. He told me that they used them in some parts of the city to make the streets and sidewalks out of them.

The headstones were engraved and inscribed with the dead person's name with holy menorahs, lions, and the Star of David and now everyone was stepping on them. Hearing this, I started to cry and I kept on crying without being able to stop. I thought that at least my father's and my grandfather's graves would be there and I would be able to come and talk to them. I never knew where my mother, my sister, my two brothers and the rest of my family were buried. I did not even have their graves to go to, either. The Polish man was standing and looking at me. I remember that he tried to calm me down by saying to me that my family is now in heaven and they were watching over me, then he put his arm around my shoulders and he said to me, "I know how you feel."

I could see that he really felt sorry for me, but he could never know how I really felt. We talked to each other and I spilled my heart out to him. After awhile he gave me some money, Polish zlotys, and he said to me, "Please do not stay here. Leave Poland as soon as possible." I wanted to know why he was saying this, so I asked him why I should leave Poland? After a minute of silence, he replied, "The anti-Semites who took everything away from the Jews, are scared that the Jews are coming to take everything back from them and they do not have any intention of letting it happen, so when they see a Jew they kill him. The police never say or do anything to punish them for it. On the contrary, they encourage them to do just that. " He also told me that some groups of the A.K. (Armia Krajowa) were killing the Jews who survived the Nazis.

I thanked him for the money and his advice and I left. I kept on walking back to the main street and when I turned my head back, I still saw the Polish man standing in the same spot where I left him and he kept on looking after me as I walked away. It felt to me that he was really watching over me like a good angel.

One of the Jewish men who was in the forest with me, and then when we were liberated together, offered to come along and help me look for my family. I was very happy that he was willing to come with me and keep me company. He was very friendly to me and I could see that he had a special interest in me. I still remember one night, in the forest, I went to sleep outside the tent, near a tree. It was a cold night and I did not have anything to cover myself with, because the Russian leader, Misha, had burned everything. In the morning when I woke up, I saw that I was covered with his jacket. I thanked him for it. In a way it made me feel good that someone cares about me.

Once he said to me, "Sonia, I have to tell you something." I asked him, "What do you want to tell me?" Then he said to me, " I saw good women and I saw bad women, but a woman like you, I never saw in my life." I asked him what he meant by it? He said to me, "You risk your life only to stick to your principles." I replied to him, "My reason for being so persistent was that I thought if I will ever survive the war and I will find someone of my family alive, I want to have a clear conscience, and I would want them to know that I never did anything that would be against our religion and our ways of living. "

He even proposed marriage to me, but I was not ready for it. He was a very nice man and we stuck together. He came with me to my city and we both wandered the streets looking for familiar faces. I was hoping that maybe I would be lucky enough to find someone of my family alive. Even if deep in my heart I felt and knew that it was hopeless, I still kept on praying and looking for someone who may have survived. I saw what happened to the city that I once knew. No Jews, no family, no friends, no life, no nothing. By walking the streets I passed a lot of

Polish people, but they did not look familiar to me. I kept on walking and looked at everyone who was facing me, and I hoped that maybe I would see someone who I knew before the war. Suddenly I saw a Polish couple coming towards me without even looking at me. I recognized them right away. When they came closer they saw me and recognized me, also. I tried to ask them if they saw anyone of my family after the war, but instead of answering me they kept on walking faster, away from me. These were the Polish people with whom my mother did business with for many years. They did not even want to talk to me. It looked to me like they had a guilty conscience or maybe they owed my mother money and they thought that I came to collect it.

I knew that the war ended, and I had no more fear of being hungry or being killed by the Nazis, but everything and everyone whom I loved was killed and I started to ask myself all kinds of questions. "What now? How can I put the pieces of my life together? Where is my place in this world? Where and to whom do I belong? How will I go on? What will I do with my life? What will the future hold for me?" and so on and on. Because I could not find one answer, not even to one of my questions, I kept on asking the same questions over and over again.

I kept on walking the streets of our city looking around and thinking to myself that once, many years ago, which now felt like a lifetime to me, I was very happy here, and tears came to my eyes. I started to remember all of the good things that happened to me in this city before the Nazis came to us and destroyed my life. Suddenly, I realized that I did not yet see Warshawa Ulica (street) where my mother had her two stores and the buildings that were ours, too. I started to think to myself of all the times that I spent there after school, almost every day, helping my mother with whatever I could and looking at her smiling face. Now I had nothing left, only a few good memories of my childhood years. I became very sad and miserable. I kept on walking and I came to Warshawa Street. I saw that some Polish people made, a frizjier (barber shop) out of one of the buildings and in the other building was a krawiec (tailor shop). I told them that these buildings belong to my family and they said that now it belongs to them. They got very angry with me and they started pushing me and calling me all kinds of names. They kept on hollering that they do not want any more Jews here and the Jews should go to Palestine. I really got scared of them and I left right away. The Ukrainians and the

Poles killed a lot of Jewish people when they came back and tried to claim their properties.

I remembered what the Polish man who I met by the cemetery said to me, to leave Poland as soon as possible. I saw that he was right and whatever he told me was true. The lives of the Jews who came back to Poland, even not to claim anything, were not safe and I decided it was not worth it to me, to survive the Nazis and be killed by the Polish or Ukrainian anti-Semites for a property.

I remember that I kept on looking back to see if anyone was following me. It was lucky for me that I was with this young man from the woods, because this made me feel safer than being alone. After a few days, the young man said goodbye to me and he went to Kovel where he had lived before the war. He wanted to look for his family. I left Wlodzimierz Volinsky and I went to Hrubieszow, where my grandparents and my uncles with their families used to live. I met some Polish people who I remembered very well from before the war. I used to come to my grandparents to visit them, and these Poles used to come into my grandparents store very often to buy yard goods or just to talk for a while to my grandmother. I tried to find out if they knew anything about my mother's family. I asked about my grandmother, my uncle, aunt, and their family. Even though I knew from the man who came to our city, Wlodzimierz Volinsky, when the Nazis were already in Hrubieszow, that told my mother and me that they were all killed, in spite of him telling us this, I was still hoping that it was not true. The Polish people who I saw told me that since the beginning of the war they did not see them and they did not know what happened to them.

I used to love this town with the people in it. Everyone used to be very friendly and nice to each other. After the war, when I came to Hrubieszow and I went to Targowa Ulica (street), where my grandmother had her business, I saw that some Polish people now occupied the business. They were scared that I would try to take it back from them. The same was with the homes that my grandmother and my uncle's family left behind. The Polish and the Ukrainians took everything and they never gave anything back to the survivors.

Thanks to the Nazis, the Poles and the Ukrainians became owners of properties and all of the other goods. Everything that they dreamed of in their whole life came true for them. They got everything for nothing, all of it free and clear.

I stayed in Hrubieszow for four days, and I slept on the street, in the park and wherever I could. I hoped to find somebody, but it did not happen. I had to face the reality that no one else from my entire family had survived, only me, and I decided to leave Hrubieszow. I started to analyze my life and the situation that I was in. I was not even fifteen years old. I did not have a normal childhood and I was all alone in the world with my whole family killed. I did not even have their keiver (grave) to go to and no miceivy (headstone) with their names. I had no pictures of us to show that we shared our lives together. In other words, I had absolutely nothing that was left of their lives. It seemed like they never existed in the world, and by the same token my life from the past and all of the years that I had spent with them were erased, also. The only thing that was left for me from my past were the memories of my very happy childhood years, which were my very best years of my life.

I started to wonder. "Why were they all killed and I was the only one of the whole family left to survive the Nazis?" Maybe there was a reason for everything that happened. Sometimes, I thought that maybe I was not worth it to perish together with my family. Or maybe, the reason was for me to live through the war in order to remember my dead family, and to build a legacy of generations so they would know that my family once existed.

I always believed in God even in the darkest days of my life, when my family was killed and even when a lot of Orthodox Jews lost their faith that God even exists. I still believed that God was watching over me and he, for sure, knew the reason for everything that happened, but with all my beliefs and all my logical thinking, it did not help me at all. I felt very much alone and without any hope that I will ever feel alive.

I left Hrubieszow and again I hitchhiked with the Russian soldiers. It was not so bad for me to hitchhike because I spoke Russian and they understood me very well. I told them that I was in the forest with the Russian partisans for four months and apparently they thought that I was also a partisan. They did not ask me if I was a partisan and I did not say anything either. In reality, I was just hiding in the forest until the end of the war. They seemed to be very happy to talk to me. They gave me some food, chocolate and they were very nice to me. Finally, I came back to Lutsk. I had never been in this city before the war, and I did not know anything or anybody there. I asked the Russian soldiers to let me off in the business section and they said okay.

The Russian soldiers drove me to the center of the city and I thanked them. I still remember that this particular day was a big business day with a lot of stands of different merchandise. The streets were very crowded. There were people all over the city. I kept on looking at the different items that they sold, but I could not buy anything because I did not have a penny to my name. I also did not have anyplace to go to, so I just kept on walking the streets. I thought to myself that maybe I would see someone I knew. Suddenly, I saw a woman with her daughter who was from our city and we recognized each other right away.

She used to be a very good friend of my mother's and she knew my whole family. Her daughter and my sister used to go to the same class in public school together. We hugged and kissed and cried and laughed and we were very excited to see each other. Then she asked me where I was staying. I told her that I just came here and I did not have a place yet. She said to me, " Now you are staying with us." She asked me where my things were so I told her that I do not have anything, only one dress in my paper bag. She kissed me and then she said, "Sonia, we are here on the market and we are going to buy a couple of things for you." I told her that I do not have any money and she said, "Do not worry, I have money", and then she told me to pick what I wanted. I started to cry without a stop. When I calmed down, I thanked her and she said, "Now smile, we are going shopping and we will have a good time buying new things for you." After we were done with shopping, we walked to her apartment, which was not too far from the center of the city. I still remember that it was a big building with a lot of apartments there.

She came to Lutsk with her daughter right after she was liberated. It was a few weeks earlier than me and actually they were one of the first people to get liberated. It was right after the Russians chased the Nazis out from the eastern part of Poland. This was why she managed to get some spending money every week from the UNRRA (United Nations Relief and Rehabilitation Administration), for herself and her daughter. She was also given quite a large and roomy apartment.

All of the apartments that the UNRRA gave to the Holocaust survivors had once belonged to Jewish people who were not alive anymore. To live in these apartments was very hard for us emotionally, and by moving into these places, it constantly reminded us of our past almost every minute of the day. These apartments or homes were left with many of the Jewish peoples belongings. Most of these things had only a sentimental value to some surviving members of the families. It belonged to the Jewish families who had lived in these homes before their death. Family pictures and personal items were left in these apartments, and they were only items that were not considered worthy enough to be taken by the Nazis, Poles, Ukrainians or by anyone else.

I was thinking with regrets, why I did not have anything of my family left, not even a picture, because when the war started in 1939, the first bomb landed on the house next to ours and our house burned down with all of our belongings. This woman, with her daughter, survived the Nazis because some Polish people kept her and her daughter in a bunker from 1941-1944. She had a lot of her personal items because she kept them with her where she was in hiding. All in all, I really considered myself lucky and I was very glad that she took me in and was so nice to me.

I stayed with her for a few months and she treated me like a daughter. I would have kept on staying with them, but it was very hard for me because she reminded me so much of my own mother and she was almost as old as my mother and her daughter reminded me of my sister. I think that sub-consciously I always thought about why my mother, and my sister were not here, and by having such thoughts I always felt very guilty. It felt like I resented the fact that I was with them, instead of being with my family, especially when they were so good to me. I always knew that my way of thinking was very selfish, but I really could not help myself. In spite of my will, these thoughts came into my mind very often and I felt very miserable and guilty because of it, even though I really did appreciate how kind they were to me and how they made me feel like I belonged with them.

One day I met people from my city who were living in Lodz. They insisted that I should stay with them. They were two sisters and one brother. The brother was married and the UNRRA gave them a separate apartment in the same building. They all survived because a Ukrainian woman took them in and kept them hidden until the end of the war.

Without even thinking, I said I would stay with them. In a way

I was very relieved, but I always kept in touch with the mother and daughter and I told them so often, that I really did appreciate how kind they were to me and how they made me feel like I belonged with them. It really made no difference to me where and with whom I was staying.

I became a refugee, without a family, without a home, without identity and without any hope. The reality of it was that I did not belong to anybody and nobody belonged to me. In other words, I was living my life without a purpose or a goal, and I was wandering from one place to another place. The war was over for a few months already, but for me my war had just begun. After I had lived through all the danger, hardship and persecution and I was spared from death so many times and in spite of everything, I did survive, and now I had to start fighting for my life and my existence all over again. I started to ask myself, "When will all of this fighting stop?" I was wondering and thinking if it would ever stop and come to an end, or would I have to fight an endless war all of my life?

The way I felt, I did not have any ambition, any desire, any strength, or any willpower to do anything like this anymore, in order to fight just for my existence. I started to reassess my life and I came to a conclusion that there was really nothing left for me, and according to my thinking it really was not worth it to put up such a struggle only to live and face life all by myself. Without my family, life had no purpose or meaning. My whole situation really did not make any sense in my mind and besides that, it seemed to me at the time very impossible to cope with all of my problems all alone. I knew that I was in a very hopeless situation.

I also knew that only I could decide if I wanted to go on living, and to try to start to rebuild my life, without even knowing how to begin, and try to adjust to it without my family, or to end it right now. It was a big decision for me to make. After a while of thinking it through, I decided that it really was not worth it to go on living. I asked myself the questions, "For whom and for what reason will I live for?" I came to the conclusion that enough was more than enough, because in my way of thinking there was nothing worse than a living death.

One day when no one was home, I swallowed a bottle of pills, but I was not lucky enough to die. Shortly after swallowing the pills, the people came home and saw me lying on the floor unconscious. They knew I did something and they called a doctor right away. Without my will or my desire, I was saved from death and I was living again. At the time it seemed to me that no matter how I tried to end all of my suffering and misery it did not work and I could not succeed. I became very depressed and I continued to have the same thoughts of committing suicide.

My life seemed to be very empty and hopeless, with no reason to exist any longer. The people who I was living with kept on telling me that after surviving the war, I should not be so eager to kill myself. They probably knew that if I tried once I would try again and again until I would succeed, and it was as though they really read my mind. I sensed that they were watching me. A lot of times, I said that I was going for a walk and somebody always said that they were thinking of taking a walk also. I remember that I always felt better by taking a walk and looking around. In my mind I still did not accept that my whole family was killed, instead I kept on hoping that they were still alive and I would find them somehow.

One day I walked the streets and again I met people from my city. They asked me where I was staying and I told them where. A few days later they came to see me, and they insisted that I come to stay with them. I always liked them, they were two sisters, and one was named Etta. They had three brothers, and two brothers had survived the war and one brother was lost in the war. If I remember correctly he was in the Polish army. My parents used to know them very well before the war.

Their family was very religious and very nice and I was very happy to see them alive. I liked their sincerity and honesty and I felt very good seeing them. I still remember that Etta said to me, "I came especially to take you to us, we all like you and we liked your family", and then she said to me, "We will try to be good to you in every way." I stayed and listened to her and in a while, I decided to move in with them. I thought it would feel like I have a family again. For the first time after the war I started to feel a little more secure, like I belonged some place again. I started to have better thoughts in my mind. I stopped seeing everything black and I started to see things a little brighter. I have to admit that after the war I never saw anything white again.

Six of us lived in the house together and in a way it was enough noise and commotion for me and I was really pleased with it. I felt more alive again. People came to visit us and there was always something going on and we all kept busy. I also tried to be occupied with doing something in order not to be able to get wrapped around in my own thoughts.

Etta was much older than me, and this made me especially happy and secure. I got along very well with her and her family. They treated me like I was their younger sister. Etta had a boyfriend who had been hidden in the same place with them during the war. She told me that he was involved in the Jewish organization, UNRRA. After the war he started to work with the UNRRA, and he also worked with the Zionist organization, the Beitar. The Beitar was a part of the Zionist movement. Their goal was to establish a Jewish state in Palestine. I remember before the war, my parents sent money to Palestine, which was why I knew about the Beitar organization. The Zionist organization was very active in helping Jewish people immigrate to Palestine.

# CHAPTER XXVI
# MY LIFE AFTER THE WAR AND THE JOURNEY
# TO
# UNKNOWN PLACES

Before the war, the Jews gave donations to the Zionist movement organizations in order to take care of the Jewish people, and to help them immigrate to Palestine. They organized different political parties. They had a religious Orthodox party named Mizrachi, a Jewish socialist organization, a communist party called the Bund, and an organization called Halutzim or Pioneers. This party was only for young men. They also had other organizations, like UNRRA (United Nations Relief and Rehabilitation Administration), HIAS (Hebrew Immigration Aid Society), JNC (Jewish National Committee), Joint organization, URO (United Restitution Organization), ZOB (Zydowska Organizacja Bojowa) and many other organizations that helped the Jews with whatever they needed help with.

One day Etta's boyfriend said that he was organizing a group of Jews to take to Palestine, which later was to become the State of Israel. He asked Etta if she wanted to go, also. I remember correctly that she said, "I can't leave my sister and my brothers to go to Palestine with you." He said to her, "Think it over and let me know", but she strongly felt that she should not go and leave her family behind. I tried to talk her into going to Palestine and I even said to her if he would ask me I would not think even twice about going and I would say yes. I kept on explaining to her that this would be the best opportunity for her to go with him now, and see how she likes Palestine. If she would like it there, she would let her family know and then the family could follow her. Eventually they would all be together in Palestine, and this way she would also be able to leave the bloody earth of Poland behind her.

No matter what I said she kept on insisting that she could not go. A few days later Etta's boyfriend came over to me and he asked me if I wanted to join the group and right away I said yes, that I would like to go to Palestine. I was thinking to myself that I do not have anybody or anything here or anywhere else and I was not leaving anybody behind, only the anti-Semites and the bloody soil. I also thought in my mind that maybe if I will get away from here it will help me forget the cruel actions of the murderers, and in time I would start little by little to accept the present and maybe I would even start to concentrate on my future.

I mentioned it to Etta that her boyfriend asked me if I wanted to go to Palestine and I said yes. I told her the way I felt by being here with these enemies, who helped the Nazis kill my family and the rest of the Jews. I also said to her that I thought that we belonged in our own country, not here, and maybe in time my memories of the past would fade away by living someplace else. On the other hand, I knew for sure that by staying here and living in these surroundings it would be very impossible not to think of what happened to all of us and every minute of every day, we would be reminded of it.

When Etta heard that I was going to go, she thought over what I said, and in a while she came to a conclusion on her own and she said to me, "Sonia, if you're going I will also go." Etta's boyfriend made all the preparations for us and when the day came, Etta said goodbye to her sister and brothers. They gave her some money. Unfortunately, I did not have anything to begin with. Etta said that whatever she had was for both of us to use, and it really did not make any difference to Etta whose money it was. She said it was ours. I was very happy and relieved when she also decided to go. Etta felt very sad for a while by leaving her family, but she snapped out of it fast enough, practically in no time. I said to her, "Etta, be happy. We are going to Palestine." Then she said to me, "Sonia, you're right." She really liked me a lot and I liked her, too. Finally, we were on our way to Palestine.

We knew that we had a very risky and hard journey ahead of us. Our leader, Etta's boyfriend, had some papers for the group, but they were not too legal. We had to hitchhike and sneak into trains without getting caught and without having train tickets, because in order to buy a ticket we had to show our passport and we did not have one. We did not have money to buy tickets, either.

When we came to the border between Poland and Germany, we made a wrong turn and instead of climbing a hill and being on the other side of the border, we ran into the border patrol. The border patrols were Russians. They checked the papers that our leader, Etta's boyfriend, got for us before we left. He knew all along that the papers were not in proper order, so, of course, the Russian patrol did not let us through. They said that we have to go back to Poland. There were about forty people in our group and everyone got very upset. After what we already went through and when we were finally at the border, they were going to send us back to Poland. We all felt very badly about it.

Our leader started to plead with the border patrol, and we all stayed together in our group without saying a word. Everyone was scared of the outcome and nobody knew if they would let us through or send us back to Poland. I was sure that everyone had different thoughts on their mind. I was feeling a little guilty in a way, that I should not have talked Etta into going with me, not that she blamed me for it. I knew that the papers were not legal, but I did not think that the Russians would make such a fuss of letting a few Jewish refugees cross the border. I really thought that they would feel sorry for us and they would not care where we were going.

One Russian guy from the border patrol kept on negotiating with our leader. I could not hear what they were talking about. After all of their negotiations were completed, which took about a half an hour, the leader gave the border patrol some money. Finally, he seemed to agree on whatever it was and said to us by showing with his hand, that we can go ahead.

After crossing the border, we were now in Germany. Our leader started to holler at me and he kept on hollering and asking me why I had to dress so nice. He started to say that it was my entire fault that we had trouble at the border. I remember that I was wearing the dress that I had made from a shawl while I was hiding in the forest. Our leader said this in front of the whole group without caring that he was embarrassing me. He said that one of the patrols wanted him to leave me there and that was why there was a hold up and confusion for us to cross the border. It was not bad enough that the leader hollered at me, now everyone in the group blamed me for the hold up, as though it was my fault and I did something wrong intentionally. Only Etta stood by my side. She kept on saying that it was not my fault because I did not do anything wrong, and they should not blame me for it. I still remember that I really felt awful. I was very glad that I at least had one friend on my side, and this was Etta.

After we crossed the border, the leader got in touch with the UNRRA organization. When we came from Poland to Germany, the UNRRA took us to Berlin. I remember they put us in a big, empty house that did not have any furniture, not even a table or a chair. Everyone had to sleep on the floor, but nobody minded it at all. Everyone was also really hungry and tired.

Right away, the UNRRA organization brought us some food. We stayed there for a few days and we rested up a little and very shortly after, we were again on our way. We had to cross the German border to get into Austria. Every step that we made was under our leader's orders, and whatever he told us to do we did. Most of the time he knew what he was doing. It was the same procedure as before.

First, we had to sneak into the train without being spotted. After the train, we had to walk in order to be close to the border, and finally we were almost at the Austrian border. This time, we did not get to the border patrol. I remember it was already evening and it got dark, but we still could see where we were going so before we reached the border we climbed a big hill and finally, we made it. We got to the other side of the border.

It was in the early part of 1945. Now we were in Austria and our whole group of people, including Etta and me, started to feel more relaxed. Our leader once again got in touch with the UNRRA (United Nations Relief and Rehabilitation Administration) organization and they came with cars and took us to Vienna, Austria. We stayed in Vienna, in a lager (camp). A few days later, they transferred us to Salzburg, Austria to a Displaced Persons Camp, a DP camp. Etta's boyfriend came in to talk to us, but I made myself busy because I really did not want to talk to him after what he did to me. I thought that he did not have to behave this way at the border and holler at me in front of everyone. In a while he called Etta to the side and he talked to her in private. I did not know the kind of conversation they had. I never asked Etta and she never told me anything, but I assumed that it must have been something serious because after they came back, Etta seemed to be upset.

Etta's boyfriend saw that I was angry with him and he really tried to be nice to me, but I felt that he was not so nice to me at the border and he embarrassed me for no reason at all, so I was very cold to him. After a while he said goodnight and went to his room. Only the leaders had their own private rooms. The whole group of ours, close to forty people, stayed in one room, which was a very big room. It looked like a hall.

They put us in another empty building that had either been a school or an office building. There was no furniture in the room, except a chest of drawers, standing in the corner near the door. Again we had to sleep on the floor.

Everyone was happy that we arrived safe and sound. We were all worn out from the journey. The organization brought us a hot meal and it was really good. We were not hungry anymore, only tired. Finally we could relax. I think everyone was glad that this journey was over, and we would be able to stay in one place for now. We all assumed that we would have to wait a while and eventually and hopefully very soon we would go to Palestine and settle down there for good. That was what the leader told us. Everyone was happy that we made it as far as we did, and everyone was hoping that very soon we would reach our final destination and this would be Palestine.

In the meantime, everyone was trying to settle down and make their sleeping quarters somehow and someplace the best way they could. Etta and I made our sleeping quarters in the corner near the door, next to the chest, that was standing against the wall. This way we had some privacy. It was a big room with a lot of people in it, and everyone slept next to each other. The UNRRA got us blankets, pillows, sheets, pillowcases, towels and everyday items that we needed. The next day they brought care packages for everyone with all kinds of things, including dry food.

Everyday they brought us cooked meals and gave each of us a dish to keep, like the soldiers in the army used. It was called a monashka in Polish. When they brought the food, we had to stay in line to get it. The first week Etta and I never got anything because we did not stay in line to get food. We were very hungry. She did not want to stay with the dish and I did not want to stay in line either. I still remember the way the people behaved when they brought the food. They pushed themselves to the front in order to be sure that they will get food. I think that a lot of Jews still had the fear in them from the Nazis that they will be hungry. Believe it or not, even now, sixty years after the war, I still have fear of being hungry and I always keep, sometimes, even five loaves of bread in my freezer, and when I am low in bread I get panicky. It feels to me like I will starve from hunger when I do not have enough bread.

Etta had some money, so we went to a store and bought some food, and she shared it with me. After a while she ran out of money and I did not have any money, either, so we were forced to stay in line and take the food that the UNRRA kitchen cooked for us. Everyday they brought our meals to the DP camp. The meals were pretty good and eventually we got used to staying in line with the dish. We started to accept everything and even like it. After all, we had enough food and we were not hungry anymore. We also had a place to sleep, and hopefully this was only a transit place. That was what we told ourselves.

Everyone, including me, had one thing on our minds and this was to leave here, and settle down someplace permanently. Everyday we were waiting and hoping that someone would come soon to take us to Palestine. There were people with us in every corner of the room. It looked like a big gathering and everyone mingled with each other. The survivors, most of the days were gossiping about everything and anything. Everyone was waiting, impatiently, to be sent to a new place and a new country that would be willing to take us in. I really wanted to go to Palestine.

My main wish was to get out of Austria as soon as possible. Every minute was too much for me. I could not look at these murderers. I knew that they were all Nazis. No matter how I felt about them and in spite of my bad feelings towards them, I had to act civilized. After all, I was in their country, but I thought in my mind that it would not be soon enough not to hear or see their ugly faces ever again.

Everyday, we kept on asking the person who was in charge of our group, when we were going to leave here. Everyday he said the same thing, very soon, very soon, and he said that we have to have more patience and wait until the time will come. Everyone hoped and prayed that the time would come soon and we would reach our destination. Every one of us wanted the same thing, to be able to settle down in one place, and start living a normal life in the best way that we could.

Etta and I were sitting on top of the chest in our corner near the door for hours, not talking to anyone, only to each other. Most of Etta's family came out of the war alive so she really did not had too much to talk about the war. They were hidden at a Ukrainian family in a village and they did not experience any hunger or killing. They practically did not see what was going on at the time of the Nazi occupation. Most of the time I was talking and she was listening, and she really felt sorry for me and we were both crying together. There was not one day that went by that we did not cry for one reason or another or one thing or another.

We always felt very depressed and miserable. It really was not so pleasant to be cooped up with so many different kinds of people in one room, day after day. I always sensed that Etta must miss her sister and brothers and I really thought that she was sorry that she left them and came with me. I assumed that the real reason that she came was not because of me, no matter what she would say. I always felt that the main reason that she came was probably because she wanted to be with her boyfriend.

After he brought us to Salzburg, Austria and the first night they had a talk in private, since that time she never saw him again. He left without even saying good-bye to her. The way he acted towards her looked like he really did not care seriously about their relationship to begin with. We never talked or mentioned his name again, but she knew that I sympathized with her and I felt very badly for her without me saying anything about it. She tried in the worst way to hide her feelings by acting like nothing happened, but I really knew better. A lot of times I cheered her up by saying something funny to her. I really did try my best, but I knew that it would take some time for her to accept and adjust to it.

A lot of Jews who came to Austria before me were in other places like a temporary camp, a place called the lager. They had two lagers in Salzburg, Austria, one called Parsch and the second lager was called Ridenburg. The Jews were more settled there. They had kitchens and separate showers for men and women.

The Jewish people who wanted to remain and settle in Austria or in Germany moved from the lager to apartments. They had plans to make their permanent home there. A lot of times the UNRRA took away rooms with kitchen privileges from the German and the Austrian citizens, and gave them to the Jewish people to move into. Because those German and Austrian citizens were Nazis in the German Reich during the time of the war, they lost their rights of expressing their opinion and they had to agree to it no matter how they felt about it.

A lot of them really were very nice people and a lot of Germans and

Austrians did not approve of Hitler's doings, but they were forced into the party to become Nazis and had to follow their leader. No matter how it happened, the fact and the reality was that they were in the Nazi party at the time of the war and they took an active part in killing six million Jews, including my whole family. According to me and other survivors, they were the same murderers, and they were just as guilty as the other Nazis were.

After the war, the Nazis lost their privileges and they could not say anything about what they wanted, or did not want, or if they liked it or not. They had to live with the Jews, in their own homes, under the same roof and they were not allowed to say one bad word to the Jews. I was not interested in getting a place at a Nazis home. My only wish was to go to Palestine and get away from these enemies as soon and as far as possible.

I was planning to live with my people and to try to rebuild my life the best way I could, and I was also hoping and praying that maybe some day and somehow I would start to live a more normal life, like everyone else.

The man who I got to know when we were in hiding in the forest came to Salzburg to the DP camp and saw me. I was pleased and very happy to see him, and I kept on saying that it was a nice surprise for me to see him again. I thought it was a coincidence that we ran into each other accidentally and completely unintentionally. After going separate ways when we said goodbye to each other in my city, Wlodzimierz Volynski, I assumed that I would never see him again. This was when he decided to go to his town to look for his family and he hoped that maybe he would find somebody alive there. I was very surprised when he appeared in front of me, and he kept on saying that he could not believe that he finally found me.

He also told me that he was looking for me all of these months since we separated. I really was very flattered and happy that somebody really thought about me. After a few days of him being in Salzburg, he kept on telling me that he likes me, and he would like to marry me, and then he asked me if I would also like to marry him. I told him that one of my reasons for leaving Poland was to go to Palestine. I also said to him if he will go to Palestine with me time will tell how our friendship will develop, and maybe it would lead to marriage, but right now my only wish was to go to Palestine.

He said to me that he really felt badly for not having the same desire like I did. He even suggested for us to get married first and maybe in time he would change his mind and we would go to Palestine together. I really knew right away that his plan would not work too well for me, so I said definitely no to it. I saw very clearly that he did not have any desire or intentions to live in Palestine, and he really tried to talk me out of going, also. I felt very strongly that after what happened to the Jews here, Palestine was the only place for Jews. He wanted to live any other place, but not in Palestine. After all of our conversations and negotiations that we had, we did not come to an agreement and we could not even reach a compromise because he had his ideas and I had mine. Finally, he realized that it would not work. He said that he was sorry that it did not work out and he left. I never saw him again. I knew that it would not work anyway, because we both wanted our own way. It looked to me that he would not give in and I would not give up.

In the meantime, life in the DP camp went on with no changes. We had the same routine day by day. We kept on waiting and hoping to hear good news, but nobody was even coming in to talk to us. The representatives of the organization were busy taking care of the new immigrants who came in from Poland. They also came with the intention of being sent to a country that would accept survivors, in order to get settled someplace.

I think that everyone had enough of wandering like gypsies, and everyone wanted a place to call their own. Every time I asked the person in charge of our group when they will take us to Palestine, he said, "Soon". He also said over and over again that we had to have patience. When he said it to me, I thought to myself that my patience ran out a long time ago. We were already in the DP camp for a few weeks without knowing what will happen to us. I myself was not only losing my patience, but I was also losing my hope that we would ever see Palestine.

A few more weeks passed and, again, there was no news of us leaving. We were still in the same place. Jews who were living in the temporary lager were coming in everyday to talk to us. Everyone was asking each other questions, such as, "How did you live through the war? Did you find anybody of your family alive? Maybe you know about this and that person?" Some Jews came just to talk about their own tragedies and losses. Etta and I were sitting on the chest near the door and we talked about our troubles and we asked each other, "What was going to happen to us? Are we going to go to Palestine or not?" The way I felt and from what I saw, the representative was always trying to avoid us and it did not look too good to me. I started to get worried about the whole situation that we were in.

A lot of Jews came in to see us and surprisingly, whoever came in, was very friendly, and they talked to us more than they talked to anybody in the room. A man came in everyday and he gave everyone chocolate, candy, food, and sometimes clothes. From the beginning I thought that he was a member of the UNRRA organization, then I found out that he was a survivor, just like we were. He started to wheel and deal with the MP's (Military Police), who were Americans, and whatever he could get from them, he divided between everyone.

One morning the leader of our group came in, and announced that they just closed the border and they were not letting any more refugees into Palestine. I became very disappointed that my wish did not come true and all of my plans fell apart. I have to admit that I had a very bad feeling about it from the beginning. It felt like I knew what would happen. I started to think to myself that if I would have known that I would not go to Palestine maybe I would have gotten married to the man I was in the woods with. I knew that he really liked me a lot, but on the other hand I kept on thinking that maybe it was not meant to be.

The British government did not permit any more survivors to immigrate to Palestine and the United States was not willing to let refugees in, either. My first disappointment was when the United States found all kinds of different excuses for letting Hitler kill six million Jews by lying to themselves and to everyone else, including to us, and claiming that they did not know what was going on. I thought that this was really very sad and after so many years it was and still is very hard for me to overcome my anger. Until this day, I still cannot accept the fact that they could have helped, if they would have been willing to, but did not.

In my mind and according to my and everyone else's thinking, I came to realize that the fact was if they would have gotten involved they could have stopped Hitler from doing what he did to us. They simply did not care at all if the Jews lived or died. It would have been too much bother for them if they had helped to prevent this tragedy from happening. My second disappointment was when America started to make up all kinds of other excuses and washed their hands of any responsibilities towards a few Jews, the only remnants of the Jewish people, who were left after the hands of the murderers.

America claimed that economically they were not too well off and they did not want to have the responsibility of the survivors. The way I was taught was that people should not always do what was only good for them, but sometimes they just had to do what was the right thing to do. According to me, it would be very right if America would, instead of thinking only about what was good for them, to think about what the right thing to do would be, which was to help the few Jewish survivors.

To my regret, I have to say that they did not think of helping the Jews before the six million Jews were killed, including my whole family, and they did not think of helping them after the war when there were only a handful of Jews left.

According to the American government, and the way they acted, it seemed to me and to all of the other survivors that they were probably thinking that it would have been better for everyone around if there had not been any survivors left at all. They showed it in so many ways that it was too much for them to dedicate a little time and a little effort in order to help the few survivors with whatever they had left of their life, to start a new life for themselves.

They probably thought, why should they bother with the Jews and help them with anything. After all, the Jews did not mean anything to them when the Nazis killed six million Jews, and they did not mean anything to them now, either, because they were only Jews. No matter what anybody was thinking or saying or doing or not doing, the fact was that if the Jews had not known Hitler, we would not need any help from anybody. We would have our families, our places, our lives and we, for sure, would not need anyone to do us a big favor and take us in. We would be able to live a normal life like we lived before the war, and before the murderers came to us and destroyed our lives completely. Now, the couple Jews who were left by accident only and with no thanks to anybody, had to be at the mercy of others and these others were too ignorant, selfish, egotistical, and apparently prejudiced enough to think, act, and behave the way they did and not to be willing in any way to offer any help to helpless people, like we refugees were right after the war. I have to admit that I was bitter against the whole world. My only thoughts and hopes of making some life for myself was in Palestine.

Suddenly, when they notified us that they closed the border, it was a shock to me and I was very disappointed, because my purpose of being here in Austria was only to go to Palestine. I did not dream that I would be stuck in Austria with the Nazis again. The reality of it was that we could not go to Palestine anymore and the United States or other countries did not want the Jews, either. I was in a strange country, I did not know anybody, I did not know the language well, and most of all, I was between enemies again, the German and the Austrian Nazis, who had killed my entire family and all of the other Jews.

I was thinking to myself, why do I have to go through all of the misery and suffering without an end to it. I really did not see a way out of this situation. The only thing that I could figure out was that no matter what I would do or how I would try to go on and make the best of it, it did not work out, and I had one disappointment after another. Everything turned out the other way around and, of course, the wrong way. I did not think that I was just feeling sorry for myself, I really knew that I was facing reality and I saw everything as it was. I saw that no matter what I did or how I tried to do my best it did not help. All of my plans fell apart and nothing ever materialized for me, to my advantage.

We were lying on the floor, not knowing what the future for us would be. Etta was more patient and she tried to calm me down by saying that everything will work out for the best, but finally it got to her, also, and she took sick. It was like she was giving up, too. She could not eat the food that they gave us and we did not have any more money to buy food. Now I stopped thinking and feeling sorry for myself and I started worrying about her. I remembered how dedicated she was to me and she always shared the food with me that she bought with her money. I kept on saying to her that I wish I could do something for her and she said to me that just being her friend made her happy. I always knew that she was also a real friend to me.

In the meantime, the man who brought us chocolate and a lot of other things kept on coming. He came sometimes, twice a day, and he started to talk to us. I found out that his name was Kadish Kaplan. He told us that he had survived concentration camp, but his wife and his two children were killed, together with his entire family. He came in everyday and he became friendlier and more open with us. He told us that a group of people who he worked with in the concentration camp made a pact that whoever would survive the war would meet in a certain city that they had agreed to. After the liberation, whoever survived of them met and from then on, they really stuck together like a family. When they came to Salzburg, Austria, they moved into a house that was deserted. The women had their rooms and the men had their rooms. The women did the cooking and the men did the other chores. Kadish got to know some American soldiers, the MP's (Military Police) and he bought whatever they had to sell, and then he distributed it between everyone in the house.

He started wheeling and dealing and bringing in groceries and clothes into the house and whatever he was able to buy he bought. One day he came in and started a conversation with us, and made a statement that the women who lived in his house were complaining. They said that they have too much work to cook for fifteen people, two meals a day plus taking care of all the company that came everyday. Kadish told us this and he mentioned that he was looking for a couple women to help out in the kitchen. We said that we do not know anybody here, without even having the slightest idea that he meant us. When he saw that we did not understand him, that actually he meant both of us, Etta and me, he came out and said it very plain that he was thinking of us. Then he asked us if we wanted to come to help with the cooking everyday and, of course, to have our meals there and after supper to return to our place, which was in the DP lager.

I remember that I did not say anything, not even one word, but Etta said, "We will let you know." When he left, Etta pleaded with me to do it for her. She said the only way she would get better would be when she would have a decent meal everyday. I started to feel sorry for her and at the same time I felt bad by saying yes. It felt and it looked to me like I would be somebody's servant and this would be very degrading to me. The other way of my thinking was that I remembered when Etta shared her food with me that she bought with her own money, so I came to a conclusion that it was my turn to do something for her. No matter how it looked or felt to me, I decided that I must swallow my pride and do it to help Etta.

The next day when Kadish came in, and asked us if we had decided what to do, I said to him that I would come to help with the cooking on one condition, that only I would do the work and Etta would also have her meals, there, because she was still too weak to do anything. I told him to think it over and if he would decide that it was okay this way, I would start the next day. He stayed and talked to us for a while, then he said to us, "I will see you tomorrow morning" and he gave us his address.

We came there and I helped with the cooking everyday. There were six women and me, and we got along very well. Etta was lying on the sofa in the living room, resting, while we prepared lunch and dinner. Everyone was very respectful and very nice to each other. We did not have any special conversations with each other and most of the time we only talked to each other when we had something specific to say. Everyone did whatever they had to do to prepare the meals.

I remember that one of the girls was in charge of the cooking and whatever she told me to do, I did. It was very quiet and I felt good about it. It seemed to me that everyone was preoccupied with their own thoughts. In a way these surroundings helped me mentally because I had people to share my feelings of misery with, people who would understand even when we did not talk about it, and we still knew what and how each of us felt. It really felt like we were reading each other's minds just by glancing at each other from time to time. Besides that, nobody talked loud and there were not as many people in the room, like in the DP camp. It was really good for Etta and me to have some peace and quiet.

After a few weeks, Etta's health improved and I was very happy that I decided to come and help with the cooking. By the same token, I really got to know everyone and everyone got to know me. We really became good friends, especially Kadish. I sensed that he felt more towards me than friendship.

One day, after supper when Etta and I went back to our place, I mentioned this to Etta that I sensed that Kadish had a special interest in me. I said to Etta that I felt that Kadish thinks of me in a more serious way, even though he never said anything to me in this respect, but I just felt it.

At the time, I did not even dream of such a thing like getting involved with a man like Kadish. In my mind just the thought of it was very impossible. To begin with, he was more than twice as old as I was. He was married and had two children before the war and I was only fifteen and a half years old. Besides that, we both were two different people with very different backgrounds, like day and night.

All in all, he was a nice man and I had respect for him, but not for a husband. In the meantime, Etta and I kept on coming everyday and I helped prepare the meals. Sometimes Kadish bought some jewelry and he gave it to each of the girls. A few times he also wanted to give me a present, but I did not want to accept it, so he gave it to one of the other girls. It was okay, because I really did not want to be obligated to him in any way. I started to sense and I felt that everyone was talking about me behind my back. Of course, they knew more than I did because he told them how he felt towards me and what his intentions were.

In a while, I started to fell very uncomfortable about the whole situation. It became very obvious to everyone in the house that Kadish thought seriously about me and the girls started to tell me that Kadish likes me a lot. From the beginning I kept on pretending that I did not understand what they were trying to tell me, and I even said that he was a very nice man and I liked him, also. One time one of the girls openly came out and she said to me very plain and straight that Kadish mentioned something about wanting to marry me. I knew right away that it was time for me to call it quits and give up my cooking profession. I made up some excuse and I told the girls that I would come until the end of the week only, because I had other plans that I had to attend to. I started to feel very strange by being there, but I told myself that it was only a few more days until the end of the week and soon everything would be forgotten.

# CHAPTER XXVII
## THE TURNING POINT IN MY LIFE

Kadish's uncle saw Kadish for the last time in Poland, before he immigrated to America. At that time, Kadish was still a very young boy. Very shortly after the uncle came to America, he got married and he had two sons. The oldest son's name was Nathan or Nuchum, and the youngest son's name was Harry or Herschel. Kadish never met his cousins or his aunt. All of the years they kept in touch with each other until the war. Right after the liberation Kadish wrote to the uncle that he had survived the war and Kadish gave him the address of where he was living in Salzburg, Austria. At that time, the uncle's youngest son, Harry (Herschel) was in the army and he was stationed in Germany or Austria, I really do not remember where. When the uncle wrote to his son, Harry, the soldier, he mentioned that Kadish was in Salzburg, Austria and he gave Harry the address just in case he wanted to get in touch with Kadish and get to know each other for the first time.

The same day, while I was still there in the kitchen, only to finish up the last day of work, and while I was talking with the girls about different things, and they were telling me that they will really miss me, somebody came to the door and kept on ringing the bell. I opened the door and I saw a young soldier standing in front of me. He said hello to me and then he asked me, in Yiddish, if he was in the right house because he was looking for Kadish Kaplan. I said yes, that he was in the right house, but Kadish was not home yet. He replied that he would wait for him. I called him into the living room and I asked him to sit down. I thought in order to be polite I will keep him company for a while. He told me that he was born in America, but his parents and his grandparents were born in Europe, in Poland. I said to him that I was also from Poland and so was my family. He asked me about my family and I replied that the Nazis had killed my entire family. He got very sad and he said to me that he was sorry to hear it. He kept on talking about the war and he asked me all kinds of questions about myself, but he did not tell me who he was or how he knew Kadish's name and I did not ask him anything, either.

In the middle of the conversation, I heard the door opening and Kadish walked in. I said, "Kadish, you have a visitor. This American soldier came to see you." Kadish shook hands with the soldier without knowing who he was because they had never met before. They exchanged a few words, then the young soldier, whose name was Herschel, said to Kadish, " I am your Uncle Manas's son." Right away they started to hug and kiss each other and they were both crying. It was a very touching scene. Finally, when both of them calmed down, Kadish introduced me to his cousin and he made a statement that he would like to marry me if I would agree to it. Even though I knew what the girls told me about how Kadish felt towards me, it still was a shock to me when he said it. I felt very uncomfortable with it.

This was the very first time that I heard it from him. I still remember that I was standing and looking down at the floor without saying one word. Kadish kept on talking, and he was saying that he likes me and that he was left all alone and I did not have anyone anymore, either, so at least together we would not be alone. This was probably a proposal. The cousin turned to me like he was waiting for an answer from me. I did not say a word and I tried to keep calm. Then the cousin said to me, "If you will marry Kadish, my father will send both of you papers to come to America".

I knew that Etta heard the whole conversation, but she pretended to be asleep. When we were on the way back to the DP camp, I asked her what she thought about Kadish's proposal, and she said to me, "Sonia, this is your life and it has to be your decision and whatever you will decide to do, good luck to you." I knew Etta, very well. I also knew that if she would think that it was right for me she would have showed more enthusiasm and I would see it on her face that she was happy for me. Looking at her I knew that she was hiding her feelings only because she did not want to influence me in any way.

When I came back to the lager I told a few other people about it. Everyone said that I was the luckiest person in the world because I would go to America and I would start a new life for myself. In spite of what everyone was saying about how lucky I was, I was thinking to myself, how come I did not feel so lucky, instead, I felt very miserable. I started to analyze my situation. I thought about my life here, and how I hated every minute of it.

I knew for sure that I must get away from here, as far as possible and now I had the opportunity to do just that, so why was I so very unhappy about it? Maybe because it was like an ultimatum and it looked and sounded like this, that if and when I wanted to go to America, I had to get married to Kadish. Of course, my dreams were to get married to somebody who I would be in love with, and I would want to have my parents and my family with me, in order to share my happiness and my joy, together with them. Only in my case, all of my dreams of having my family, my parents, my happiness, my love, and my joy of getting married were not ever going to materialize and to my regret it did not turn out the way I wished for at all. I really thought that under these circumstances that I was living in now, it was not worth it for me to survive the war. Hitler with his Nazis took everything away from me. Even if they did not kill me and I survived the war, I never felt alive from then on.

In spite of everything, I started to think about what Kadish's cousin said to me about the so-called package deal getting married to Kadish and going to America or I had another choice, to stay here in Austria with the Nazis. I really started to think about it very seriously and analyze my situation. I faced the truth, and I came to a conclusion that the reality was that I did not belong anyplace. I was very young and I did not have anybody to depend on or to give me some advice. I did not have anyone even to give me an opinion so I had to decide this by myself. Finally, in spite of my better judgment I came to a conclusion on my own, and I made my decision to get married to Kadish, even if it was only for practical reasons.

The first reason was to leave the enemies and come to America. The second reason was that I told myself that because he was much older than I, so he would be my father, my mother, my sister, and my two brothers. In other words, he would be my entire family. At that time in my life, to have a family was more important to me than anything else in the world. I made up my mind that I would accept his offer. Of course, I would have never married him before the war. I would have never even met him because we lived in very different worlds and besides that I would never marry a man old enough who could have been my father. After two months of briefly knowing each other we got married, it was in 1945. I started to accept the present, and I started to believe that it was meant to be this way. I really tried my best to live a normal life, as well as the circumstances allowed me to. I still remember the day of my wedding and the clothes we were wearing.

Kadish was five feet tall. He wore a light blue suit with Galafay style pants, like pedal pushers. I wore a black dress to my wedding, because that was all that I had. Looking back I realized that the black dress was very proper for me at this time and in the mood that I was in. Besides that, there was no place to buy clothes or anything else. It was right after the war and most of the stores were closed. The only place we could buy some things was on the black market, but we did not know anyone who was selling clothes.

After some time I found a dressmaker, who came from Vienna, Austria to Salzburg, Austria and she had a few women who she made some clothes for, and they recommended her to me. I liked her work and after I picked the style and the material she made some dresses for me, too.

I have to tell you about my wedding ceremony. The way my wedding started was that the rabbi did not want to come on his own free will because Kadish was married before and he had a wife and two children. The rabbi did not know if his wife was still alive and if she would come back, because these things had happened quite a few times after the war. When this happened both parties had to get a divorce and then they could marry whomever they wanted to. The rabbi did not want to jeopardize his position to perform a marriage ceremony without a death certificate of Kadish's first wife. Everyone knew that the Nazis did not issue death certificates. They just issued death for the Jews without any legalities. I remember that Kadish was upset when the rabbi did not show up, but in a way I really felt good. All of the guests sat and waited for the rabbi to appear.

Two of Kadish's friends, who were living in Kadish's house, were very big men. They went to the lager and they got the rabbi to come, practically by force. He came against his will and he performed the ceremony. The wedding took place in the house where Kadish lived with the other people. I remember it was a big house and every room in it was full of people. Everyone had a good time. There were a lot of guests.

The house was full of survivors who came to the wedding. No one was invited, people just came.

The women who lived in the house made all the preparations for the wedding. They cooked and baked all week and there was a lot of food and drinks. That was how it was in Europe before the war. I still remember how unhappy I felt the whole week before the wedding and I could not stop crying. I felt very much alone and very confused and a lot of mixed thoughts came into my mind. Even when I knew exactly the real reason I was going to marry Kadish, I still had a doubt in my mind and I kept on asking myself if I was doing the right thing or not. Deep in my heart I felt that nothing was right, but I also knew that no matter what I would do, it would not be good and I would be a loser, one way or another. I guess that I was too determined to be able to get away from the Nazis and leave Austria.

I remember that once Kadish said to me that he knew that we were not a match for each other, but he kept on saying that he would be good to me, as though he tried to reassure me that everything will turn out for the best. I thought that even he knew that we were not right for each other, and it did not look like this marriage was made in heaven.

I did not do any of the cooking or baking for the wedding, like it did not concern me. The others who lived in the house prepared everything and Kadish took care of the whiskey. The guests, mostly the men, drank L'Chaim, to life. They drank so many L'Chaim's that they started to get too happy. Even the rabbi had a few too many L'Chaim's. He loosened up and danced and sang all night long. He really had a good time.

Everyone was eating, drinking, singing and dancing, but I was staying in the kitchen most of the time, looking through the doorway to see what was going on at my wedding. It felt like I was at someone else's wedding, not mine. By watching what everyone was doing I realized that they had enough to drink. I remember that I took the cases of whiskey, which were in the kitchen and I hid them. Kadish came into the kitchen to get a few bottles of whiskey and he could not find them, because they were not where he had put them. He asked me where the whiskey was, and I said to him, "No more whiskey. All of you had enough to drink and most of you already had too much to drink." Kadish looked at me for a second with an angry and surprised look, and then he walked out of the kitchen without whiskey.

After so many years, I still remember what he said to me. When the wedding was over and everyone left he said, "You were the first woman to tell me how much I should drink and you were the first woman who I listened to," and he did not drink too much anymore. In all of the years that we were married, I really never saw him drink to a point of getting drunk. All of the guests celebrated the wedding until morning and they seemed to be happy. Everyone had some breakfast and little by little they left to go back to the lager. Kadish made a reservation in Bad Ischl, in a hotel, and we went there for a few days. I remember that this was the first time that we were alone since we knew each other, and this was also the first time that both of us had a very open, honest and truthful conversation with each other. I felt that in order to start some kind of a life together, we had to face the reality and not live in a world of pretenses, hidden feelings and mixed thoughts.

We opened up and we told each other the way we felt about this wedding and the reasons for it. I started to talk and I reminded Kadish that before we got married, I told him that I did not like him and he was not a match for me, and he said that he liked me enough for both of us. We had an understanding that the reason I got married to him was to go to America, but I guess he knew my reason all along, because I told him so many times before the wedding.

I felt more relieved after the whole conversation that we had. In a way I felt much better by bringing it out in the open in order for both of us to know how we stood with each other, even if we knew all along without saying too much of anything. I thought that this way was the right and the honest way to do it. We also agreed not to talk about it again. Now we were married and we both had to try to make the best of it, for one reason or another, no matter what it would take to do it. We had to try. We both promised each other to try our best to make this marriage work, and that we should also have mutual respect and consideration for each other.

## MY LIFE IN SALZBURG, AUSTRIA

In the year of 1945, after we got married, the UNRRA gave us a place to live in a home with a Nazi family. We moved in there, but I really was not too happy to live with Nazis and see them everyday of the week, but I did not have another choice than to make the best of it. In the same way, they did not like to have Jews in their house, either, because they were Nazis. The man was an Oberbauerer, a main engineer and he told us that he was forced to become a party member of the Nazis.

He was a very nice, elderly gentleman and I liked him right away. He treated us with respect. His wife was a housewife. She was a very beautiful woman, and she spoke very softly, but with resentment in her heart and in her voice towards us. The first minute she saw us, of course, she disliked us because we were Jewish and we were going to live in her house. At the time, the Nazis did not have any rights to say anything about this, and they had to accept what the government was doing.

We had one big room and kitchen privileges. In spite of the government orders and the rules that they had to observe and follow, such as that they were not allowed to harass the Jews who were living in their house, meaning us, the wife was a hateful Nazi and an anti-Semite. She could not stand us because we were Jews and she harassed us in any way she could. What a shande (shame) it was for her that she had to live with Jews in spite of her will and desire, but her shameless and hateful feeling towards us was mutual, because I could not stand her, either. She was a Nazi and an ugly person and among all the other things, she was a Jew hater.

Right from the beginning, she was very nasty towards us, especially towards me. The building had four apartments and Austrian families occupied them. When I walked out of the house in the morning, I used to meet other people from the building, and in no time we started to be friendly towards each other. They were Austrian citizens and they were nice and polite towards me and I acted the same way towards them. Some of them even sympathized with me and they condemned the Nazis for their actions towards the Jews.

They used to ask me, "How is Mrs. Gossner behaving towards you?" and I told them that she was not nice to us at all. She made it very obvious that she hated to have Jews living in her home. She treated us like nobodies. One word led to another and they started to tell me about what happened to her.

They told me that one day an unexpected tragedy hit her home. She had only one child, a son, and suddenly he got killed. They also told me that her son was an engineer, like his father. One day he climbed tall mountains and while he was standing on top of the mountain a piece of the mountain broke off, and he fell to the ground, and was killed instantly. Since that time she became very bitter against everyone and everything, including her husband. Her son was her only child.

The neighbors told me that after her son's death, she took in a dog and the dog kept her company. When we moved in, I saw that she gave all of her attention to the dog and treated the dog like a child. It seemed to me that she gave all of her love to the dog that she would have given to her son. I never saw her talking to her own husband. The neighbors also told me that she blamed her husband for her son's accident.

She never wanted her son to become an engineer. She claimed that her husband talked her son into it. I was sure that it was not her husband's fault that their son was killed, but she always blamed him unjustly for it even though it was his son, also. Since that time, she was never on speaking terms with her husband. She never forgave him and she held a grudge against him for no good reason at all. A lot of times I felt sorry for her, and no matter how mean she was to us I still kept on forgiving her because of the loss of her son.

When our friends rang the bell to come to see us, she did not let them in. We had to share the kitchen, so when she was done cooking, she locked the kitchen door and I could not go into the kitchen to cook my meal. She said that I had to cook when she was cooking. This reminded me every minute of the day of being in the ghetto surroundings with the Nazis, and I started to get scared all over again because I really did not need another Hitler.

The first minute she started to boss me around and tell me what I should do and what I should not do, I got very angry at her, but I did not say anything. The anger started to build up in me and I knew that I would not be able to be patient enough with her for too much longer. Eventually, there would come a time in the near future when I would have enough of her treatment and of her bossing me around and I would be forced to strike back.

My husband always said to me that I should not pay attention to what she said or did. Of course, most of the day, he was not even home to hear her calling us names and giving me a hard time by doing all of the nasty things to me and irritating me to death. When he was home, he did not have to use the kitchen or hear her ugly name calling, because she would watch herself with him around. She thought with me she could do and say whatever she wanted to. Because I did not answer her, so she assumed that I was just a goody goody.

Every time she saw me going out, or coming in, she muttered something under her breath. A lot of times I heard her talking in the hallway to her husband about us. It sounded very funny to me because usually she never talked to him, she only talked to him when she had something nasty to say about us. She talked to him and he was probably too scared of her to contradict her, so he just stayed and listened to her.

I heard her calling us, "fafluchte Juden and fashmutzte Juden", meaning cursed Jews and dirty Jews. This was the Nazis way of cursing towards the Jews. One day, finally, it got to me and I decided that I had enough of her insults. I was in my room and I heard her talking in the hallway to her husband about me and she kept on saying that the Jews were this and that.

This time she really pushed me too far and I really had enough of her nasty attitude towards us. While my husband was out of the house, I remember that I walked out of my room and I saw her standing in the hallway in front of the mirror. In spite of the fact that she was a head taller than me, I managed to grab her by the hair and I pushed her head against the mirror. The mirror got smashed into little pieces. Then I smashed the glass kitchen door and I opened it from the inside. I took her pots with all of her food and threw them across the floor. It splashed all over the kitchen floor, walls and every place else.

I remember that when my husband and I moved in we had two closets in our room, but we did not have too many things to put into the closets. One day my landlady asked me if I would do her a favor and let her use one of the closets for her clothes. In order for me to be nice I agreed to it without even thinking that she could have something else on her mind. She knew exactly what she was doing, but to me it seemed like she just needed a closet for her clothes.

Each time we had company she found an excuse to come in and spy on us, pretending that she was taking some clothes out of her closet. From the beginning I did not catch on what her intentions were, but after a while I started to get annoyed with it and I started to notice that every time we had company she came in. Because I could not prove that my theory was right, I just did not say anything to her and I let it go.

When this big blow up happened and as long as I was on the go,

I grabbed her things from the closet that was in my room and threw them in her face. She was screaming and crying, but I did not stop. She was screaming and I was screaming and I kept on throwing all of her clothes out of my room. When all her things from the closet were thrown out into the hallway, on top of the broken mirror and broken glass from the kitchen door, and the food all over the kitchen floor, the place was a disaster and it looked like a hurricane hit it. I guess that all of the frustration and anger that had built up in me for such a long time finally came out. I ran over to her and I really wanted to kill her. If it would not have been for her husband, who grabbed me from behind and I remember he pushed me towards my room, I probably would have killed her because when I got so angry I got very strong. I went into my room and tried to calm down. After I calmed down a little, I walked out and I saw her in the kitchen cleaning up the mess, which I had made. She was on her knees on the kitchen floor, cleaning and crying and talking to herself. When she saw me she started to run away. I grabbed her by the arm and I looked straight into her eyes, then I said to her in German, "If I will hear one bad word from you or if you will ever do anything spiteful or disrespectful to us or my friends, I will kill you. Do you understand?" She said, "Yes, I understand". By looking at her I could see that she was really very scared of me.

From this time on, there was peace and quiet. From this time on she went on her tippy-toes. I never wanted to be good with her again. My friends came when they wanted to and they were let in by her most of the time. She greeted them in a very friendly way with a smile, even though she did not feel like smiling to a Jew. She was probably scared that in case she would not behave, they would tell me and I would get angry at her again. Even the rabbi who married us off came to us every Saturday night. He liked the way I baked challah and pletzel with onions and poppy seeds. I had learned to bake by helping my mother with her baking.

I remember that when I was a child, I always wanted to learn as much as I could from my mother, and I kept on watching her when she was cooking and baking for the Sabbath meals. We kept on living at the Nazi's home in Salzburg, Austria, and I hated every minute of it, but there was nothing we could do, only to wait for the papers to come in order to be able to leave the Nazis and go to America. In the meantime, life went on and I got pregnant with my first baby. Unfortunately, when I was in the fourth month of pregnancy I started to hemorrhage. My doctor lived right near me, so I managed to walk to his office. He examined me and he said I was going to lose the baby. He also told me that there was no time for me to go to the hospital. I remember when I was on the examination table, he put me to sleep and when I woke up he told me that I had a miscarriage and he had to perform an abortion. The doctor's name was Doctor Schallen. He was my doctor until I left Austria, to go to America.

Very shortly after my miscarriage I became pregnant again and I was under the doctor's care all during the time of my pregnancy. This time there were no complications in my pregnancy. I was not even seventeen years old when my son, David, was born. It was in February 1947. We named him after my husband's father, Dovid, and my father, Boruch Moshe. In the Jewish religion, we named a baby after the dead members of the family. This was the way of remembering our beloved dead people. My daughter, Gloria, was named after my mother, Gittel, and my husband's mother, Sima. My daughter, Ellen, was named after my father's mother, my grandmother, Esther, and my husband's grandmother, Rochel.

Before my son was born, my husband was scared and worried that I would not know how to take care of our baby, and in a way, he was right in this respect. Besides that, he lost two children in concentration camp by the Nazis, so he was over protective with this baby. Before I came home from the hospital with the baby, he never gave me a chance to find out how and if I would be able to take care of my baby, so when the baby was born, instead of at least letting me try to do it myself, without even asking me or telling me what he wanted to do, he hired a registered nurse and she took care of the baby. In this way my husband had piece of mind. Of course, my feelings did not count with him at all. He thought only about what he liked and what would be good for him. Instead, I was never given a chance, even to try to be a mother to my baby on my own.

In spite of everything, I liked the nurse very much. She was German, but a very nice person. She was more of a mother to my son than I was. In a way, I was very happy and relaxed that she was so good to my baby and she really took good care of him. I knew that she had more experience with babies than I did. The fact was that I did not have any experience at all, after all, it was my first baby, but I really could not help myself, thinking that I could learn to do a good job of raising my baby if I would be given a chance.

I just could not forget the way my husband acted and I kept on remembering the way my husband made all of the decisions by himself without consulting me. It looked like the baby was only his and I had nothing to do with it. In spite of it, that I resented the way my husband acted, I was very pleased with the nurse. Besides giving her a weekly salary, I always gave her nice presents, also. We became very good friends and we talked to each other a lot. She always understood me and many times she sympathized with me.

She never liked my landlady, because once she made a remark and said to my nurse that she should not take care of a Jewish baby. The nurse got very upset with her and when I asked her what was wrong she told me what my landlady said to her. At the time, when the nurse told me this, I remember that I got very angry. I was ready to get into an argument with my landlady, but the nurse stopped me. I still remember what she said to me. She said, "Sonia, what do you expect from a Nazi? A Nazi will always be a Nazi." The nurse was a nice person and she could not believe what the Nazis did to the Jewish people.

# CHAPTER XXVIII
# THE PREPARATION FOR THE JOURNEY TO
# AMERICA

We were still waiting for the papers to arrive that would allow us to leave for America. My husband's uncle in America was working very hard through the organization, HIAS (Hebrew Immigration Aid Society). They said that they had to investigate everyone before they were able to issue the papers and bring refugees into the country. In spite of the fact that the government was not responsible for our well being because we would have a sponsor who was obligated to take care of us, it still took four years for the American government to approve our immigration to America.

Kadish's uncle had to sign an affidavit that he would be responsible for us and he would find us a place to live and a job for my husband to make a living, in order not to be a burden to the American government. The government did not want any responsibility of the few survivors who were left alive by accident only because the Nazis had overlooked them.

In the meantime, even before the papers arrived and I knew we were going to America, I was very curious to know ahead of time how the American women looked, if they were fat or skinny. One day I decided to write to my husband's uncle and aunt and I asked them to let me know all the things that I was asking about. After a while I got a letter from them with all the information that I requested, and they told me that every woman was on a diet and most of the women in America were mostly skinny. At the time my weight was one hundred and seventy pounds. When I heard how the women were in America and me having all of the weight, it did not sound or look too good to me, and I knew that I had to do something about it. I knew right away that I really needed to get prepared in order to come to America and look presentable. Now I had a purpose of making preparations and getting myself in better shape than I was in. I knew that I must lose a lot of weight as quickly as possible.

After the liberation, when I came to Austria, besides weighing so much from eating almost nothing but corn and potatoes in the forest, my face was also infected from the dirt and mosquitoes, which were there at the time that I was in the forest. When I came out of the forest after the war, I still could not get rid of this infection. No matter how many creams I used, it did not get better, it even got worse. I really did not know what to do anymore with the awful infection on my face. The only thing I knew was that I had to do something about it before I was going to America.

I went to a doctor and he put me on a diet to lose weight. He could not do anything about my infection, but he did recommend me to a cosmetologist in order to clear up the infection on my face. I still remember her name. It was Helena Rubenstein. I went to her twice a week and after a long time of getting all kinds of treatments, finally, my face cleared up. Between losing sixty-two pounds and my face starting to look normal again, everyone gave me compliments that I looked pretty. After my face was back to normal, I still kept on going to Helena Rubenstein, but only once a week, until I left Austria to immigrate to America.

I also knew that very soon we will have to leave for America and I thought that it would be better for me to learn English in Salzburg, Austria than wait until we came to America. It also would be much easier for me to come to America and know the American language, in order to be able to communicate with the people there. Besides that, I knew that I had more opportunities to learn English in Austria than I would have in America.

One day I made up my mind that before the time will come for us to immigrate to America, I should know English. I decided to hire, through recommendation, an English teacher who was a German professor in college. Of course, he spoke German to me. He was very nice and very polite, but in my mind I kept on wondering what was he doing during the time of the war, when the Nazis were in power. A lot of times he told me that I have to concentrate more in order to learn the English language and he was right.

I wanted to learn to read, write and speak English, but it did not penetrate in my head fast enough because I could not concentrate on learning. The reason for this was that in the back of my mind I did not think of him as being my English teacher. Sub-consciously I thought of him as being one of Hitler's Nazis and it made me angry. When I thought of this, I immediately lost my concentration. My mind was always wandering from one thought to another. I learned to understand English, but I could not speak, read, or write English. I really was not too happy with my accomplishment because I felt at the time that I had not tried hard enough to concentrate. I probably did not, but I just could not help myself.

We started to make all the preparations for the journey. I knew that when the time would come it would be very hard for me to say goodbye to all of our friends. We were very close with each other because we were all in the same situation. Jews without families, without countries, without having anything left from the past, only some remnants were left of us. We all looked for somebody to be able to communicate with, and have understanding of our feelings. That was why the survivors tried to stick with each other because we shared the same hardship, the same pain, the same misery and the same losses. When we got together we always talked about the past. It was and still is a very painful conversation for us, but we thought that by bringing it out in the open it made us feel better. They always had a saying that "misery likes company". What we really wanted to find in each other was company for our misery. Most of the time we talked about our dead families, friends, neighbors, and how their lives were taken away from them for no good reason at all. They were murdered only because they were Jewish.

Most of the survivors heard about me and they knew my name. When they came to Salzburg, the first stop was to see me. I never said no when anybody needed help, financially, emotionally or otherwise, because from the minute I was able to understand, my parents started to teach me to help people who needed my help. They also taught me that "even when somebody throws stones at you, you should throw bread at them". This was the Jewish way of living and doing certain things, especially with the very religious Orthodox Jews, which my parents were. They believed in doing a mitzvah (good deeds).

While we were in Austria, besides having to leave all of our friends behind, it also would be very hard for my baby and me to say goodbye to the nurse. My son loved her very much and he was very used to her because he was with her all the time. He was with her more than he was with me. When he was sick, she sat with him all night. I loved my baby, but I really did not feel a very strong dedication to him, while the nurse took care of him in Salzburg, Austria. Maybe I was too young or maybe I knew he was in good hands, or maybe I was scared to handle him, because my husband said that I was unable to take care of our baby, and he told me that something bad could happen to the baby when I would take care of him.

Anyway, my husband did a very good job of putting so much fear in me that I started to believe what he said. With the nurse taking care of our son, my husband felt more relaxed and more sure that our baby will be in good hands. I thought that he was wrong, by playing boss and making all the decisions by himself, and taking away my rights of raising my baby. Since it was my baby, too, I should have had something to say in this matter. I never could forget the way I felt and I never forgave him for it, either.

Principles were always very important to me. According to my way of thinking, he had to consult me and we had to make this decision together, instead of not even asking me how and what I think about it. His actions made me very angry and I always had bad feelings towards him. In spite of my feelings, all in all, I was very happy with our nurse because she was very dedicated to my son. When she took this job, she told her boyfriend that she would wait to get married because she wanted to be with our son until he left for America. Of course, her boyfriend was not too happy about it, but he loved her, so he agreed to this and he waited until she was ready.

Because of my poor health that I developed at the time of the war by Hitler's Nazis and later in the forest by being undernourished and living in filthy and contaminated surroundings, my whole body was in pains and aches. The doctor prescribed for me to go to Bad Ischl in the summer and to Bad Gasstein in the winter. Bad Ischl was a summer resort and I was under the doctor's care when I went there. He prescribed for me to take certain kinds of special mineral baths and I did. Little by little it started to help me. I felt better day-by-day. Wintertime, I went to Bad Gasstein for a few weeks because the air from the mountains was very healthy and it did me a lot of good. It took me a long time, but finally my health improved and I got stronger. Wherever I went, the nurse with the baby went with me, also. She knew Bad Ischl very well because her parents lived there, and even on her day off, when she went to see her parents, she always took my son with her and he really enjoyed it.

The nurse was really a very big help to me by taking good care of my baby. I did not have to worry about my baby, so in this way I was able to take better care of myself. I remember that at the time, while I lived in Austria, the economic and financial situation was not too good there. People were out of work and the Austrians were looking for some income.

When I moved into the building after a very short time I got acquainted with the neighbors. I did not know if they had joined the Nazis at the time of the war or not, but they were polite to me and they treated me with the greatest respect so I was friendly to them, also. One day, some of the neighbors asked me if I wanted to buy dishes to take to America. I said yes, and I also told them that if they knew anyone who wanted to sell something, I was interested in buying.

Very soon, from mouth to mouth, the word got around and they approached me with different items that they were interested in selling, things like crystal, jewelry, Persian rugs, furs, silver candelabras, silverware and many more items. Probably, they were all the things that were left in the Jewish homes after the Nazis killed them. The Austrians took everything and kept it for themselves. I bought a lot of things that they showed me and that I liked. We had money because when my husband's cousin came to see him he gave him some money, then when he came to say goodbye to us before he was sent back to America, he gave us all of the money that he had left and told us to buy whatever we wanted to. Every time one of the neighbors wanted to sell something for cheap and I liked it, I bought it from them. I knew that it was Jewish goods that they stole from the Jews, but I thought that it was better that it should be in my possession than in the hands of the Nazis.

My other reason for buying all of these items was that most of the religious things that I bought reminded me of my parents and of the antiques that we used to have in our house. I knew that when the time would come and we would get to immigrate to America we were allowed to take everything and anything with us that we wanted to without paying for shipping charges. I bought as much as money allowed me to, and finally, we started to pack up everything by wrapping all the breakable items with newspaper. My husband did all of the packing, and of course, he did not stop complaining, not even for one second. I kept on pretending that I did not hear a word of it, but most of the time his complaining made me very nervous and by the time he finished packing I was a nervous wreck. In a way I thought that he was right and he made good sense.

He kept on saying that we do not even know where we were going to live or if we will even have a place big enough for us, and I was dragging extra junk with us. That was what he called it. In one way I knew that he was right, but in another way, I thought that was what made me happy, so I figured that I would worry about what to do with it when the time would come. In the meantime I was happy with all of the things that he kept on calling junk.

We had about four big, strong coffers (packing cases) of all kinds of items. I thought that everything that I would bring to America would be the memory of the old country. According to my thinking, I felt very strongly that I was doing the right thing, no matter what my husband or any of my friends said. They all thought that I was too determined and it seemed to all of them that it was ridiculous for me to take what they called, all of the junk, to America, but I did not feel this way at all. The way I felt was that I was holding on to something of my past. What most important to me was that I would carry out my thoughts no matter how it would work out, but I kept on hoping that in the end I would be proven right, after all.

The survivors started the immigration by 1947 and continued until 1951 and even later. They emigrated from many different countries and they went to other countries in order to reach their destination and be able to settle down. This was the major immigration period when most of the survivors got their visas to emigrate. At this time, the first transport of survivors that left from Austria to go to America was in November 1948. The second transport with survivors left sometime in December 1948. We were called to the consulate and finally we received our visas in December 1948.

We waited almost four years for our visas. Finally, the visas came and we were very excited and happy that we were going to America. Some of our friends got their visas at the same time and we would be traveling together. I was very happy that finally we would leave the murderers behind us, and maybe in time the wounds would heal a little, by not being reminded every minute of the day what the cruel Nazis did to our Jewish people and to our families.

Very shortly after getting the visas, we were on our way to America. We were practically one of the first groups of immigrants after the war to leave Austria. At the time, my son was almost two years old. I was not too scared about going to a new and unknown country, but I was a little worried. I started to have very mixed feelings about the whole situation, sometimes I was happy, and sometimes I was sad. I also was a little puzzled because I was all alone and my husband had a big family in America. I really did not know how they would behave towards me. I only could hope and pray that they would be supportive enough to offer their help and friendship, especially to give all of us some moral support.

After all, it was a big change for me. In my early life I had too many changes already. I was not even nineteen years old at the time and I went through a lot of changes. First, in 1936, my father died. Very shortly after that my grandfather died. On September 1939, World War II broke out and the Russians came to us. In 1941, the Nazis pushed out the Russians and occupied the eastern part of Poland. In 1942, during the first pogrom, the Nazis killed my whole family and I became an orphan. In 1944, after the war, I came back to Poland. In 1945, I arrived and lived in Austria. In May 1945 my marriage to Kadish took place, and I became a wife. In 1947 I became a mother when I was only seventeen years old. Now, I was going to another country, and I wondered if this would be my last change in my life or not. I felt very tired and all worn out from all of the changes, and all of the uncertainties of not knowing what lies ahead of me. I kept on wondering what the future would hold for me, and my family.

The only thing that I could do was to hope for the best. I did not know how it would work out. I did not know the country, the people, the language, and besides that I had a baby to take care of. I knew that we were going to a new land. We were going to America to try for a better life, but not knowing what lies ahead of us, and what we can expect there, was a little scary. I, myself, also was more or less sure that I would have plenty of problems to solve and I would have a lot of questions to ask about a lot of things that I would not understand, but I kept on telling myself that in time everything would straighten out and it would fall into place.

I knew myself, that I was a very determined and ambitious person and the more obstacles we would have, the harder I would try to overcome them, and nothing and nobody would stay in my way, no matter what. In spite of the fact that my husband was more than twice as old as me, he never took any part of being the head of the family. He always left it up to me to worry and solve all of the problems by myself. This was the easy way out for him, not to take any responsibilities on his shoulders. Instead, he always mixed in where he should not, and always contradicted me in order to show everyone how nice he was, and I was the big black wolf.

I really did not pay too much attention to his insults because they did not mean anything to me. I always thought that by insulting and criticizing me in front of people he belittled himself and I thought if that made him feel important, let him have the privilege of doing so. I always did what I thought was best for my family anyway, especially for my baby.

# CHAPTER XXIX
## THE IMMIGRATION TO AMERICA AND THE BEGINNING
## OF MY LIFE THERE

We came to America at the end of December 1948, from Bremen Haven, Germany, with the ship, the SS Marine Marlin. This was not a passenger ship, but a cattle ship. Until then, they only used this ship for transporting cattle on it, so you can see that it was not a luxurious ship at all. I still remember how hot it was in the cabin and the pipes were almost on top of our head. I slept on the third bunk on top, and my son slept with me in the same bunk because he wanted to sleep near me.

We shared a room with a lot of people. The men, the women and the children had separate rooms. It took almost three weeks to make the journey to America. It really was a very hard time for us to be cooped up in such conditions for so long, but nobody complained, on the contrary everyone took it very well. Most of the people on the ship who were sailing with us were feeling okay and the sailing did not bother them at all. They enjoyed being together and socializing with each other. Unfortunately, this was not the case for me.

From the first minute, as the ship started to sail, I got seasick and all the time we were sailing, I just could not eat anything and I kept on throwing up. The heat on the ship and the poor ventilation made me sick and my stomach was upset all the time. I looked awful during the time of sailing. Throughout my entire journey on the ship, I never went into the dining room. I remember that my husband used to bring me something to eat and drink. I tried to eat, but most of the time I could not look at food. I got nauseous right away, just by looking at food. I remember that there were a few other people who felt the same way that I did. When I came out on the deck I met them sitting there. We talked for a while and then I had to go back to my cabin to lie down. I really forced myself to join everyone, and sometimes I tried my best to sit on the deck a little bit longer. Everyone took care of my baby, except me, but he was happy.

All of the people on the ship knew him and even the ship crew loved him. They came to look for him everyday and they brought him candy and chocolate and everyone played with him. He really was a beautiful baby. He had light, blond, curly hair. He looked like a girl and he always had a big smile on his face. I was not too happy, the way I felt. I could not socialize with anybody because most of the time I thought that I felt better just by lying on my bunk. In spite of how I felt and that it was not a smooth sailing for me, I still did not care because we were going to America, to the Goldeneh Medina. That was what we called America, the land of gold.

While I was still on the ship, I started to write a letter to my son's nurse. I told her that Putzale, that was what she called my son, David, really missed her and we all missed her, too. I told her that I would write to her as soon as we settled down. I asked her to write to us and let us know what was going on in Austria, and how she was doing.

Finally, we arrived on Ellis Island. I remember when I was standing on the deck with the other immigrants, and from the distance I saw a red building and the Statue of Liberty. It made me very happy. When the ship docked in New York Harbor, we had to go through a registration and after the registration was over, everyone started to leave the ship. There was a lot of confusion and commotion. It was very hard to say good-bye to everyone. After all, we knew each other for almost four years and we were like family to each other in Salzburg, Austria. We made very sure that we had each other's addresses where we could be reached in order not to lose contact with each other and to be able to keep in touch.

Different people picked us up. Some survivors were picked up by their organizations and some survivors were picked up by their sponsors. I think that everyone, including me, felt sad because we had to part. We really did not know when we would ever see each other again, maybe soon, or maybe never. Nobody knew what the circumstances would be for us. I think that none of us was certain of what the future would be, and how we would adjust to our new place and our new ways of living here.

My husband's cousin, Nathan, the uncle's oldest son, and a

representative of the HIAS organization came to meet us. I still remember that they took us to a restaurant for dinner as soon as we arrived. I just looked at the food and I got nauseous. My stomach was still very upset from the sailing. I remember it was evening when we arrived in Philadelphia. I was sitting in the backseat of the car with my baby and he fell asleep. I kept on looking out of the window and I saw all the streets were full of trash. I started to think to myself, that was how America looks like, with trash all over the streets? I was very surprised to see this because in Europe, we were not allowed to throw a cigarette butt or a piece of paper on the street. If a policeman would catch us, we would have gotten a fine for doing it. It seemed that in America, they could put trash all over and it was okay. In my mind it really did not make any sense, and I became very curious to know why such a country like America looks so dirty.

Finally, after a while when my curiosity took over, I said to the representative, in Yiddish, "Excuse me, I want to ask you something." He turned towards me and I said to him, "This is what America looks like?" He replied, "What do you mean?" I told him that I saw all of the streets were full of trash and it looked awful. He started to laugh and then he told me that tomorrow is trash collection day, and the city trucks were collecting the trash here, and after that, the city workers were cleaning up the streets.

When he explained it to me I understood how it was done here and how their trash system works. I guess every country had a different system. In Austria, where I lived for four years, every building hired someone to take care of their trash. We did not see any trash on the sidewalk, but in America they were doing it different.

Finally, we arrived in Philadelphia, on the street where my husband's aunt and uncle had their luncheonette and on top of it they had an apartment. The uncle and aunt, the cousins with their families and a few of the neighbors were all waiting for our arrival. Everyone said that they were very happy to see us. They kissed all of us and they wished us good luck in the new country.

According to me, it was not what they said, it was how they were saying it that seemed strange to me. I felt that they were only putting up a front by saying all of these things. I thought that this was the proper way for them to behave, at this time. I had a feeling that they really did not mean what they were saying, and they felt a lot of resentment towards us, especially towards me. After all, I was not their cousin, only my husband was. I also sensed that they did not like me, even though they said, "Welcome to our family". What they did not know was that I did not like them, either, because they were two-faced people and I felt it right away.

To me, when someone spoke nice in front of me and talked bad behind my back, these kinds of people were very ignorant and they were cowards. They did not have guts to tell me how they felt about me straight to my face, so right then I decided that two of us can play the same game and I started to act very charming with a big phony smile on my face. Even though I always knew that "two wrongs don't make one right", at least for the time being, I had to put on an act.

I still remember that after such a long journey every one of us was very tired. After all of the introductions, everyone left and we were ready to go to sleep. The uncle and aunt took us to our living quarters. They gave us a room on the second floor, on top of the luncheonette. The room was pretty small for us, but at the time I did not care. I thought to myself, now we are in America, and soon we will start to build a new life for ourselves.

On the second day after we arrived, in the late morning, a newspaper reporter came and interviewed us. Because my husband or myself did not speak English and the reporter did not speak Yiddish or Polish, the uncle translated the questions that the reporter asked us from English to Yiddish and our answers from Yiddish to English.

My husband did not want to talk about the war. It was very painful for us to talk about the past so I talked a little and in a while I got very upset and angry. I got angry at the whole world and I said exactly the way I felt and what I knew happened. I told the reporter that almost all of the Jews were murdered and after the war there were left only a few survivors. The reason for it was that no one wanted to help the Jews and stop Hitler from killing them before it was too late. In spite of it that the whole world knew about the Holocaust no one tried to prevent it from happening and instead the world pretended to be shocked about hearing the horror and the tragedy of what happened to the Jews.

Now, suddenly, everyone was very concerned and they started to ask how this could happen and everyone became very sympathetic towards us. I thought then, and I still think now, that we could have lived without their sympathy, but the six million Jews could not and did not survive without their help. I think that a lot of countries were in a position to help innocent Jews, if they would have been interested in doing so.

Everyone probably thought, "After all, they were only murdering Jews". According to the world, the Jews were not counted as human beings and that is why the Jews were dead even before they were killed. Human beings with a brain had a choice to choose between being good or being heartless and selfish. All of the countries leaders apparently chose to pretend that they did not see anything, they did not hear anything and they did not know anything. If one human being would have had consideration for another human being, and we would have had a little help from the world, they would have been able to prevent the murdering of six million Jews for no good reason at all. It took only one insane man to murder all the Jews. It would take only one good world leader to stop him.

We needed help then, not sympathy now, because all the sympathy in the world would not bring all of the murdered Jews and my family back to life again. I told the reporter that it was very nice to come to America, but it would have been even nicer to come to America together with my family that I had before the war. If America or another country would have helped and tried to prevent this brutality, my family would be alive now.

I was sure that I was not the only person to understand this and to know that this, to my regret, was unfortunately a true fact. Then the reporter asked my husband and me if we were happy that we came to America, and of course, just to avoid any bad feelings right from the start, we said, "Yes". The reporter also asked us if we were going to see the Mummers Parade. I did not know what he meant by this, so the uncle explained to us that today there was going to be a parade and they will pass by here.

They started in the center of the city and they marched all day. They had orchestras playing very loud. When I heard the orchestra I walked out in the street. It was on the street next to the luncheonette. A lot of people were lined up on both sides of the street and the parade kept on passing by, the people in the parade were dancing and singing and it was very lively. I still remember that I held my son in my arms and a lady stood next to me. She kept on talking to a man in the parade that was dancing near us and he was very happy so she asked him, "Did your wife allow you to join the parade?" He looked at her and then he said, "The reason I am here is because I do not have a wife to tell me what to do or what not to do, and that is why I am so happy". I understood every word of it and we were all laughing. The parade was really nice and I enjoyed it a lot because I had never seen a parade like this before.

I thought to myself that all the uncertainties of coming to a strange land, to live with different people, and to start to adjust to their different ways would not be too easy for us. I have to admit that it was a little confusing and threatening. Everything was and looked much different here than in Europe in many ways, including the people and their ways of living. No matter what, I was still almost certain that the life here would be much better than the life we had left behind, with the Nazis in Austria. I did not expect too much, only to have my freedom. Even though I did not know what lays ahead of me, I was sure that I would be determined enough to make the best of it, because I was beginning a new life for myself and for my family. After all, we were in the Goldeneh Medina, the land of gold, in America.

Most of the immigrants who came to America were settled in the big cities. It was a big change for them because many of the survivors came from small towns and small cities. That was where we lived all of our lives when we were in Europe. In most of the European countries, their cities and towns were small, compared to America. The reason for settling the survivors in big cities was that a big city offered more opportunities for people, especially for newcomers, and the survivors had a better chance of finding a job. All of us had to learn the lay out of the city. We had to get acquainted and know where to shop, how to go to the doctor and a lot more. Besides this, we had to adjust to the American people and their different ways of living, talking and communicating with each other. It really was very hard for us because the Polish Jews lived a very different life. The Jews in Poland were more relaxed than the people in America. They had more patience with each other and towards each other, they cared about each other, they helped each other and most of all, the families were very close and dedicated to each other.

I have to state a fact that in spite of living in America for sixty years, I am still waiting to see a little more of a united way for people to live. The way I remember my childhood years living in Europe, even if our ways of living and doing certain things were very primitive, but our standards of morality, religion, friendship and togetherness was held on a very high level by us. The way I think, we lived a very rich life, even if it was not financially and materialistically high, but in other ways our lives were much richer and fuller than any place here. We made the best of everything with whatever we had, and we always valued things that we could not buy for all of the money in the world.

## MY FIRST FRIEND IN AMERICA

I remember that very shortly after we arrived in America, and I was sitting in my room, which was on top of the luncheonette, the baby kept on crying constantly and I did not know what to do. The baby was crying, mostly because he missed his pacifier that he lost on the ship while we traveled to America. I bought all kinds of pacifiers, but it did not help, he just wanted his. Everyone heard the baby crying, downstairs in the luncheonette and they asked the uncle, "Whose baby is that crying?" The uncle told them that his cousin, with his family, just arrived from Europe.

I still remember that I sat on the bed in my little room that they gave us, I held the baby and we were both crying. I did not know what to do with him. This was actually the first time for me to take care of the baby all by myself since I left Salzburg, Austria. The first night when we arrived, the whole family came to see us, but since then nobody even bothered to come and ask if we needed any help. The only people who I saw was the uncle, but he was busy in the luncheonette all day, and the aunt was mostly in the kitchen, which was downstairs next to the luncheonette.

Of course, my husband was a free spirit, he was never around when I needed him. As soon as we arrived here he became an explorer and he started to explore America. I sat in our room with the crying baby, and I did not know what to do to make him stop crying.

Suddenly, I heard footsteps, and then I saw a girl coming up the stairs. She was about my age. She immediately started to talk to me, and said, "Hello." I replied back to her and I said, "Hello", too. The next thing that she said in Yiddish was, "My name is Boyt and I want to be your friend." I thought that I was dreaming. I really thought that it was not possible. I just came to America a few days ago and I have an American friend already. I started to cry even harder from happiness. I felt so relieved, happy and lucky and I just could not believe that something good would happen to me, because before I met her I felt very much alone and very miserable.

As soon as she said that she wanted to be my friend, it felt like God sent me an angel to take care of me. It made me feel that somebody still cared about me, and I was not completely alone. I felt, right away, that we would become very good friends. She actually was the first person in America that offered her friendship to me. I remember exactly how it happened. Boyt sat down on the bed and she took the baby from me and in seconds the baby fell asleep. While the baby was sleeping, Boyt started to ask me if I minded talking about Europe, because she was born in America and she told me that she was never out of the country. Boyt made a statement that she never had any connections with European people, and that was why she did not know anything about European countries or the people who lived there.

Boyt stated a fact that she had never met or socialized with people from other countries. She only knew Americans. She also mentioned to me that she would like to know a little about the European people, their habits, their hobbies, and their general way of living. I remember that I said to her, "Boyt, whatever I will remember from my childhood years, I will gladly tell you because I was only ten years old when the war broke out." I also told her that most of my memories of my early life were wrapped around with my family childhood years and that was what I remembered the most.

I was happy to start a conversation with her because she really spoke a good Yiddish and we could communicate with each other very freely. I liked Boyt right away. I still remember her very well. She was a very nice person and she had a very loud laugh, and she also spoke loud. I always spoke in a very low voice. In Europe we were taught to speak, softly, because it was more dignified, but now I was in America and I knew that I had to follow the crowd. When Boyt made a remark that I speak too quietly, she also told me that in America everyone talks loud and I should try to talk louder. I listened to her and I did not take it as an insult. Instead, I took it as a friendly suggestion. I thanked her for it and I started to talk louder. While the baby was asleep, we sat and talked about the countries I had lived in, in Europe. I told her that I was born in Poland and I lived there until after the Second World War, first with the Russians when they came to us in 1939, then the Nazis came to us in 1941. I still lived in my city, only in the ghetto by the Nazis.

After the war, I left Poland and I went to Germany for a while, then I came to Austria and I lived in Salzburg, Austria, for four years, with the Austrian Nazis. I told her that in Austria it felt to me, like I was still by Hitler. Boyt asked me if I minded talking about the war. I told her that I was very sorry, but I really did not like to talk about the war. I also said to her that I did not think that anyone could describe all of the happenings, and completely make somebody understand the pain that I felt, and the hunger that I suffered with the Nazis. I would have given everything for a piece of bread. Besides being hungry all of the time, I had the constant fear of knowing that I could get killed any second of the day. I asked, "Boyt, how can I make somebody understand this, someone who never experienced this themselves?" Then I stated a fact that, " Even after I was living through it myself, sometimes it was even hard for me to believe that this unbelievable thing could and did happen to me and to the rest of the Jews."

Boyt saw that I was getting very upset and I started to cry, so right away she changed the subject. Since that time, she never asked me anything about the war anymore. Apparently, she knew that I was not ready to talk about the war. She thought that in spite of her interest of wanting to know, she would wait until I would be ready and willing to talk about it.

Little by little, I started to trust and have more confidence in Boyt and I realized that she really was my true friend and not only curious to know about the war. I started to open up and we talked about the war almost every day. I talked to her and I told her what I went through during the war only because I wanted to spill my heart to her. In a way it made me feel better by getting it out in the open and it relieved the tension for me. I felt from the first minute on, when I met Boyt, that she would be my best friend. I felt that she was genuine and sincere and she really sympathized with me. I knew that when I would need a shoulder to cry on, I would have it in her, my friend, Boyt.

## MY INNER STRUGGLE WITHIN MYSELF

My husband had a lot of family in America, who lived in different cities, like Philadelphia, New York, Chicago, Hartford, Connecticut and in Arizona. Some of them were born in America and some cousins immigrated to America before the First World War started. When they heard that we arrived, very shortly after, many family members came to see us. They probably wanted to see how the refugees looked.

They looked me over like I came from another planet, like I was from out of space. They did not even try to act nice. None of them spoke Yiddish, so I could not have a conversation with them. In a way, I was glad not to be able to talk to them. Besides that, I knew that they were out-of-towners and they would leave in a couple days, and I would not see them too often. It really was fine with me.

My husband's family, who lived in Philadelphia, just about twenty people, I knew for certain, that they would constantly be on my back. They were very nasty to me from the beginning. I tried my best to be nice and diplomatic to them, but they probably thought that I was a young, dumb kid who did not know anything better and I would be a broomstick for them.

What they did not know was that because of what I lived through in my young life, I matured very fast and I knew exactly what was going on in their mind. I also knew that I was waiting for the right time and the right place, then I would show them the real me, who would not be a broomstick or a pushover for them, because this was not my personality. They did not like the way I dressed and they told me so. They criticized the way I was taking care of my baby, and they made remarks about everything and anything I did. According to them I had two faults, everything that I did and everything that I said.

They kept on and on and on, criticizing me without a stop. If it was not one thing that they did not like, it was another thing. They always managed to find something to complain about and tell me how wrong I was when doing it. They never said one bad word about their cousin, my husband. No matter how I did not like it, and no matter how I felt like telling them that they were very nasty to me, I still did not say anything. I made up my mind that even if it killed me, I would be patient and keep quiet until the right time would come. I kept on telling myself that the right time would definitely come very soon.

They called me greenhorn and they gave themselves permission to insult me only because I was not their cousin, but my husband was, and that was why they did not bother him in spite of the fact that he was a greenhorn all of his life.

In other words, they were very nasty and rude to me and it aggravated me very much. They spoke to each other in English about me and they thought that I did not understand what they were saying. I could not speak English, but I understood every word of it. I never told them this because I wanted to know what they were saying and thinking about me. I stored everything in my mind, and I was waiting for the right time to tell them off.

I told myself that I did not care what they thought of me or what kind of impression I was making on them, but the truth was that it irritated me to death, because according to them I was guilty without a chance to be proven innocent. The first minute they saw me, they disliked me right away without even getting to know me better.

The only thing that I understood was that the situation that I was in did not look to be a good one. I knew that I had to face reality. I was a stranger in their country and I was all alone. I also knew that I had to use diplomacy in order to avoid any bad feelings on their part. We used to have a saying that "when you need the thief you cut him from the rope". I knew that I needed them. I also knew that our future depended on them, so I swallowed my pride and I kept silent for the time being. I tried to be very patient with their attitude towards me, but this was not the real me.

I was and still am a very proud person and I never took any insults from anybody in my life. I always lived my life the way I was taught by my parents. I stayed away from people who tried to influence me in the wrong way. I lived by my own rules, moral values, and principles, which were very important to me. I always had a special and different way of doing things. I tried to live my life according to my religious upbringing, in an honest, decent and respectable way. Some people did respect my honesty and truthfulness, but others did not appreciate my openness. It really did not matter to me who liked me or not.

The most important thing to me was that I had to please myself and be happy with myself. I always was a very independent person and I always minded my own business. I did not like people who were only thinking of themselves and never lending a helping hand to others. I always had my own way of expressing myself, even when others did not agree with me. I never tried to live up to someone else's expectations, I only tried to do what I thought was right to do. I felt very strongly about being myself and not pretending or acting that I was someone else. The fact was that I never wanted to be someone else, only me.

I will never change my personality, because right or wrong, believe it or not, I was and still am very proud of myself and I feel good about myself. No matter what and who tried to change me, they did not succeed and they never will.

I always stood by my principles, but sometimes under certain situations and predicaments that I was in, I did use diplomacy in order to avoid disagreements and bad feelings. I was patient enough to wait for the right time to express my opinion, and I think that I was fortunate and very lucky to know when the right time was for me to speak up, and take care of my problems my way.

After being in America for two weeks already, for the first time the cousin's wife invited us to dinner. First, she showed us the house. It was a very nice house with nice furniture and everything was furnished in good taste. I kept on giving her compliments that everything was beautiful and very tasteful. I remember that she turned towards me and then she said to me, "Sonia, when you will be in America as long as we are, you will have a nice house, too. " I started to think to myself that I have to be in America fifty years to have a nice house? Me, without even realizing what I was saying, said to her, "I want a nice house sooner." As soon as I said it, she got very angry with me. Then she started to holler, and kept on hollering that, "The greenhorns were coming to America and right away they wanted everything." Of course, everyone who came to dinner agreed with her. I was sitting at the table, like on pins and needles, and I felt the tension from all of them. The dinner was good, but the atmosphere was very tense, and I felt like I was sitting on a volcano and waiting for an explosion.

I felt like I was in the ghetto, by the Nazis, and I got very upset by her screaming at me. I sensed that they were judging and criticizing me every step of the way. I thought that it was very impolite of them to invite me to dinner and make me feel like they were doing me a big favor, and treating me like I was a nobody. In their mind they thought that I had to be very thankful for every little crumb that they were throwing me, and according to them, I did not have the right to want a nice home or to live a normal life. In their eyes, I was just a greenhorn. I knew that everyone was watching every move that I made and they corrected every word that I said. They hollered at my baby, that he should not touch anything, even when he did not touch anything. I still remember that I really tried my very best to finish the dinner, instead of walking out.

When they invited us again, I said no, and I did not go. Of course, because I did not go, my husband did not go to their dinner, either. The only reason that he did not go was that he knew better than to go against my wishes. In private, I was not such an agreeable person and he really could not do things that would degrade and humiliate me by going to the dinner without me. He only did it when I kept quiet because I thought that I had to behave like a lady and not fight with him in front of other people.

I was sure that they did not invite me to begin with. They had to invite their cousin and I just had to tag along and they made it very obvious, that this was how it was. All of the time they really thought that I was too stupid to understand or get insulted. The situation got worse and worse.

My husband did, and said, all the nasty things in front of them, just to make them happy. By the same token, he was happy, also, by thinking that now he has the power to do and say to me whatever he wants to. He started to become surer of himself. After all, he had his whole family behind him and I did not have anyone to back me up, so he decided to join them and be against me. I was thinking of leaving him right away, but I knew that nobody would help me because we came through a sponsor, not though the American government. I knew that I was in a very bad predicament and I also knew that I was stuck here for good. There was no way out for me because I had to think about my baby.

After thinking it over, finally, I came to the conclusion that no matter what, I was going to keep quiet until the time would come and hopefully the time would come soon and I would be able to repay everyone for their so-called kindness towards me, especially my husband for being so disrespectful and ignorant. Instead of sticking with me, he stuck with them in order to buy their love. He did not care how I was feeling, instead he tried to please them by humiliating me, and that was why they did not have any respect for me and they treated me like I was a nobody.

What he did not understand was that the more he was against me, he was against himself because the more he tried to buy their love by humiliating me, and by being so mean towards me I hated and despised him more and more everyday. My husband agreed with them and was on their side all the way.

Everything that they all did to me stuck in my mind and I knew that sooner or later I would take care of it and it would be my way, and my way was always that I got angry, but I was also getting even. No matter how long it took, I knew that the time would eventually come and my husband with his family would be repaid by me for everything, in many, many ways, mostly my husband. The only thing that I was hoping for was that it would be sooner, than later. In the later days they found out very quickly that the joke was on them, after all.

The cousins had a nice big house and beautiful furniture, but I thought to myself, "What about us? What about my family?" According to them, we did not deserve anything, after all, we were just intruders here. This was their country and they did us a big favor to let us come here, which was what they thought. What they did not know was that I never would or wanted to come here to begin with, and that I would have been more than happy if I would have never gotten to know them. I also would be much happier to live in my home in Poland, with my own family.

If we had not known Hitler, to disrupt and destroy our lives, I would not have to listen to anyone telling me that the greenhorns wanted everything. For their information, my family had just as nice of a home as they had, maybe even nicer. When the cousin's wife said it to me, it made me very angry and frustrated, and I kept on thinking and asking myself, "This was why I came to America, to his nasty family who don't have any feelings or consideration for the couple survivors? They were not even nice enough to show a little sympathy and some respect for me. This was why I came to America to live on the second floor, on top of a luncheonette in one room with my baby? This was why I got married to Kadish, in order to come to America, and this is what I thought, that he would be a friend in my life? Instead, he was my enemy."

Besides all of these things, I did not know the language and I came to a strange country. The people looked and acted very selfish, ignorant, disrespectful and strange. On top of that, I had to learn a way of acting and I mean acting, because most of them did not know how to be themselves. I had to learn a new way of dressing and a new way of communicating with others. The few weeks that I was already in America, I noticed that everything that I was saying and doing, I had to use diplomacy, and I had to become a diplomat and say things that people wanted to hear, instead of saying how it really was.

According to me, the people here were very selfish and not friendly at all, not like where I was brought up. They were not like the Jewish people in Poland. Even the survivors after the war, who were full of pain and hurt, were still friendlier and closer to each other than I could expect here. I did not see it here in the Goldenah Medinah, which was supposed to be the Golden Land, and I began to doubt if I made the right decision. In fact, I came to realize that everything that I did was wrong. It was very wrong for me to pay such a high price and to give up a lot, like my freedom and my self-respect just to be able to come to America, but I also knew that I could not turn back the clock. Of course, I never expected all of this to happen and unintentionally I fell into it. I did what I did and it was much too late for my regrets because now I had a baby to worry about and to take care of.

Many of the Jewish people in America did not speak Yiddish and the surroundings seemed to me to be very different and strange. I did not say anything, but I was very miserable and unhappy with the whole situation. Not even one of my husband's families, except his uncle and aunt, gave me any encouragement that it would, in time, get better and we would be happy here. The fact was that they could not have cared less if I was happy or not. On the contrary, they treated me like I really did not count and that I was not important enough. In their mind, they told themselves that I was the intruder here and they acted like they were the bosses over me.

They always seemed to be angry with me, maybe because they all knew why I got married to their cousin, and maybe that was why they were so mean to me. It probably seemed to them that I used their poor cousin for my purposes, only to come to America. They probably thought that after me being in America I would leave him, which would be the right thing for me to do, but I did not have any intention of doing it. I got married for better or worse.

Besides that, I did not think that my reasons for getting married to Kadish should and did concern them and it really was not any of their business to begin with. I thought that they did not have the right to mix into my life, to judge and criticize me. The way they behaved towards me made me very angry, but I still kept my anger to myself and I waited patiently to see how it would develop, and what the outcome of it would be. I remember that I was sitting in the luncheonette with my baby and the customers were curious and anxious to see a refugee and to speak to me.

Most of the time, the American people were born in America and they had very little contact with European people who had come after the war. They started to ask me all kinds of questions, like, "Why did you survive the war and not your family?" They asked me, "Do you feel guilty because you survived?" I told them that I did not feel guilty because I did not do anything wrong. They kept on asking me about the war and how I survived, and what we had to eat, and I told them the truth, that we hardly had enough bread and a lot of Jewish people died of starvation.

I still remember, to this day, that one of the customers was standing and listening to the conversation and then he said to me, "Yes, in the time of the war, in America, there was a shortage of sugar and we had to use saccharin, and we could not get any meat so we had to eat chicken every day of the week." Apparently, he did not care about what I had told him. The only thing that he was concerned with was that these poor people, here in America, were very unhappy that they had to eat chicken everyday, instead of meat and they had to use saccharin instead of sugar. What a shame it was for them.

I thought to myself that they were really very ignorant and selfish. Also, when they started to ask me how the Nazis treated the Jews and I started to tell them about my past and what I lived through, they really did not believe me, not even one word that I said and they said straight to my face that I was exaggerating. Once, a neighbor told me that I had a very good imagination and I should write stories. She really did not believe anything that I told her about the ghettos, concentration camps, death pits, and gas chambers. She told the other neighbors in the building that if they wanted to hear a good story, they should speak to the refugee, meaning me, and that I had a talent to make up stories. Since that time, I never talked to anybody about my past again.

I realized that it was really unbelievable, especially to the people who did not experience this. They really could not believe or feel the same pain or sympathize with the survivors. Instead, they thought that they were doing us a big favor by bringing us over to America and giving us some support until we would try to put whatever was left of our lives back together. Most of the survivors were sponsored by a member of their family that was taking the responsibility of the coming survivors and their well-being. In this way, the American government did not have to, and did not do anything for the survivors.

I was glad that I made up my mind not to talk about the war. When somebody asked me anything, I pretended that I did not hear and right away, I changed the subject. It seemed to me that by having less discussion with them it was much better for me. I thought that the people in America, at the time of the war, when they had to use saccharin and eat chicken everyday, really thought that this was a real tragedy and a disaster for them.

They were so preoccupied with themselves and they were so narrow minded that they really did not care, and were not concerned about the things that were going on in the world, especially what was happening to the European Jews. When they heard something about Hitler and the Jews, they really did not believe it, and they said that it was propaganda. I think that maybe the media did not know the truth, but the world leaders knew that Hitler was murdering the Jews in cold blood.

When someone asked me something about the war, I said that the best ones died and the worst ones lived and most of the time I said very plain that I did not want to talk about it, and I meant every word of it. Still, until today, I do not get into these conversations with anyone. I never wanted to bring back my past because it was and it still is very painful for me. Only by talking about it, it feels that I relive it over and over again. In spite of my feelings I thought that after sixty years after the war, it was the highest time for me to tell the world about all of the happenings to me.

Most of the people, even until today, did not want to believe or they did not understand the Holocaust. The reason they did not feel our pain was because they were not put in this position to experience such suffering, like mass murder, sadism, murder of the families, murder of men, women and children. I would have liked very much if it only would be my imagination, like the neighbors thought that I was imagining everything. I have to say, with regret, that it was the bitter reality in my life and I was a living witness that all of the cruel, unbelievable things really did happen and six million Jews perished, including my whole family of eighty-six people.

In the meantime, I got a letter from my son's nurse and it made me very happy to hear from her. Besides that, my son still missed her and I missed her, too. She was like a friend to all of us. The nurse wrote to me that she saw my landlady in Salzburg, Austria, Mrs. Gossner, and she told my nurse that her dog got run over by a car and got killed. Mrs. Gossner also told the nurse that I put a curse on her and that was why this happened to her dog. My son's nurse asked me to write to her about everything that was happening here, in America. She asked me to let her know if I was happy coming here. I wrote to her and told her when I will settle down here I would let her know if I was happy here. The only thing that I really knew was that I had to make my happiness myself, and hopefully, maybe, in time I would wind up being happy.

## MY UNCERTAINTY OF MY FUTURE IN AMERICA

Boyt came a few times a day and she was the only person who I really started to like and trust. When I talked to her, I felt like I talked to a friend and when she asked me something about the war and I told her about our suffering, she got very upset to hear what I had lived through. I kept on talking to her and a lot of times we were both crying. I talked about my family and I really poured my heart out to her. She kept on saying that she felt sorry for me.

Boyt really sympathized with me and I knew that her feelings were sincere. Boyt really was a good person, besides that, she was educated and she knew what was going on in the world. They had newspapers with the world's news, and everyday there was news about the Nazis on the front page. She read the papers and she believed what they were informing the people about, the war and everything that was happening during the time of the war. If the people would read the news and believe that it was true, they would have known what was going on in the world, especially with the European Jews, during the Nazi regime.

Boyt and I communicated with each other very well, mostly because she spoke Yiddish, and besides that, Boyt was a very smart and friendly person and I always sensed that she understood me. It seemed to me that she was always reading my mind because she always knew what I was thinking and before I started to talk to her about one thing or another she said to me, "Sonia, it will get better, you'll get used to it." I remember I said to her, "Boyt, I will never get used to two-faced people like the cousins and I will never get used to being treated like this." She said to me, "Don't pay attention to them."

Besides that, I asked Boyt, " What will happen to us here? What will our future be?" I asked Boyt, "For this I wanted to come to America, to take all of the insults and humiliation from all of them, and to live in one room, together with the baby?" I said to Boyt that these conditions were not what I expected. The reason I came here was to start a better life for my family. The fact was that for this I did not have to come to America, instead I could have stayed in Europe with the enemies. I told Boyt that I really did not know how long I could keep quiet and not say anything to them. I knew myself, that when I will start to talk, I will say things that they will not want to hear. Boyt said, "Sonia, you must be smart and have patience and everything will work itself out", and I said to her, "Boyt, I will try my best. I do promise you that I will try."

Boyt lived across the street and we walked to each other's house a few times a day. Boyt was a hairdresser, and one day she decided that I would look better with short hair. I agreed with her, so she gave me a haircut and she showed me how to put on make-up. One day, she took me shopping and I bought a few dresses, which she helped me pick out and she told me what styles they were wearing in America. She helped me a lot. In no time I started to dress and act like other Americans, and I forced myself to become Americanized. I started to look like a new me. I even got a lot of compliments from a lot of neighbors. Boyt told me that now I looked better than the cousins did.

When my husband's cousins saw that, I would not have to depend on them for everything, they did not like it at all, in a way, thanks to Boyt, I did not need them for anything anyway. Not that the cousins did much of anything for me to begin with. They started to tell me that I depend on Boyt more than on them and they became jealous of Boyt. I never asked the cousins for anything. They really thought that they would have me, who they called greenhorn, to boss around and criticize every step of the way, but to their surprise, it did not work out the way they really planned.

They really thought that I did not understand how they treated me and they thought that they could say and do whatever they wanted to, and I would not mind the way they acted towards me. They thought that when they spoke in English, I did not understand, anyway. What they did not know was that I did understand, and whenever someone said something nasty to me or about me to each other, I did not want to socialize with them anymore.

The only people who I really trusted were the aunt, the uncle and Boyt. Whenever I got upset with something or somebody, I confided in them. They used to say to me, "Sonia, it is not important enough to aggravate yourself over it." I started to think about it and then I saw that they were right. The uncle said to me, "Sonia, wait until you will become a citizen, then you will be able to ask them, are you a citizen?" This was because a lot of them were not citizens, even though they lived in America for a long time and maybe they went for citizenship, but they did not pass the test. The uncle said that when you will ask them this question, they would stop bothering you. Besides that, a lot of them could not even speak, write or read English in spite of the fact that they were living in America for a long time.

The next morning, the uncle took us to the city hall to apply for citizenship. We registered and they told us that we have to wait five years to be sworn in. In the meantime, during the five years, we had to learn to read, write, and speak English in order to answer all of the questions that they will ask us. They gave us books with questions and we had to study them. I remember that I started to feel a little better.

On the way home, I was really excited and I felt important that eventually I would become an American citizen. It felt good to me to look forward to it. In a way, it felt to me that in time I would belong someplace, and I would be able to have a voice in a country like America and build my future here. I also knew that the constitution says free speech, so I thought that some day I would be able to express my opinion. Of course, usually I would not wait for someday. To me, there always was no time like the present, but here in America I had to act like everyone else for the time being. I thought to myself, "Why was I thinking about someday when I have to worry about today first?" I knew that today did not look too good and I did not know how tomorrow would be and I was pretty much disgusted with everything.

## THE UNEXPECTED SURPRISE

A few weeks passed with us being in America, and I mentioned to my husband that we came to America and we lived under worse conditions and circumstances than we had lived in Austria. Living here, on top of a luncheonette in one room, with a lot of steps to walk up and down, with the baby in my arms, was not so easy. These conditions did not make me too happy and I did not feel too safe, either. He did not know what to say to me because he did not know any more than I did. Some survivors who came to America the same time we came, but who the American government was responsible for, were settled in apartments. They were supplied with food, with utilities and all of the necessities that they needed. They were also given jobs in order to try to make a living.

They were taken care of, with the help of social workers, until they could stand on their own two feet. It was a big help for them, but the only thing was that they had to settle down wherever the government wanted them to and they could not pick where they would live. In other words, the government was controlling every move the survivors made, like you were in the army.

We came to America through a sponsor, my husband's Uncle Manas (Max) Goldstein, and my husband's aunt. In this way, Uncle Manas was responsible for our well-being, but it did not look to me or to my husband that he was taking his responsibility towards us too seriously. Even though Uncle Manas seemed very nice and kind, it looked like he really did not care how we were feeling, good or bad, or if we were happy or miserable. He just did not say anything to us or showed us that he was making any efforts to help get us situated. Everyday, I kept on wondering what the next day would bring. I thought to myself, it would probably be the same as the day before. I was already too tired, disappointed and very doubtful that I would ever feel and be an independent person or that I would ever have the opportunity to manage my own life, instead of everyone telling me how to live and how to do things. I kept on mentioning it to Boyt and she kept on telling me the same thing, to be patient. She really did not know what else to say to me.

One day the uncle said to me, "Sonia, I would like you to come with me." He left my husband and his son, Nathan, in charge of the luncheonette and he took me by the hand. He said, "Sonia, I want to show you something." I walked across the street with him and he unlocked the door of a house and we both walked in and then he said to me, "This is the house for your family to live in. Now you have to pick the paint and the wallpaper and after everything will be done, you'll move in."

It came like a shock to me. I really did not expect this. I started to cry from happiness. The uncle was very touched, also, and he said, "Sonia, you suffered enough." The reason he knew what we went through was because his son, Harry, the soldier who came back from Austria, told him everything about what he saw.

The American soldiers, after the war, saw the concentration camps, the death pits, the ghettos and they also talked to the people so the soldiers found out, first hand, what really happened. They found out about the unbelievable and inhuman acts and all of the happenings that were caused by the Nazi regime. When the uncle's son, Harry (Herschel) came home, and he told his parents what he saw, they were very disturbed by it, to hear about such brutality. The uncle felt very bad hearing this and he was very sorry about what we had to go through in our life, and then he said to me, "From now on I will try to see to it that you and your family will be happy here." He also told me that before we came to America, he picked one of his nicest houses and made the tenant move out, then he hired a contractor to renovate the house. He told me that he wanted to make everything in the house in perfect condition so that we should really like it and be happy. I remember that I kept on running from one place in the house to another. I was very excited and I really could not believe that only our family would live in such a big house.

This was one of his eleven houses that he owned and he fixed this one up for us because it was in the best neighborhood. I remember that it was like a project and all the houses were semi-detached. We could hear everything that was going on in the other half of the house. In a way, nobody could feel lonely. I remember there were two rows of houses and a narrow street in the middle. When we stood in front of our house we could see what the neighbor across the street was doing in her house, but the house that the uncle gave us had a closed porch in the front and nobody could see what was going on in our house.

The uncle told me that the workers had already worked on this house for two and a half months. They finished with the renovations and everything was done, except for the papering and the painting. The uncle also told me that he was especially waiting for us to come to America, so then I would be able to pick the paper and paint according to my own taste. The aunt never mixed in with what the uncle was doing. She let him make all the decisions and she was happy with them and did not mind it at all.

I have to mention that the minute I met the aunt and uncle, I liked them right away and I sensed that they also liked me. In fact, when the uncle told me that he fixed up the house for us, I asked him why he did not tell us before. He replied to me that he first wanted to meet us, especially me, and he first wanted to get to know me better. When the uncle said this to me I was very happy that somebody from all the family cared and apparently liked me. This was the uncle and the aunt and they knew that the feeling was mutual.

I also liked their two sons, Kadish's cousins, Harry (Herschel) the soldier whom I met in Salzburg, and the other son, Nathan (Nuchem), who worked with his father, in the luncheonette. I was always close to Harry and he was like a brother to me, besides this, he was the first member of the family who I met when he came, as an American soldier, to Salzburg.

The house had nine rooms, a closed porch, and a fenced in back yard. After everything was done in the house, the cousins called the post office to deliver the four coffers, which were stored there, with the Persian rugs, the dishes and the other things that we brought from Austria. The post office delivered everything. To tell you the truth, I had the satisfaction of being right, by bringing all of these things to America. Now we had a big house and plenty of room to put everything in place. I was very glad that I did not let anyone influence me in any way. The next thing was to look for furniture. I was a little worried if the cousins would let me pick what I liked and I hoped that they would.

One morning, my husband's uncle decided that we should go shopping for furniture. I was a little concerned about it. I hoped that there would be no bad feelings between us, because we went with the uncle's daughter-in-law, where we had the first dinner in their house and she told me that I had to wait a long time in order to have a nice house like hers. She and her husband, the cousin Nathan, were supposed to go with us. Apparently, none of them knew the uncle's plans. He did not confide in them and told none of them what he intended to do for us. The uncle probably did not want any interference from anyone and he did what he felt he wanted to do.

My husband and I were the only ones to be surprised in a wonderful way. Of course, they had a surprise coming to them, also, but it was not such a happy surprise for them. I was sure that the daughter- in- law was not too happy with the whole situation. What a shame. No matter how they felt they really did not have any say in this matter, because the uncle made these decisions and whatever he said and did had to be okay with all of them.

One day, they picked a time that was convenient for them and they decided to go shopping with us for furniture. The uncle did not go with us, but before we went, he said to me, "Sonia, don't worry about the prices, just buy what you both like and be happy. " I knew that he meant what he was saying. The uncle had to co-sign in case my husband would not make the payments, so the uncle would have to make them himself. I knew that he was not worried about the payments. The uncle was fairly rich and he never talked about money. Even if he would have to make the payments himself, I was sure that he would not mind it at all.

Finally, my husband, myself, and the cousin with his wife, went together, to pick furniture. They knew all the best places and they also knew where the best prices were. It took us a few days and I picked what I liked. My husband's uncle said to get what I liked and the cousins liked what I picked, also. That is what they said. At that time I felt very overwhelmed with all of the unexpected surprises. I really could not believe that something wonderful could and did happen to me and after being in America only two months I would have a beautiful house with beautiful furniture. Besides that, I would start to be my own boss. Finally, I started to feel free and good for the first time in a long time.

After we picked everything out for every room, I was happy. We started to unpack the coffers with the Persian rugs and we laid them out in the rooms and it really looked very nice. I thought to myself, after everything will be arranged and the house will be all done and furnished, then I will say to the cousin's wife, "You see, I did not have to wait too long after all, in order to have a nice home. I have it in two months of being here." I could not wait to start to repay all of them for being so mean, nasty, and disrespectful to me, and for all of the misery that I went through in these two months because of them. Now thank God, I was happy.

All of the wonderful things that happened to us was thanks to the uncle and aunt, and how generous they were to us, not just with money, but having so much consideration for us. They thought that after what we went through by the Nazis we deserved something good in our life. Only the aunt, uncle, and their sons, especially Harry, the soldier, felt this way. From my husband's whole family in America, only they showed friendship and understanding towards us and I was very grateful to them for all of the things that they did for us.

I do not exactly remember how long we had to wait for the furniture, but finally, they delivered the furniture and I started to arrange everything according to my taste. I then unpacked the coffers with the dishes and I put the nice things in the dining room breakfront. After arranging and putting everything in place and having all new things, the house looked beautiful. It really looked to me like a palace. I had all of these expensive things that I brought from Austria and I displayed them in the living room on the end tables and they really looked good. I always liked a lot of mirrors in the house and I mentioned this to the uncle. He told me that if I like mirror I should get them, so I ordered wall-to-wall mirrors.

Whoever came in, said that everything looked beautiful. Even the cousin's wife said that our house was nicer than her house, and she also said that our house was decorated in better taste than her house was. For the first time it looked to all of them that I could do something right. At the time, when she gave me all of the compliments, I thought that she felt a little embarrassed by thinking that I really do not know how to do anything right. I think that my husband's whole family was very surprised to find out that this so-called, by them, greenhorn, has good taste and she is not as dumb as they thought she was meaning me.

We even bought a television. It was one of the first televisions that just came out in America. No one of my husband's family or the neighbors had a television yet. I remember it was a Zenith with a round screen. I also remember in Austria, when we were living in Salzburg, I used to go, practically everyday, to the Keno (movie theatre). At the time, in Europe, the movies were mostly silent pictures. I did not mind it because I used to love movies. My husband used to make a joke out of it. He used to say that he would put a keno (movie theatre) into the house, so maybe I would stay home sometimes for a change. I always liked a good movie. Now I was in America and I felt like I had a keno (movie theatre) in my home.

The television was very important to me. It felt good to see all of the different programs on it, even though, at the time there were not too many programs on television available, but it was okay because I wanted to see the news and know what was going on in the world. It also felt to me like I was not alone, instead, I was surrounded by a lot of other people. I invited some neighbors who I liked to come in and watch television with us. Of course, my husband's uncle, aunt and cousins who lived only two blocks away from us came everyday.

When the house was all fixed up and I had more time for myself I started to look for a day school in order to learn English. My husband did not want to learn anything and he did not even care if he would become a citizen or not. He used to say that he knows enough, even though he really did not know too much of anything. Most of the Jewish people in America did not know how to speak Yiddish and they spoke only English. It was the other way around with me, I knew Yiddish, but I did not know English.

Right from the beginning, it was very disturbing to me not to be able to carry on a proper conversation in English. I thought that it was time for me to learn English, and I decided to attend a class that they had at noon, only for newcomers. I remember that I did not have any place to leave the baby with, so I had to take him with me. He was only about two years old at the time and like any other baby, he did not want to sit in the seat. Instead, he walked over to everyone in the class, talked to them, and disturbed their concentration.

No one said anything to me, but I myself thought that it was not fair to the others to distract them and not let them concentrate. After two times of coming there, I decided to stop attending the classes, but I knew that I had to learn to speak, read and write English, in order to be able to communicate with others. I wanted to be one of them and not be an exception or an outsider. Besides that, I always wanted to learn and know as much as I could, even when I was only a young child.

My husband was the opposite of me and he never wanted to learn anything. He did not have any education at all. The only thing that he could do was to read a Jewish paper, which was written in Yiddish. What he was interested in was to be involved in all kinds of business and to try to make money. According to him, money was the most important thing in his life. It was his idol. The fact was that we both liked very different things.

One day I mentioned it to Boyt that I was no longer attending the English classes and I told her the reason for it. She understood me, and she even said to me that it was very nice of me, not only to think about myself, but also to have some consideration for others. She saw that I was not too happy to give up the English classes, but at the time she did not say anything to me.

One day she came to me and said, "Sonia, how would you like it if I will teach you English?" I was very surprised to hear this question. I asked her if she was a teacher, too, besides being a hairdresser. Then she said to me, "I don't have to be a teacher to teach basic English." I immediately said to her, "If you are willing to teach me, I for sure, am willing to learn." A few days later she brought some books over and we started the lessons.

I was very determined to learn English and every free minute I had I studied English. Boyt lived right across the street from me so it was easy for her to come. She came to me a few times a day and she gave me homework and then she checked everything. She was like a real English teacher to me. She became very formal and she said to me, "From now on I am not speaking Yiddish to you," and she started to speak to me in English only.

I understood every word that she was saying to me, but I could not answer her in English, so she told me the answers, and then she made me repeat them a few times. It really did not take me too long, about three months to learn to speak English, thanks to Boyt. Eventually, I was able to express myself and I was able to take a part in a conversation in English. I would not say that I spoke well, but at least people understood me and little by little I spoke better and better. The more I spoke English, the better I learned to express myself. I kept on practicing my writing and also my reading.

When I came from Austria, I had an international driver's license, but I wanted to get my American driver's license and I knew that I had to be able to answer all of the questions that they would ask me in English. I also knew that I had to study for my citizenship papers, so I made up my mind that this came first, to know the English language better. I kept on studying every chance I had, and I tried to learn all of the questions that they would ask me. I tried very hard to memorize everything and eventually, little by little, everything finally started to fall into place. When I thought that it was time for me to try to get my license, I made an appointment to take my driver's test and to everyone's surprise, including mine, I passed the test right away. I was very happy about it and now I started to concentrate on the house.

As soon as I was done with fixing up the house and no matter how I felt towards my husband's family, I thought that I would let bygones be bygones for the time being. In spite of the way I felt about them, I invited them for a visit. They all came to see us on a Sunday. From then on, before they left, I invited them for the next Sunday for lunch and we spent Sunday afternoon together. I always had in my mind, and I was almost positive that sooner or later they would go back to their old tricks and they would again start to make nasty remarks about me.

Most of the time, I stayed in the kitchen doing the dishes because I really did not want to take a part in their conversation and listen to their criticism. I never could forget the way they talked to me and about me, from the very first beginning, and I still carried a grudge against them, but I could not bring myself to a point to be mean and pick an argument with them. According to my way of thinking was that "two wrongs do not make one right". I thought that because they were wrong, I did not want to stoop to their level and act the same way that they did, because it will make me wrong, also.

In spite of how I felt, I started to think that it was time to show my husband's family my hospitality, and I invited all of them for dinner. I really wanted to show them that I was a better person than they would ever be. I called them up and they agreed to come on Sunday because they were all in business and on Sunday their businesses were closed.

They all came to us, about eighteen people. I guess they were all curious about what kind of a cook I was. I still remember that when they came, the table was set in the dining room, which was big enough for twenty-four people. I think that they were surprised that I did something right because they called me the greenhorn all the time. Come to think of it, that since we moved into the house and I was on my own, and I made my own decisions about doing things, I gave them a lot of surprises. I think, little by little, they started to realize that I was not such a dummy after all. In spite of my better judgment, I was very sweet and nice to them. After supper, they all had a conversation in the living room. Most of the time I was in the kitchen doing the dishes. In Europe, the custom was that when we invited guests nobody was supposed to help with the dishes.

The first few times when they came to our home, they behaved very well and they even gave me compliments. They kept on saying that the house looked nice and clean. They kept on telling me that they accepted me and took me into their family, even though I knew better, because I remembered the way they talked about me and treated me. I never let them know that I was very angry with them, and I understood everything that they were saying about me in English. I thought to myself that now they were nice to me so I would be nice to them. From this time on, I invited the whole family for dinner every Sunday and they came. I adopted the philosophy to think that "today was the first day of the rest of my life."

To tell you the truth, for the first time in so many years of not having anyone who thought that I was part of their family, even if I did not believe them, it still made me feel good. I always knew that none of them wanted to accept me for some reason or another. I thought that maybe they were jealous of me, because I was much younger than they were and to be very honest I really did not care what or how they thought about me. I felt that as long as they started to behave, I was happy.

The only people from the whole family who I really liked were the uncle, aunt and their two sons, my husband's cousins. They were genuine and sincere people and I knew that they cared about our well-being. They showed it in so many ways and they tried their very best to make us happy. There is an expression that "actions speak louder than words." They did not say too much, but they did a lot of good things for us.

I always told them that I appreciated their generosity because I always knew that they did not expect anything in return. I also always knew that whatever they did was out of the goodness of their heart. In spite of it, that they did not want or expect anything in return from us, we still willingly paid back to the uncle and aunt, every penny that they spent on us in bringing us to America. I always thought that they were the greatest, but I sensed that the other members of the family were not sincere and sooner or later they would start, again, to act the way they always did. They would make themselves at home, in our home, without even thinking that I had a right to be there. I was sure that very soon they would be back to their old, and nasty ways of treating me, and of course, they would have my husband to back them up every step of the way.

They mentioned a few times that I just came to America only a short time ago and I already have a nicer home than they have and I have nicer things than they will ever have. I knew that they were jealous, but it did not bother me at all. I still invited them to our home and they came every Sunday for dinner and for a while they behaved more or less like guests. In a while they became too comfortable, and they started to loosen up and act like their real selves again.

They looked around in the house, and whatever they saw and liked, they asked my husband if they could have it. Of course, right away, he said yes, without even consulting me. He wanted to play boss over me in front of them. He really did not care how I felt. When nobody was around he was not such a big boss over me. He always knew the boss he was in private, but I assumed that according to his thinking was, that he would rather be a boss over me anytime he could, no matter how it backfired on him, instead of not being a boss at all.

I remember that I was very angry with them for coming into our house and having a nerve not to care if I liked it or not, and take whatever they wanted to. They knew if they would ask me if they could have it, I would say to them that I did not drag everything all the way from Europe for them. I still did not say anything to any of them, until one day something happened and right then I decided that I had enough of this behavior from them.

I remember this incident very clearly. It was when the cousins took us for a ride to show us the city. I was sitting in the backseat with my baby and the cousin's wife was sitting next to me. She looked at my ring for a while and then she said to me, "Sonia, your ring is beautiful." It was a golden ring with a big, black onyx stone, a signet. I remember that after the liberation when I got some spending money from the Jewish organization I bought this ring.

This was the first thing that I bought for myself after the war and I wore it since then. I always loved this ring and I wore it all the time. It had a very sentimental and a special meaning to me. The cousin kept on saying that she liked my ring and I said, thank you. My husband was sitting in the front seat and when he heard her saying that she liked the ring, he turned around and said to me, "Give me the ring." I thought for a minute, "Why does he want the ring?" I really could not understand. I never took this ring off my finger before, but in order for me not to go against him I obeyed his wishes, I took the ring off and gave it to him. Right away he gave it to her and she thanked him for it, then she put the ring on her finger. I felt like killing both of them, but instead I kept quiet. From this time on, I made up my mind that enough was enough.

After this incident, from then on when they came into our house and when they said to my husband, "I like this and this, can I have it?" before he even could say anything, I said to them, "Yes, you can have it, but you have to take your cousin, too." I told them very plain, "Do not ever come into our home and ask your cousin for anything. In this house I am the boss, too. Whatever you see and like will stay here from now on. I hope that I made myself very clear and we understand each other."

This was the very first time that I struck back and I spoke up. My husband still thought that he was in Europe where a wife was treated like a maid and the man was the king. Maybe he was the king with his first wife, but he was never a king with me even before we came to America. On the contrary, he always treated me very nice while we were in Austria, otherwise, I would never go anyplace with him.

In spite of me telling them off, they did not get angry with me and they kept on coming to our home like nothing happened. The reality of it was that they really did not care what I said to them. According to their way of thinking, I was not important at all. They did not listen to me or pay attention to what I was saying. They took the right to keep on telling my husband, who was their cousin, how much money he should allow me to spend, to tell me what to buy, what to cook, when to go out and when to stay home. In other words, according to them he had the right to treat me like a slave.

When they came to our house, no matter what I did for them and how I treated them, they never appreciated anything and instead they still had thoughts in their mind that I was a nobody and they were coming to their cousin, Kadish, only, and they were not also coming to me. After all, I was only the slave for them to cook and listen to their nasty remarks. What they did not know was that in front of people I was a lady, but when nobody was around my husband was getting from me what he deserved and more.

A lot of times when they came and they saw something new, like a knickknack, they said to my husband, "The greenhorn needs such an expensive knickknack?" meaning me, and then they asked him, " Why did you let her spend so much money?" They said this in front of me, like I could not hear, and my husband agreed with them. He said that he really did not want me to buy it, but I argued with him, like he was trying to defend himself by lying to his cousins. The truth was that he was never with me when I went shopping, and I never asked him what I should buy or should not buy.

The fact of it was that he never told me how much money I should spend, but in front of the cousins he played a part like I was the bad one, and I was not listening to him. Of course, the whole family sympathized with him. Poor little him, and of course, after they left I gave him the biggest argument for lying about it to the cousins.

Sunday, when they all came to us and after supper, the main topic of conversation was me. They kept on calling me greenhorn and they kept on teaching their cousin, who happened to be my husband, how to treat me. It always looked and felt to me that he was treating me badly in front of them, especially to irritate me, like he was taking revenge on me. It always felt to me that he had a grudge against me.

He knew when he had his chance of striking back at me, so he took it and he really did a good job of aggravating and belittling me by not being on my side and not sticking with me. When I decided to get married to Kadish, he knew exactly that it was only because I wanted to come to America. Kadish always knew my reason for marrying him, because I told him before we got married, and I was very honest about it. Now I was in America and I had Kadish for my husband plus his whole nasty family on my back. I started to think that I really did not make such a good choice, or a good decision, to marry Kadish and come here to be with his family and be abused by them. The other reason for marrying a man more than twice as old as I was, was, because I thought that he will be like a family to me and he would treat me with love, respect and consideration for my feelings. That was what he promised me before we got married. Instead, he treated me without any of the things that he promised.

# THE BIG BLOW UP

I remember that every Sunday when the family left, besides having a fight with my husband, I was always upset and very aggravated with myself. I always thought to myself, "Why was I keeping quiet in my own home when they were embarrassing me? Why did I let them treat me with such disrespect?" Finally, it hit me and the most important thing that happened to me at that time was when I decided that their nasty behavior towards me would not work with me, anymore.

One particular Sunday, while they were all still in my house, I did not say anything, but after they left, I decided that enough was enough, no more being nice. All week I was very upset, but I made my plans about what I was going to do and how I was going to act when they will come next Sunday. I knew very well that it was a very big and serious matter and of course, I did not, and I could not know how it would turn out, but I knew for sure that it would be a breaking point, one way or another, only it would not be this way anymore. Finally, Sunday arrived and they all came. I still remember it was cold outside and everyone wore a coat. I took their coats and hung them up.

The table was set and everyone sat down to eat. I never sat down with them because I had to take care of my guests, my so-called company. They started a conversation with my husband and even though I was in the kitchen, I could hear every word that they were saying to him. It really sounded like a broken record. They asked him how much money he let me spend and what I did all week. I do not even remember what he said. The only thing that I knew was that this was the end of our friendship, which there was never any to begin with. I did my best to finish supper, but most of the time I tried to stay in the kitchen so I would not have to look at their faces.

I remember that I was very upset because I knew what I was up against, and I was all alone. In spite of it, I made up my mind that whatever the outcome will be, if I will win or if I will lose, I knew that it will not be the same, because definitely, I will not take this kind of treatment from any of them anymore, not even if my life and my future depended on it.

When they finished supper, and they came into the living room, everyone sat down, and they started to make themselves comfortable. I remember that I came out of the kitchen and I sat down on one of the steps in the living room, and then I started to talk very plainly and in a very low voice. I told them that this was their very last time to come into our home and think that they were coming to their cousin's house only and I was the slave here. This was their very last time that they were going to mix into my life and teach my husband how to treat me. This was their very last time to call me greenhorn and give me such disrespect. I told them that I was sure that they would be very disappointed not having me as a victim to control anymore and treat me like I was a nobody.

Then I said to them, "Well, now I have news for all of you, that the reason that you succeeded in doing all of these nasty things to me was only because I let you do it. Now your privileges are taken away from you, by me, and now your meddling in my life is finished, and you will never have a chance again to insult me, call me names, and tell my husband how to treat me, because I think, as a fact, I know that he should feel very privileged and very lucky to have a wife like me, and another thing, he should thank Hitler for it, because Hitler was the matchmaker." I also told them that I had a lot of patience with them and I swallowed my pride too many times and I gave them too many chances of behaving in a more human and civilized way towards me, but no matter what, it did not work and they kept on thinking that they will get away with it, because in their mind I was too stupid to know any better.

Then I took their coats and threw them in their faces and little by little they started to leave. My husband started to holler at me that I was throwing his family out and kept on hollering, and he kept on saying that his uncle gave him the house. His uncle was the last one to leave and he heard what my husband said. He turned towards me and said to me, "Sonia, I gave the house to both of you and you are right for throwing all of us out. We all were wrong by treating you like an outsider." Actually, the uncle and aunt never said a bad word to me or about me, on the contrary, they were always nice to me.

The minute we came to America, I always considered them as being my friends. I have to mention, that I remember, that the uncle did not say too much, but I always felt that he saw and understood a lot about what was going on and deep in his heart he always knew that I was right. In spite of it, he could not mix in and express his opinion until it came to the blow-up from me, because it would mean that he was going against his family.

My husband still tried to overtake me by playing boss, but I put him in his place right away. I told him that he had a choice to go with his cousins or live here and behave like a person, not like a dictator. I also told him that if I will ever hear a disrespectful word from him again, I would pack my things and leave him with his family. He knew me well enough, to know that whatever I was saying I meant every word of it and that I would do it, too. My husband was really very surprised by my actions. I remember that he asked me what happened to me. He said, "You never said a loud word before", then I said to him, that, "I have a good teacher, you, and you taught me to open my mouth."

In a while, without the advisors and manipulators from his family, he started to get used to the fact that I was not such a dummy or such a goody goody after all. He saw that I would not accept bossing around or disrespect from his family or from him anymore. As long as it was out in the open, he knew to behave. He never bossed me around before we came here. When we lived in Austria, he was always nice to me, but here in America he wanted to show his family that he was the boss over me. Besides everything else, my speaking up for myself came as a big surprise to him, also. He never thought that I would ever have the nerve of going against all of them all by myself.

After a few weeks, the family started to call me and they plain pleaded with me that I should let them come back. They told me that they did not realize what they were doing and they kept on apologizing to me. They also promised me that they would never make this mistake by interfering in my life again. I was very sure that they always knew exactly what they were doing, but they probably thought that a stupid young girl like me does not know any better, and they could say to me whatever they wanted to. They thought whatever they would say would be okay with me because I was too stupid to get insulted. I knew all along that in time they would find out who the stupid one was, them or me.

After they kept on apologizing to me so many times, finally, I forgave them and this time we became almost like friends, but I could never forget all the humiliation and aggravation that they put me through. Still and all, we got to know and understand each other better and they started to talk and treat me with the greatest respect. Most of Kadish's family were pretty smart people and we really were able to communicate very well with each other. From time to time, they even mentioned that they still felt guilty and ashamed about the way they behaved towards me.

After they got to know me better, they realized that I was very careful with spending money, not that it should be any of their concern what I was doing with our money. I always liked nice things because I was brought up with them in my parents' home. Now, since I could afford to have them, and I thought that a nice home would make all of us happy, I thought, "Why not have a nice home and nice things?"

I thought, after what I went through, I deserved to be happy with something. To their surprise, they found out that it really was not me to be careless with money, instead, it was their cousin, Kadish, who could be and was always careless with money. They always said to me that "I was making gold from nothing and my husband, their cousin, was making nothing from gold." I thought that it was a nice compliment that they gave me, and especially coming from them, I was flattered.

After a while and with a lot of effort on their part, I started to believe without a doubt that they really liked me. They always said to me, "Kadish is our cousin, but we love you more than him."

From the time of the big blow-up that we had, they never mixed into my life again. I remember when I was a child and my father taught me a lot of things, one of them was that he said to me, you always have to try to make a friend out of an enemy. I really tried very hard with them, no matter how they were towards me. In the end they transformed themselves from being my enemy to become my friend. I think that I never gave up on them completely, because I felt that I really wanted to have someone to be my family or as close to being like family as possible.

From then on, every time my husband had something to complain about me and wanted to tell the cousins, they told him that they did not want to hear about it. The reason I always knew about my husband's complaints to them was because they told me. When they did not want to listen to him, he got angry with them. I really was very happy the way it turned out. It felt to me that I have a family in my life again that was on my side now. In a way it made me realize that I was not alone anymore and I started to feel more content with my life.

My husband had to get used to it that he was not the king in the house and I was not his maid or slave. These days were gone forever. He was in America now, where the women were more independent and nobody was the boss in the family. A marriage should be an equal partnership. Both had the same rights to express their likes and dislikes, and both of them had the same right to decide what was best for their family. In a way, I was fighting city hall, but in the end I came out a winner.

Everything got straightened out, I got into my daily routine and I tried my best to have peace and quiet. I knew that if I would let it go any longer with his family interfering, I would never be able to control it. There were almost twenty people in my husband's family just living in Philadelphia, not too far from us, besides all of the distant members of Kadish's family, and I was the only one. Even my husband was on their side. They were the leaders and he was their loyal follower.

I knew in my heart that it was my husband's fault for not protecting me from them, and not only did he not protect me, instead he sort of gave them courage and he joined them in being against me. I thought that by him being on their side, it gave them more power and they took the right of treating me so disrespectfully. It also seemed to me that I had to fight a war all over again, only for my existence and for my peace of mind. I tried my best just to have peace and quiet and to be left alone. I really did not think that I asked for too much.

My husband was very disappointed that he would not be able to boss me around anymore, and in a way his personality and his behavior changed completely. He used to be very loud and happy, especially when I had company. He showed off that I, the slave, was doing what the boss wanted me to do. He always knew that in the presence of people, I would never contradict him. On the contrary, I played a very good part pretending that I did not even know that he was so mean and disrespectful to me. After he understood that this would not work with me anymore, he became very quiet and withdrawn. He acted like he lost his position and authority over me. I was never his possession and I knew that I would never let him or anyone else treat me like a slave or a nobody ever again.

I came to realize that in order to survive in this world I had to have enough courage, willpower, and determination. I had to put a lot of effort in and have patience until the right time would come. I thought that if I really would try hard enough, eventually I would overcome every obstacle that was standing in my way and in the end I would succeed, and I would come out of it a winner, after all, no matter what it would take. Apparently, by my way of acting I accomplished what I intended to.

After everything settled down I thought that now was the time again to write to my son's nurse. I sent her some pictures of my son, who she called, Putzale. I also sent her pictures of me and Kadish and his uncle and aunt. In the letter, I asked her if she wanted me to send her something special from America, and if she got married. I also wanted to know how the financial situation in Austria was. In a few weeks, after she got my letter, she wrote to me and thanked me for the pictures and mentioned that she really did not need anything and was just happy to hear from us. She also told me that she did not get married yet. We kept in touch with each other for many, many years.

When my son, David, was three years old, I became pregnant with my daughter, Gloria. I asked everyone who the best gynecologist in Philadelphia was. Everyone said Dr. Israel, but they also told me that he was not too polite to his patients and he talked very little to them.

In spite of what people said about his personality, I knew that this really was not important to me, because I was looking for the best doctor and right away I made an appointment to see him. The first few times he talked to me, only to the point about my medical visit. He knew that I came from Europe and that I was a Holocaust survivor. In a while he started to get friendlier towards me and every time I came for an examination we talked about everything and anything.

He told me that every year he went to Europe and he also stopped in Salzburg, Austria to see the International Festival. I told him that I lived in Salzburg for four years and every year I also saw the festival. That was how we started our first conversation together. We talked about the operas and operettas, and all the other festivals that took place in Austria. He really started to like me and he probably felt sorry for me because in some conversations that we had, I mentioned to him that I had lived through the Nazis and World War II.

He kept on telling me to take care of myself during the time of my pregnancy. It felt to me like he knew something that I did not know. He never mentioned anything to me that something was not going right with my pregnancy. I think he knew that I would have complications. I never asked him if there was anything wrong with my pregnancy, instead, I kept on saying to him that I was okay and I told the doctor, " Just please see to it that the baby should be okay."

Before my daughter, Gloria, was born, I went into labor very unexpectedly, because I was only in the seventh month of pregnancy. I still remember that I was rushed to the hospital by police car. At this time in December, the roads were very slippery, like a patch of ice, and no taxi wanted to come to take me to the hospital. When I arrived in the hospital, the doctor immediately gave me a spinal. I could see everything that was going on. When the baby was born the doctor himself wheeled me over to the telephone and he called my husband and I told him that we had a daughter. I do not know why, but Dr. Israel really treated me very special.

My daughter, Gloria, was born on December 31, 1950. I could always depend on my friend, Boyt, for her help and support. Gloria was born prematurely and was a seven-month baby. She was in an incubator for twelve weeks and after I brought her home she weighed five and a half pounds. It was touch and go with her.

When I got pregnant with my second daughter, Ellen, I remember that I was very sick all the time during the pregnancy. Dr. Israel came to my house for a visit quite a few times to take care of me. Every morning my husband left the house to go to work, and I was home with my two children to take care of. I was pregnant and sick and I could not even get out of the bed. My friend, Boyt, was there for me again. She stayed with me and she took care of the children and me. I remember that she even cooked dinner for us. In spite of having her own family, she did not go home because she was afraid to leave me all alone, and she stayed with my children and me until my husband came home. This went on for weeks while I was pregnant.

Every week, my husband had to go away on business for three days. Boyt used to come in every morning to check up on me. One morning when she came in, and when I told her that I was hemorrhaging, which happened at the time of my pregnancy, she knew that something was very wrong. She saw that I looked very pale. Without even asking me, right away she called a taxi and took me to the hospital. The doctor probably came as soon as they notified him about my condition, but I did not see the doctor or anybody else because I lost consciousness.

When I woke up and I opened my eyes, I saw that Boyt was sitting near me. I was still drowsy, but I heard her saying something to me. In the beginning I could not understand what she was talking about, then I heard her mentioning my name again and I started to concentrate. She said, "Sonia, they thought that you wouldn't wake up from the operating table. You kept on hemorrhaging for two and a half hours. They kept on giving you blood transfusions. They gave you nine transfusions and it did not help." Boyt said that all the time she sat in the waiting room, until the doctor came out of the operating room and told her everything that happened.

He also said that the only last thing that he could do for me, in order to save my life, was to take the baby by Cesarean and perform a hysterectomy on me. At this time, I did not even know what a hysterectomy meant, so I asked Boyt and she told me what it meant. She also told me that I would not be able to have any more children. Boyt remembered that once I mentioned to her that I wanted to have four children, like my mother had. She felt badly for me that I would not be able to have my wish come true. I was still drowsy, but I remember saying to her that I was glad, and I would not be able to go through all of this, all over again. Then she said that the doctor told her to tell me this as soon as I will come out of the anesthesia and when I was still drowsy, so it should not be such a shock to me.

When I was taken to the hospital, for this emergency, my husband was not around to give consent and I could not give consent because I was unconscious. The doctor saw that I was not going to survive if he would not perform a hysterectomy, so without anybody's consent, even when he knew that he was really jeopardizing his career, he performed a hysterectomy on me. At the time when Boyt was still sitting and talking to me and I was already fully awake, I remember that the doctor came in and the first question that I asked him was, "Doctor, what was wrong with my insides?" He replied that, "Nothing was wrong with your insides."

I remember like it was now, that he sat down on the bed and started to talk to me and he told me that I was in great danger. He told me that if he would not have performed the hysterectomy I would have bled to death, and I would not wake up from the operating table. He also told me that he did not have the right to do this without our consent and he could lose his license because of it. I thanked him for saving my life in spite of his knowing that he was jeopardizing his career by doing it. I also told him that I would never forget what he did for my children and for me.

Then I asked the doctor to give me the papers and I signed them right away. After the doctor left, I gave Boyt the address and the telephone number where my husband could be reached. She called him, and he left everything and came back. When my husband came to the hospital, I filled him in on what happened and then he, too, signed the papers. He was very happy that I came out of it alive, thanks to the doctor. Dr. Israel was one of the best gynecologists in Philadelphia. He really liked me and he jeopardized his career in order to save my life. I thought then and I still think until today that it was a very noble and unselfish thing for him to do.

I also thought that if Boyt had not come in that morning to check up on me and if she had not taken me to the hospital right away, I would have hemorrhaged to death in my home with the baby inside me. Also, thanks to Boyt and to Dr. Israel, everything turned out for the best. Very shortly after, my husband notified his cousins and they came to the hospital to visit me. When they found out that we signed the consent, they got very angry at both of us and all of them started to holler at us about why we signed the consent form. They told me and my husband that we could get a lot of money from this case because he was not allowed to perform the operation without mine and my husband's signature. We both said that we did not need this kind of money. The cousins' got angry and they said that we were both greenhorns.

When they called us greenhorns for showing our thanks, and showing our appreciation to the doctor for saving my life, I got very upset and angry with them, because the doctor really did not have to do it. Instead, he could have just let me bleed to death. When they stopped hollering for a minute I started to talk, I asked my husband's smart cousins, "Tell me. How much would I be worth if I would die on the operating table? And how much would your cousin's life be worth, to raise three children all by himself?" Right then they got quiet and they did not say another word anymore.

All the time, I really could not believe how the people here in America thought and acted to each other when it came to money. To them, money was the most important thing in their life. To them, money was even more important than life itself, not talking about principles, values, appreciation, gratitude, and most of all, conscience. At that time I thought about the war and the Nazis and how we lost everything, including the lives of our families, friends and neighbors. I also thought that I would give up everything in the world for their lives if only I would have had a chance to prevent and spare them from their death. The way I felt was that everyone could make money when they were alive, but nobody could get their life back when they were dead.

My husband and I felt very thankful and I thought to myself, if we would listen to my husband's family, it would haunt me every minute of the day and night, and I would have it on my conscience for the rest of my life. I do not remember how long I was in the hospital. My doctor came in a few times a day to examine me. I could see in his face how happy he was that I made it. He also reminded me that after the examination when he told me to take care of myself, I always said to him, "I will be okay, just doctor, please see to it that the baby should be okay." Then he said, "I am very glad that you are really okay."

In a while, I was sent home from the hospital and my daughter, Ellen, was still in the incubator for a few weeks. I remember when I came home and I saw my two children, David and Gloria, I felt very happy and very thankful that I was alive. When my second daughter, Ellen, was born January 16, 1954, I was a little more mature and I had more confidence in myself. I tried to do a good job of raising my children, but no matter how much confidence I had in myself, I still felt better having my friend, Boyt, around me, even though I did not need her help as much anymore. It still felt good to know that I had someone to depend on, who really cared about me in case I needed help.

# CHAPTER XXX
## MY LIFE ON THE FARM AND ALL OF THE HAPPENINGS

Just about the same time when my daughter Ellen was born, in the beginning of January 1954, my husband decided that he wanted to build a chicken farm and a house in Mays Landing, New Jersey. When the house was finished being built we moved from Philadelphia to Mays Landing on Route 50, between Mays Landing and Egg Harbor City. We had ten acres of land and a lot of space to move around. Besides that, there was a lot of fresh and clean air and not too much traffic, not like in the city. We both felt that it would be better to raise our children there.

I remember that we were one of the first families to move on Route 50. After us, twenty-six Jewish families settled down there. All of us were from Europe, and all of us were survivors who had lived through the Nazis. Every family built a house with a chicken coop and we became chicken farmers. We all had new homes on the farms, and everyone at this time made a nice living by farming. In no time we got friendly with each other and we became like one big happy family. In a way it was very good for us because we understood each other.

Everyone was almost the same age and almost every family had small children. Because we wanted to see one another more often, we decided to get together every week in a different house. We had some refreshments, played cards and we had discussions with each other. Mostly we talked about our past. Each of us had a story to tell about our lives, and the awful happenings to us by the Nazi murderers.

A lot of times we went shopping together. Almost everyday we took a walk, and we would stop at a neighbor's house on the way, just to say hello. It really was very nice. The children grew up together and they really got along very good. At least once a week, I got some neighbors together and we went to see a movie, especially when there was playing a wartime movie. I always took my children to see these movies, also, because I wanted them to know what their parents went through at the time of the Nazi regime.

No matter how painful it was for me, I still went to see every movie that came out about Hitler. I felt that I should not ever try to forget what happened to my family. It really was very emotional for me, but I thought in my mind by seeing and reliving it, over and over again, it kept the memories of my family alive. I thought that my neighbors felt the same way, too, because we were all survivors and we all had the same things in common, the awful memories of the past which will stay with us forever.

Since we were all Jews and we had our own community on Route 50, we all decided to build our own synagogue. I donated the aporoiches (Torah Curtain). It was a special curtain for the Holy Ark where the Torahs were kept. I had the aporoiches (Torah Curtain) especially made in New York. The aporoiches was inscribed in golden Hebrew letters, with my parents' names, and it was donated by me to the synagogue in memory of my dead parents. It felt to me that I kept my parents names alive by seeing the aporoiches every time I came to the synagogue. I learned, in my parents' home, about the Jewish laws, traditions and customs and I also wished that my children should learn the same in my home in order to preserve our Jewish spirit and religion and be proud of it.

I still remember that on one of our meetings while we discussed different things I mentioned that the children have to learn about the Jewish religion. It took a while for the members to decide, and finally it happened. One day all of our Jewish families decided to hire a Melammed (rabbi) in order to teach our children Judaism, and we did. The Melammed, (rabbi) came to the synagogue twice a week. Right after school the children gathered in the synagogue to learn to davinnen (to pray), and the Melammed (rabbi) also prepared the boys for their Bar Mitzvah. In the old days in Europe the girls did not have Bat Mitzvahs, but here in America the girls have this ceremony.

The synagogue was also there for the Jewish families to be used for getting together and playing cards and many times we got together just to socialize. On Friday night and Saturday morning, most of the Jewish families came to synagogue to pray.

We had many parties and get togethers in the synagogue. It was not a very big synagogue, but it was enough for our community on

Route 50 and for all the parties that the members of the synagogue had and everyone helped with whatever they could. Every member of our synagogue was involved with each other and everyone cared about each other, like a family. That was how it was on our Route 50, when we moved from Philadelphia. Everyone was a friend to each other.

Besides my new friends, who I lived together with, on the same Route 50, Mays Landing, I always stayed in contact with my friends from before, the people who I knew in Salzburg, Austria. We all came together to America and we kept in touch with each other for years and years. I always invited them for a visit and we were very happy to have them in our home and they were happy to come.

I had a big house, a lot of ground and whoever came to us felt comfortable. I was always happy to see them and they were happy to see us. We always reminisced about the old times in Salzburg and no matter what we talked about, out of nowhere, we started to talk about the war, the Nazis, our dead families and all of our losses that we had in our past life. I did not think that anyone of our survivors could or would forget what the Nazis did to us. The Nazis left me without anything or anybody, nothing to show from my past life, not even a family picture, only sad memories.

My husband's cousins came to Mays Landing every so often, to see me. I was very nice and polite to them, but in a way I was more formal than friendly with them. I never had too close of a relationship with any of them. Maybe I never forgot how they treated me from the beginning or maybe, because I never completely trusted them or believed them that they really cared about me.

When they came, I knew that this time they were not coming to see their cousin. I knew that they were really coming to see the children and me, because they saw their cousin, my husband, in Philadelphia. He used to stop to see them twice a week when he was in Philadelphia to take care of his business.

Most of my neighbors on Route 50 came to visit me. They just took a walk to see how I was doing, and to gossip for a while. Sometimes I did some things for them because I drove, so I took them shopping and sometimes we went to the movies together or we took a ride to Atlantic City. I think the way it looked was that I lived a pretty normal and happy life. Deep in my heart though, there was only loneliness, sadness and painful, bitter memories, especially on holidays when there was no one left of my family to celebrate with.

One day we got a letter from the government that we should appear in court and by the end of 1954 they called us to be sworn in for citizenship and we became citizens of America. To tell you the truth, I was really worried that I would not be able to answer all of the questions, in spite of studying a lot. The judge did not ask my husband any questions, luckily for him because my husband said that he never wanted to learn anything and did not study. The judge only asked him if he was happy to come to America and he said, "Yes." I still remember what the judge said to us. He said, "It is an honor and a privilege to have you for citizens of America." Apparently, it was customary for him to say it, in order to make us feel good. After being sworn in, I felt very relieved that finally my worries about not knowing the right answers to the questions were over.

I still remember that I felt very important at that time and I was proud to become an American citizen. My son had to wait until he was eighteen years old to become a citizen because he was born in Salzburg, Austria, and he was an Austrian citizen.

In the year of 1954, we had a lot of changes. Most of them were very important happenings in our life. In the beginning of January, the year of 1954, my daughter, Ellen, was born. In 1954 we built the chicken farm with a house on Route 50 in Mays Landing. In the same year, we moved from Philadelphia to Mays Landing. At the end of 1954 we became American citizens. The most important thing for me was that we were all healthy and the children were happy living on the farm.

All in all, no matter how, everything fell into place and I went on with my daily routine, I still thought very often of my friend, Boyt. I remembered all of the many things that she taught me. I remembered how many times she said to me, "Sonia, you have to learn to stay on your own two feet. Sonia, you have to learn not to depend on anybody." She kept on repeating the same thing to me over and over again.

I remember that when something came up and I said to Boyt that I cannot and I would never be able to do it, she would say to me, "If somebody else can do it, you can do it too, and better." When I came to live in Mays Landing and when I really thought of asking someone to do me a favor, I began to think about what Boyt taught me and then I tried to do it myself.

From then on I really started to adopt a philosophy, which Boyt, my first and best friend in America, kept on telling me. You can believe it or not, but all of my life I have lived by these rules, and most of the time it has worked for me. I decided to try not to ask any favors or anything from anybody. I tried to help myself with raising my children, going shopping, and I learned the lay out of the city. I learned to drive and I had my own car so I moved around very freely.

My attitude was that the less I will bother my friends, the better they will like it. Besides that, all of my life, I liked to be independent because since I could remember, even when I was a very young child, I was always determined to do most of the things by myself. I always had enough confidence in myself that I will do a good job. In spite of my confidence in myself, coming to America and having everyone telling me that I did not do anything right, this shook my confidence and the belief in myself. Thanks to Boyt, I got my confidence back and I started to believe in myself again.

The only person who I asked to do me a favor was Boyt. When I was in trouble I always wanted Boyt beside me, like I felt safer with her around. I did not even have to ask her to do me a favor. As soon as I told her my problems, she offered, right away, to help. When my daughter, Gloria, had to go to the hospital in Atlantic City for an operation on her eardrum, Boyt was by my side. At the time we already lived in Mays Landing, and Boyt was still living in Philadelphia. She left her husband and her daughter home and came to be with me before the operation and stayed with me until after the operation. When she knew for sure that everything was okay with my daughter, Gloria, and when the doctor reassured her that there were no complications, only then, she went back home.

Boyt was a real genuine friend. We understood each other. I always confided in her and I always told her my deepest secrets because I knew that it would stay with her. I know that I did not talk about Boyt too much, but I want to tell you that she played a big part in my life from the minute I came to America. She was the first and the only true friend to me. We kept in touch after I moved to Mays Landing and she visited me all the time and I visited her in Philadelphia.

Suddenly, she got very sick and developed kidney trouble. She suffered quite a long time with it and finally, the doctor could not do anything for her and she died. I was very heartbroken to lose my friend, but I could not do anything about it, just like when my father died when I was only six and a half years old and just like when my grandfather died when I was only nine years old and just like when my mother, my sister and two brothers and the rest of my family were murdered, when I was twelve and a half years old. I could not do anything about it, either.

After Boyt's death I was very depressed all over again. I felt lonely and very miserable. I thought to myself, now I lost my best friend in my life. I could not understand why these things were happening to me, but they did and there was nothing that I could do to prevent them from happening.

# CHAPTER XXXI
## MY FINAL DECISION

In the older days, in Europe, in most of the Jewish families, the husbands were responsible for making a living and providing for the family, and the wives were responsible for the home and children. Even by being now in America, some European men still followed the same way of living. One of these men was my husband. I did not go out to work. I stayed home with my children and my husband took care of making a living.

I remember certain times when my husband's business was not too good and I suggested taking a babysitter for the children and I wanted to look for a job. My husband said definitely, no. He also made a remark that he did not want me to be the breadwinner in the family. He always said to me that whatever he will earn, we would have to live on it.

My husband had a good business head on his shoulders and he always provided for us, financially, but I was never happy with my life. I really felt that in order to be happy was, when you belonged to someone and they belonged to you, and you have somebody to share your life with, like to share your happiness and share your misery with. The way I understood was that this would be your parents with the rest of your family, and a good marriage partner in your life. I was not lucky enough to have either of these things. The Nazis murdered my family and my husband was never around for me. He was not like a husband, instead he was like a border or a guest in the house. The only thing that he shared his life with was with his business, not with the children or me. He always did what he liked and wanted to do without thinking that he was even married, or that he had some obligation and responsibilities towards our children and me. Instead, I never, in the twenty-two years of being married to him, saw him going out of his way in order to do something for us. The fact was that whatever he did was only for himself, without thinking of us.

He left the house early in the morning and came home late at night and when he came home the children were asleep, and he always said that he was too tired to listen to my complaints. On the contrary, he always thought that I had a very good and easy life. Of course, according to him I was sitting home doing nothing and the three children of ours raised themselves and the household took care of itself, also, and the farm with the chickens was no work either, which I had to take care of. The result was that no matter how hard I worked from morning until late at night it did not mean anything to him.

My husband never appreciated anything and he was never happy with what he had, instead he was always miserable, but for very different reasons. His happiness depended on how much money he could make and in his mind he felt that the more money he would make, the more important and noticeable he would become.

He had an inferiority complex and it did not matter what I said to him or how many times I told him that to me, the money was not important. I kept on telling him that he should not work so hard and devote all of his time to only making more money, and instead he should be a husband to me and a father to our children. No matter what I said to him nothing penetrated in his head and he did exactly what he wanted to do. To him, to make more money was the most important thing in his life. It was more important than his family and anything else.

After so many years of trying to talk sense into his head without getting any results, finally, I stopped telling him anything. I realized that no matter what I would say, it would not help and he would not listen to me anyway. The only thing that I would accomplish by telling him what to do would be to get into a big fight and everyone would get upset, including my children. I came to realize that I was fighting a losing battle and I finally came to a conclusion that no matter what I will say or what I will do, it will never work with him. He was a selfish person who thought only of himself and nobody else counted in his life, only he, he and he. After thinking it over, I knew that I had to stop trying to change the unchangeable.

It was like an obsession with him only to live for having more and more money. He was good in business when he thought it through, but when he started to get careless with his investments because of his determination to succeed, it did not work out his way. When his drive took over to the point that most of the time he got into the business without thinking or looking ahead, the result was that he lost most of the money that he made before. There were many times in all of the years, when I really tried to give him some good advice, because I always had an instinct for business, like my mother used to have in her business, but he never listened to me anyway.

He was very determined and eager to do it on his own without any help from anybody, especially from me. He wanted to prove to everyone that he was the best in his business world, and that he was succeeding. In the end he proved the opposite and then he put the blame on me. The outcome of it was that no matter what I did he always had something to complain about, just like Hitler did. Hitler put all the blame on the Jews for his mistakes. The result was that my husband not only ruined my life, but by his actions and his behavior towards me and by his own doing, he ruined his life, also. Because of the way he treated me, I repaid him in many ways and sometimes he really got more from me than he really expected.

The only thing that I was happy with was that I never lost my sense of humor and even though nothing seemed to be funny, at least I had myself and I could laugh and joke at myself and about myself. Most of the time the joke was on me anyway. I always thought of my life as being a big endless joke.

The man who was old enough to be my father, who I got married to, with the intentions of having in him my whole family and a friend in my life, who promised that he would be all of these things to me, turned out to be a complete stranger. He was my husband, by name only. I never had a husband to talk to or to go out with. I never felt that he was my friend, he was like a guest in the house. I kept on making excuses to everyone that he was busy and I pretended in front of my friends that it does not bother me, but in reality I just played a "happy-go-lucky" part. Like they were saying, "we had to laugh outside even when we were crying inside, because when we laughed the whole world would laugh with us, but when we cried, we were crying alone."

I went on vacation, I dressed, I went to parties, I went to funerals, just like everyone else, but I did not feel like everyone else because the difference was that everyone else went with their husband, their families, but I always went by myself, and I was always alone.

I cried for my family that was murdered, and that I would never know where their final resting place was. I made parties and I invited many friends, but the ones who I really wanted the most, I knew would never come. To my regret because of Hitler's cruelty and murder my children never got to know their grandparents or cousins or aunts or uncles and they also never had any of these family members in their life.

I always invited people to my house, and it was lively, and I always liked to go to crowded places with music and loud noises. In a way I was happy with the noise, like I tried to lose myself. This was my way of dealing with my problems, even until today. I always kept on pretending that everything in my life was very normal, and I really tried to be as happy as I wanted to be. With all the pretenses, most of the time it did not work, because the spirit in my life was not there.

Most of the time, I thought it was not worth it to pretend, but I did not have another choice. I had to raise my children and try to live with my terrible situation as well as I could. I did try my best to adjust and to make my happiness with what I had, because every time I faced the reality and I started to see things as they really were, I became more miserable and more depressed. I knew that I must snap out of these thoughts and feelings because my children needed me, so I told myself, " Thank God I have nice children and I should not sin and be happy with what I have." My children never saw their father. I was a father and a mother to my children. He was never around when we needed him. The only thing that he did for us was to make a living. This was when the business was going good.

I realized that from the very beginning my marriage was a big mistake. We were two different people from two different worlds, but it was too late for regrets. The way I felt, I blamed it on the Nazis because they destroyed my life and my faith in everything. I felt bitter and did not even hope for a better life for myself. I was thinking of leaving him so many times, but when I thought it over, I saw that it was hopeless.

I did not have any place to go, I did not have any living soul from my whole family to go to, and I could not see how it would be possible for me to manage with three little children all by myself. I knew that I did not have a way out of this situation. Finally, I gave up hoping for anything better anymore and I sacrificed my life only to exist in this world. According to my thinking, everyone came first in my world, and I always came last. My parents taught me, that in order to become a good person, we have to do, first, for others, before we were thinking of doing anything for ourselves.

The only good thing that came out of my marriage were my children. The only thing that mattered to me was that my children were okay, and that they have a home with a father and a mother in it. Of course, there were many times when they heard us fighting and they got very upset by it. I always tried my best to be quiet and not to answer. I took all the harassment and humiliation from him because I did not want to break up the home, as long as the children were still small. Most of the time I hid my feelings, my thoughts, and my anger just not to get into an argument. Under these circumstances, that I was in, I did not have another choice, but to try the best way I could to talk myself into it that I live a normal life like everyone else, if it was only to put up a big front. I had my daily routine like everyone else.

I worked all day in the house, washing, cooking, cleaning, mending, doing laundry, and baking. In a household with five people in it, I was always busy. Besides this, I had to take care of the chicken farm. I was busy from the minute I got up in the morning until late in the night. I remember when the children came home from school, the minute they walked into the house, they ran to the cookie jar, which was always filled with cookies that I baked every week. The children had their daily routine, also. After they came home from school they had their snack, then they went out to play for a while.

After supper, they did their lessons, and then they watched television. They knew when they had to get ready for bed. After the children went to sleep the house was quiet and I started to relax a little. I remember that my biggest pleasure was when I walked into their rooms to check on them. I stayed for a while and looked at them and when I saw them sleeping so peacefully I smiled to myself and I felt a lot of love in my heart. I really dedicated all my life to them. In a way my children were the most precious things in my life. It seemed to me that I wrapped my life around them. At the time I thought that I was doing the right thing, but as the years passed me by, I started to take count of my life. It took me a long time to realize that I had one life to live and I had wasted it for no good reason at all. Now all the regrets would not bring back my years and my life that I wasted and lost by not living it, only existing in the world.

Even now, a lot of times, out of the blue sky, for no special reason at all, I become very depressed and I am crying for days without knowing why. I did many things in my life against my better judgment, mostly to please others. Sometimes they turned out to be right and sometimes I made the wrong decision and I became very disappointed.

No matter how I tried to lose myself in crowds, loud noises, and busy places and no matter how much I was surrounded by my friends, I always felt that I was alone. After so many years of talking to my husband and warning him that if he would not change I would divorce him, nothing penetrated in his head and he still always felt sure that I could not or would not survive without his financial support.

Once again, I started to reevaluate my life, and once again I saw how it really was. For many years I took all of his abuse and I started to ask myself, "For what? Only just to have a roof over my head?" That was why I lived with a man with whom I never had anything in common with, except twenty-two years of misery. I knew that I was very wrong for wasting my years for nothing, but it was too late for regrets.

After twenty-two miserable years of being married to him, I reached the point that I had enough and finally, I did divorce him. After the divorce went through, the judge ordered him to pay a certain amount of child support and everything that we owned together should be divided equally between us. For the first time in a long time I was happy just to have my freedom. Even after the divorce, from the beginning, he was sure that I would come back to him. He knew that everything that we owned was on his name only. In spite of what the judge ordered for him to do, he still thought that he could do whatever he wanted to do. I told him that I did not want anything from him anyway.

The way I was thinking was that I did not earn the money and I did not work anyplace that I got paid for. Besides that, I was determined to prove to him and to myself that I will make it without his financial support. I have to admit that I was very scared to start to find a way in order to support myself. My husband always held me back from doing anything else besides housework and raising the children, in general, just being a housewife. That was why I never worked, because he said a woman's place was in the house. Most of the European men did not consider this as working. I never learned a profession and to tell you the truth I really did not care. I felt that at least he could do one thing for the family and this was to make a living for us.

After so many weeks since the divorce, I was forced to give up the house because it was too big of an expense and I did not have any income at all. My children and I had to move into a small apartment, leaving most of the furniture in the house. Next, I started to concentrate on getting a job, any job, in order to be able to pay my bills. It was not easy for me without any skills or profession to be able to get a decent job. In the situation that I was in and under the circumstances, I did not have too much of a choice. I had to try to adjust to my new life, accept it, and make the best of it. After all, it was my choice, my decision, and my doing to get a divorce.

The only job that I could find at the time was in a factory where we lived in Mays Landing. This was my very first job, in the plastic factory. I remember that it was a very hard and complicated job for me, but I knew that no matter what, I have to work. I was not too happy working there so I started to look for a better job.

Luckily for me, people who really knew me and they liked my truthfulness and honesty recommended me to their friends. I got a good job as a manager in a hotel. I told them that I did not know anything about managing a hotel or any other place. In spite of it, they hired me anyway. I learned about managing very quickly. Finally, I felt that now I could stand on my own two feet. I realized that all of the years I really did not need a crutch to lean on and I became an independent person.

What a shame that I never even tried to find out if I could do more than just be a housewife. I thought to myself that I could not bring back my wasted years of my past, and instead, I had to concentrate on the present and my future. I started to feel good about myself, and I started to feel like I belong in the world again. I felt free from all of the pressure and by the same token I felt good that I was able to control my life, and make my own decisions.

My ex-husband saw that it did not turn out the way he wanted, so he became very serious about the whole situation and he asked me to come back to him. He even offered to sign everything over in my name, but I thought that all the money in the world was not worth it, and it was not enough to pay for my freedom. So you see, he always thought that he was winning. I guess he won all of the battles, but in the end I won the war and I came out a winner, after all.

If nothing else, I got back my dignity, my pride, my self-respect and my freedom. Most of all I got back my piece of mind. After the divorce he always said to me that he wished that he had listened to me. He knew that it was much too late for him and I always said to him that, " Even though Hitler did not kill me, you saw to it that I should have a slow death." In my case, it was and still is a lifetime of torture, because the way my life turned out to be was nothing but constant misery. I really think even now, that it was not worth it for me to survive the war. I know that my life was, is, and always will be an endless war. I guess that I do not have another choice, but to fight it to the end of my life.

# CHAPTER XXXII
## MY LAST EPISODE

I cannot and I will not ever forget my past of growing up all alone without my family. I also have a lot of regrets for not having a normal childhood and a educational upbringing. This always was and still is one of the many reasons that I have been very unhappy and depressed most of my life. It always seemed to me and I always felt that I wasted my life by not having an opportunity to develop my mind and my talents.

When I start to think about my family, my childhood, my wasted life, I get carried away within my thoughts. Right away, I tell myself that I have to shake off my bad feelings and start thinking of happy things, but in spite of my will, I just cannot forget my past. I know that I had lived through the Nazis, but for what? For what reason? Only to have more misery in my life? I always tried to talk myself into good thoughts, but I just could not succeed and I guess I never will because Hitler saw to it to give me a lifetime of misery in every way he could.

No matter how I tried to forget what I lived through practically all of my life, without one peaceful day, I cannot erase the awful memories of my mind. I guess we do not choose memories, memories just come to our mind suddenly. The way I felt was that my body lived through the war, but not my mind. It always felt to me that I really lived in two worlds, the world of then, when all the unbelievable things really happened, and the world of now, when I kept on pretending that everything in my life was going well and my life was very normal. This was, and still is, just pretenses because I never felt alive after Hitler's war, and nothing ever went right for me since then.

I have been liberated for sixty years. As I got older and my children were married and they were no longer living with me, I was left all alone without any of my family. Sometimes I think and wish that the Nazis who caused all this awful tragedy and the allies who were not interested to get involved to stop this tragedy before it even started, should feel all the pain and sorrow the way I felt all of my life and still do until this day.

I always felt that not even Jewish American people here have the same feelings or understood how we survivors felt and still feel a lot of pain in our hearts. In a way nobody really wanted to believe that all the things that really happened were true. Almost the whole Jewish nation was erased from the world, almost like they never existed.

It was very hard for the survivors, especially when we were raising children and there was nobody left of our family to share with us our happiness or our sorrow. There was nobody to depend on in case we needed help. I personally did not even have one member of my family left alive, just to say a good and an honest word to me. I am all alone in the world and I will always have pain, sadness, and loneliness in my heart. That is why I always knew that no matter what life would offer me, good or bad, I would laugh alone and I would cry alone.

I knew that I was liberated from death, but I personally never was free and I always had fear in me. I was and still am a constant worrier because most of my life I had to take care of everything by myself. I started to be independent when I was not even twelve years old at the time of the Nazi regime when my whole family was murdered. I did not have another choice because I did not have anyone left to depend on, only myself.

The pain of my loss stays in my memory and in my heart forever. The only thing that I could do in my life was to try to make the best of it, and keep on pretending that everything is okay. The world has an expression, that "when life gives you lemons, you have to make lemonade". Believe it or not, life gave me more than my share of lemons and I made more than enough lemonade. Most of the time, I got more than I could handle. It seems to be funny, but this was and still is my personality. I always did put a little humor in my life. I cried a little, I laughed a little, I sang a little, I thought a little, and in this way I amused myself a little. Otherwise, I know for sure that I would never be able to survive and live until this day.

Looking back as far as I could, I do remember that my best years of my life were before the war started. With the beginning of the war, my life, my plans, my happiness and everything else was over for me. After the war, I tried very hard to make some kind of a life for myself, but everything turned out the other way around. My whole life was and still is a very big disappointment to me. I can sincerely say that since after the war, in my adult life, I did not have even one day of being happy. I felt that I was not living, and it felt to me that all of the years I just existed in the world, but never lived in it.

I could go on and on and on, but I would go back to the same conclusion, that no matter how good I was playing my part, "happy go lucky", the reality of it was the opposite and this was because my childhood was taken away from me, my family was taken away from me, my years were taken away from me and my life was taken away from me. I would really try to think of happy things and I would start to feel happy, but my happiness changed instantly to sadness and I would start to cry. After I lost my whole family, I always felt that I lost my life also, because my family was my life. I survived the war, but my life was destroyed. Everything that happened to me was because of the Nazis. The awful tragedy of the Holocaust happened only because we were born Jewish, and because the Jewish people believed in God, and the Jews had a different faith and religion. According to the Nazis, that was why they did not deserve to live, even though we never did any harm to anyone in our lives.

It is really beyond the human mind and imagination and it is really very difficult to understand or accept, how one human being could commit a crime like this, just because the Nazis did not like the Jewish way of living. I think that everyone including the Jews had the same right to live the way they felt as long as they were not doing any harm to anybody else.

According to Hitler he blamed the Jews for everything that happened to him. He was evil, and a coward and he could not admit to himself or to others that whatever happened to him was his own fault.

I always wondered that out of my whole family, why was I the only one to survive? Why me? Maybe God had a reason and maybe his reason was to leave at least one member of my family, in order to build a new generation, and in that way the Jews would keep on multiplying and they would not be erased from the world. In spite of the Nazis brutality they still did not succeed in erasing all of the Jews, as Hitler planned to do, to make Europe and the world Judenrein (free from Jews).

Even with the help of the cold-blooded murderers who killed six million Jews, Hitler still failed to accomplish what he planned to do. It backfired on him. We were and will be a Jewish nation with God's help, and we will exist in this world forever. Even though Hitler destroyed our families and he destroyed my health and left me with my inner fears, which I cannot shake off, but I am living. I have problems with my health and I was and still am suffering with my back pain because of what the SS man did to me when he threw me on the railway track and broke my spine, and I was diagnosed with a ruptured disc in my spine. It also split my lip and I have a scar remaining on my lip until today. Besides these injuries, since this time, I constantly have headaches.

Right after the liberation, I discovered that I had arthritis. Then I was diagnosed with an abnormal heartbeat and since that time I have to have a cardiogram every six months. My whole body is in pains and aches. I have to live with these pains all these years, every minute of the day because of the Nazis and all the brutality and suffering that they put me through. In spite of everything, and no matter what happened to me, I still outlived Hitler and his Nazis. Hitler did not win. All of his life he was a failure, and thank God he failed with his plans of making the world Judenrein (free from Jews).

I have to mention that much of the history during World War II, when the Nazis came to power, was based on the Jewish suffering by being in the ghettos, concentration camps, death camps and all of this was under the Nazi regime. According to everyone else's knowledge, and mine, all of the things that happened with no good reason at all were beyond human imagination. They were horrible and unbelievable, inhuman doings. I know that because I, myself, lived through this suffering and I experienced all the pain, terror, and brutality that the Nazis inflicted on me.

I thought in time that I would be able to forget the awful past and I would live for the present, but it did not happen so. I cannot forget, not even for one moment, everything that happened, it is still staying in front of my eyes, and I see it like it is just happening, instead of that it really happened more than half of a century ago. It feels like it was engraved in my mind and in my memory and there is nothing I can do about it. I guess that it will stay with me and keep on hurting me until the end of my life.

I know now that I will never forget the war and the awful tragedy of the Jewish suffering and their death before their time, especially the eighty-six members of my family. Looking back to my past and remembering how I felt when my father died in 1936, before Hitler came to us, I think now that he was the lucky one to die a natural death. He died in peace and dignity, and he did not have to go through all of the humiliation, pain and horror that my mother and the rest of my family went through. Then, in the end the Nazis murdered them anyway. I think, not only the Nazis have to be blamed for everything that happened, but the German people are guilty for listening to Hitler and helping him commit such unbelievable, cruel and inhuman acts towards us.

He did not like our religion, our culture, our way of dressing, or our language because we were different. I think that the main reason why Hitler did not like the Jews was because the Jews were always very independent people, and most of their ways of living and doing things was to do what they believed in and what they felt they had to do in order to be good people in the eyes of God. They had a right to do, and live the way that seemed right to them and not to worry if the others would like their ways of living or not.

Hitler lived his life by hating everyone and everything. He hated his teachers and blamed them for him not doing well in school. He hated his father and everyone else who he thought were much more important and more successful than he would ever be. He knew that he was a big nobody and a failure all of his life. He always put up a big front and he always tried to belittle everyone else in order to make himself feel important. That was why Hitler blamed everyone for his problems and mistakes. Most of all he blamed the Jews because he knew that the Jews always took care of their problems themselves. They lived their life in the way that seemed right to them. They never did any harm to anyone and they always minded their own business.

Hitler wrote the book Mein Kampf (My Struggle) while he was in prison and in his book he stated that he would make Europe Judenrein (free from Jews). He told the world about his plans, but nobody paid much attention to him. When the war with Hitler broke out, I was very young and I blamed everything on Hitler's Nazis. In the later years after the war, when I got older, I started to watch the documentaries about World War II and I became more knowledgeable about the war situation.

I came to realize that not only the Nazis had to be blamed for it, but according to my thinking, the whole world took a big part by doing nothing to prevent this tragedy from happening. The fact was that the world knew what was happening to the Jews and they let it happen.

I think that it was a disgrace that people did not care about other peoples' lives and they let one crazy, insane man kill six million Jews, not to mention all the other people who were slaughtered together with the Jews. While it happened, nobody paid attention to it. When Hitler started to carry out his plans of murdering the Jews, the daily newspaper called the Free World continued to print on the front page the stories of the Nazi brutality towards the Jews.

They kept everyone informed on every detail of the Holocaust. From the moment it started in Germany in 1933 until the Second World War broke out in 1939, when the Nazis invaded Poland, they kept on informing the world until the end of the war in 1945. The European underground and the espionage groups told the people of the Nazi atrocities, and they knew of Hitler's orders to exterminate all of the Jews, and make Europe Judenrein (free from Jews), but nobody paid the slightest attention to it.

Not even one nation opened its doors to Jews. I think and I feel very strongly about this, that if the nations leaders would have been against Hitler's brutality this never would have happened, and in no way would Hitler be able to eliminate six million Jews by murdering men, women and children in cold blood. I would like to ask the whole world and so called good people where were they, when they knew what was happening to the Jews, when the Jews were chased out of their homes and businesses, when they were discriminated against, humiliated, when they were shamed and degraded. Where was the whole world with the good people when they knew that the Jews were taken to the death pits, to be slaughtered like animals, including my own family. Where was the whole world with the good people when they knew about the concentration camps, crematoriums, ghettos, oblavas, pogroms and everything that was happening to the Jews.

Yes, I will tell you where the whole world with so-called good people were, and what they were doing to help in order to prevent the death of six million Jews. They did exactly nothing. Yes, they all knew what was happening, and yes, they were in a position to help and stop this unbelievable horror, but they just did not care enough, not even to lift a finger to help. Instead, they pretended not to know what was going on. It was much easier for all of them to be a silent bystander. Yes, the whole world knew about the inhuman crimes and everyone closed their eyes, ears and minds to it and suddenly everyone became blind, deaf and mute and let practically all of our Jewish population be erased off the face of the earth.

This so-called war, which was between Hitler and the Jews, in my opinion, this was not a war. It was Hitler's hatred and his private battle against them. The Jews could not fight or defend themselves with their bare hands because they did not have the slightest chance of surviving the armed Nazis. The Jews knew that it was hopeless and they marched to their death without having another choice or alternative. All of the people can call this a war, but I would call it terrorism because one terrorist can kill a lot of unarmed, innocent people.

This murdering of the Jews was going on in Poland from 1939 to 1945, not to mention that it started with the persecution of the Jews in Germany in 1933 and the world kept on pretending not to know about it. I think that they deserve credit and a gold medal or even a platinum medal for being such good pretenders. All of this was really very unbelievable, and I also think that it was really too long of a time, almost twelve years, to keep on pretending.

According to my thinking, it was a disgrace that most of the people did not care about others. Instead of helping us when we needed someone's help desperately, and especially when all of our Jewish lives depended on that help, most of them just cared about themselves. I think people should stand by each other and help each other in need, because nobody knows whose tomorrow will be. "Tomorrow the shoe can be on the other foot." The world also has an expression that "one hand washes the other", because nobody has a crystal ball to know what the future will hold for them.

Hitler could not, and would not be able to do what he did, if he would have had obstacles standing in his way, meaning, that if the world would have taken an interest and be against Hitler's murdering the Jews, he would never be able to succeed.

There is a saying that one person can make a difference and I think that it is true. In fact, Hitler was the one person who made a difference by eliminating six million Jews, a religious and cultural group that existed for almost 6,000 years, a group that lived in peace and harmony between themselves and their neighbors. Hitler was the one person who decided to get rid of them. Oh yes, he made a big difference from six million alive Jews, to six million dead Jews.

What a shameful thing it was that out of the whole world of leaders, not even one person was interested or considerate enough to stand up against Hitler and say no to him. "No, you are not going to murder innocent people, no, this was not right, no, we will not let you do it." If one person in the whole world would have said no to Hitler, I really think this would have made a difference and six million Jews would be spared from death, including my family.

This was the greatest tragedy of the Holocaust. Hitler's war towards the Jews began in 1933, six years before World War II started. There was plenty of time and opportunity to save the European Jews from the Nazis, but all of the countries, and their leaders, who were in a position to help, stood by and did absolutely nothing. That was the real shameless truth because Hitler could not, and did not, murder six million Jews all by himself.

In a way, the world helped him carry out his plans by not getting involved to stop him. Instead, he did not have any interference from anybody. I think that it was a real horror story to understand that everyone let this evil and insane man, carry out such evil acts against the Jews. One insane man destroyed all of our lives in many different ways.

If we would not have known Hitler, I would have a life and I would have my family in my life, instead of being left all alone in the world. So much had happened to me in my life, when I was not even ten years old, and the war broke out. It was Hitler's personal revenge on Jews because of his jealousy, envy, hatred and that was why he did not like us. He thought of us as being a threat to him.

We, Jews, did not bother anyone, we lived our lives our way, and we had a right to, because the world belonged to everyone. We believed in God and in the Ten Commandments. We always helped someone in need, because that was how we were taught all of our lives. I kept on wondering and I am still asking the same question over and over again. "Why wasn't anyone willing enough to help us? Why didn't the world of leaders, and the people think that the Jews have the same right and they also deserve to live in the world like everyone else? Why?"

Yes, I did live through the war and sometimes I think that maybe it was mazel (luck) and maybe it was my shikzal (destiny), or maybe somebody died in my place in order for me to survive. I think that definitely it was my personal belief in God, because to live through so much danger that I went though and being spared from death so many times, over and over again, meant to me that there was a higher power in this world. Sometimes I cannot help thinking that maybe I was not worthy enough to die with my family, because when they died, part of me died with them.

To live with these memories is a living death. No words can describe the pain that I always feel by the loss of so many lives for no good reason at all. I was the remnant left of the human horror.

After the Holocaust, everyone with a little conscience and a little human feeling had pity on us and they showed some compassion. I felt that instead of having pity on us now, it would have been much better to have help then, when we needed it desperately before this tragedy happened. If and when we would have gotten help, then, we could have survived and so many innocent lives would have been spared from death.

So you see, the way I feel is that getting help then would have meant an awful lot. It would make a difference between life and death, but pity now does not mean anything to us anymore. Now the world is telling the story of the Holocaust, the mass killing and the genocide of the Jews. According to me, it would have been better if someone had tried to prevent this tragedy from happening and not have a story to tell. The Jews did not want to make history.

They only wanted to live in peace and dignity with their families, friends, and neighbors, just to live and survive without hurting anyone or being hurt by anyone. I do not think that we were, and still do ask for too much. To be very honest, I have to admit that practically all of my life since after the war, I am very angry and bitter against the leaders of the countries at that time. When the Nazis kept on murdering the Jews none of them even tried to stop it. They really thought that it was not important enough for them to get involved. They probably thought, after all, they were only murdering Jews.

It is really beyond my understanding that a man like Hitler could influence so many others. He was a big failure during his years, he was a school drop out, and never received a diploma from any school, he had poor grades and quit school. All of his life Hitler needed a scapegoat, an excuse for his failures. He was lazy. He hated capitalism, socialism, communism, and democracy. He hated everyone and everything and this was the personality he had. Uneducated, unskilled, without a friend in the world and his only concern was about carrying out evil crimes against the Jews. This evil man was allowed, by the whole world, without interruption, to do what he planned to do all of his life.

I have to admit that this is really very hard for me to understand, how the whole human race could stand by and let it happen. It was not just a Nazi crime according to me, but it was a major crime from one human being to another and I am asking a question about how could people not have even one shred of decency to care about other human lives. Instead, everyone looked the other way and gave Hitler complete freedom, like a green light, like they told him to go ahead and murder as many Jews as he wanted to, to go ahead and make Judenrein. It looked like everyone was agreeing with Hitler. That was how it was, and that was how it turned out to be. Hitler was smart enough to see his chance and his opportunity, so why not take it? He saw that no one stood in his way, so he kept on and on and on with killing, until he almost made Judenrein (free from Jews). He came very close of achieving what he was dreaming to do all of his life. Hitler knew that nobody in the world would care what he would do to the Jews, and he really proved his point in this respect.

Looking back on what I went through I cannot even believe, that after all this suffering it was still possible for me to come out of it alive, and to have courage to go on living without even having a special will or desire to live. I experienced all of the pain and sorrow, which I cannot erase from my mind. A lot of times I ask myself the question, "Why did the Jews not fight for their life?" I was trying very hard to understand why, since they knew that they would be killed anyway.

I think that probably the answer was that the Jewish people were not fighters, they were not killers, they do not believe that one human being should kill another human being, and I know that the Jewish belief in the Ten Commandments that says "Thou shall not kill" was truly believed by Jews. Most of all, the Jews had faith in God that he will help them. I do not know any answers to any of these questions, but the fact was that the Jewish people took all the horrible humiliation and degradation from the Nazis, instead of fighting them. Maybe they thought that if they had to die they did not want to have blood on their hands.

Or maybe the reason that most of the Jews went to their death, like sheep to a slaughter, was because they did not have a choice. The Jews did not have any arms to defend themselves. What could they accomplish without arms against the Nazis machine guns, grenades, and German shepherd dogs? If even one Jew would try to resist them, as a punishment, the Nazis shot hundreds of Jews because of it.

Some Jews tried to go against the Nazis, but not too many succeeded. The way I understand, at least they died with pride and dignity. I have to admit that since after the war I always have it on my mind, that if the Jews would fight back, maybe some of them would have come out of the Holocaust alive. Maybe. A lot of times, during the years of the war and even after the war, my thoughts and my feelings are very mixed. I never could come to an understanding of what would have been better for the Jews, to fight for their lives or go to their death without resistance.

I hope that all of these terrible things will never happen again for the sake of our new Jewish generation. I hope that we will never have to live through anti-Semitism, racism, prejudice attitudes and violence. I hope all of these things will disappear in time, and we will not be discriminated against anymore, just because our customs and our beliefs are different from others. I hope that the Jewish people will be treated equal and not be categorized because of their faith and religion. I hope, in time, we will be treated like people, not just like Jews.

My family, my friends and my neighbors were all people. They had names, dreams, and hopes, just like everyone else, and they had the same rights to live in this world just like everyone else, and share their lives, laughter and happiness with their families, just like everyone else. Suddenly, the awful tragedy happened and their lives were taken away from them, for no reason at all.

I also hope that the tragedy of the Holocaust and the brutality of the Nazis towards the Jews will make people realize that all this killing and murdering was for nothing, after all. I think that people need to treat each other with respect and dignity, just the way they want to be treated themselves. The Ten Commandments always taught us, "do not do anything to others that you do not want them to do it to you."

I really hope that in time, when the people will realize that every person is equal, no matter what their race, religion, and nationality is, and they will become free of prejudice, and hatred of differences, only then the world will be a better place to live in.

Yes, the war is over, but what the Nazis did to me and to all of the other Jews stays with me forever, and will until the day I will die. I see it in front of my eyes every minute of the day, and I still keep on asking the same question, "How could it be?" Most of my years I try to ask myself how, and why, and for what reason did it happen? The only explanation that I have is that Hitler was jealous of the Jews and he was threatened by the Jews existence. The Nazis did not fight a war, but they fought the helpless Jews.

This was not bravery, in fact this was cowardice. I will never forget the inhuman actions of the Nazi regime. They left me with all the scars that will never heal. Besides Hitler and his followers who did all of the murdering, there were others who took a part in all of this cruelty. We have to remember to mention the Ukrainians and the Polish, anti-Semites whose actions made them feel very good to be a part of the acts of violence, also. I am sure that they felt very important to be informers for the Nazis and betray the Jews in order to trade Jewish lives for some rewards from the Nazis.

Even now, until this day, there is still plenty of anti-Semitism and there are prejudiced people against Jews. They have hateful feelings, nasty attitudes and dislikes for the Jews for no reason at all, only because we were born Jewish. These people, without a conscience, without any feelings for other human beings, were grateful to Hitler for solving the problem of the Jews, by killing six million defenseless human beings. These people were anti-Semites all their lives. Most of all, I will never forget the generosity of the whole world and their leaders for their consideration and willingness of not helping and not caring for the Jews, whether they lived or died, instead of letting Hitler achieve his goal.

No matter how Hitler and his followers tried their best, they still did not accomplish their purpose of making Europe Judenrein (free from Jews). The way I see it is that in spite of the Nazis efforts and their followers and all of the evil things that they did to the Jews, their plans failed and it only showed how hateful and scared Hitler was of the Jews. The facts show that I was right after all.

First, he killed all the professional Jews because he was a little narrow minded man, then he killed the intellectual class, then he killed the young men, and then he tried to finish off by killing the rest of the Jews. All of this killing and all of the brutality that he did to us did not make Hitler a hero, it made him a coward. In spite of his wishes, he lost the war and he lost his life, also, together with his supporters. The final conclusion is that no matter how Hitler tried to erase the Jews off the face of the earth he did not succeed.

Yes, we are all victims of the Nazis horrible crimes, but in spite of it, one third of Jews managed to outlive Hitler and the Nazis. The Nazis wishes and all of their best efforts to make Europe Judenrein (free from Jews) did not materialize. I think that nobody has the right to decide who shall live and who shall die. Only God has this right. Hitler and the Nazi regime played God and they wanted desperately to erase all the Jews, but it did not quite happen the way they planned.

No matter how down the Jews were and sometimes still are, we will keep on rising up with God's help. We will overcome all the obstacles and in the end we will succeed and be winners, after all, in spite of our enemies. The handful of Jewish survivors, the remnants that remained homeless, single Jews, without a place and without a family saw to it that the Jewish people should exist forever by building a new Jewish nation. I am one of them. No matter how my life turned out to be for me, nothing else but a constant battle and a hopeless, endless war, I never gave up, and I continued to keep on fighting for my existence practically all of my life. In a way I consider myself lucky enough that I survived and I was given a chance to build the second, third and fourth generation of Jews.

I am also very happy that I outlived the Nazis. I do feel very privileged that I was able to contribute something of value to the world in spite of my personal tragedy. I did take a part in rebuilding the Jewish population. I have three children, six grandchildren, and three great grandchildren.

This was my contribution to the Jewish people. I feel that all of my suffering by the Nazis, and even after the war, was not a complete waste. In spite of everything that I had to go through life all alone, I still think that I have come a long way, somehow, to manage to put the left over pieces of my life together and go on living, even though my life's dreams, and my hopes were shattered. In a way I hope that I did something useful by surviving the Nazis and especially that I was given a chance to be able to keep my parents and the rest of my family's names and their spirit alive. In many different ways, they will remain in my heart and in my memory forever.

I also wish and hope that the world will never forget the awful tragedy of the Holocaust and the loss of six million Jewish lives, including the death of my family for no good reason at all.

Kadish and Sonia Kaplan in Salzburg, Austria in 1945

Kadish and Sonia Kaplan in Salzburg, Austria in 1945

Sonia and her newborn son, David, in Salzburg, Austria

Sonia and her newborn son, David, in Salzburg, Austria

Sonia with next door tenants living in the same apartment
building in Salzburg, Austria

Sonia and Etta in Austria with another survivor in 1945

Sonia after the war at a health clinic in Bad Ischl, Austria

Sonia in Salzburg, Austria

Sonia in the park

Sonia with other Holocaust survivors

Sonia's daughters, Gloria (on the far left) and Ellen (third from the left) with company from New York on Route 50, Mays Landing, New Jersey

Kadish, Gloria, Sonia and David Kaplan in 1957 in Mays Landing, NJ

Holiday Dinner in 1960, in the Kaplan home on Route 50, Mays Landing, NJ

Sonia in an evening gown made by her

Sonia with her children, David Kaplan, Gloria Kaplan Heaton and Ellen Kaplan Wetzel in 1996 in Temple Emeth Shalom, Margate, NJ, at grandson Matthew's Bar Mitzvah

Torah Curtain donated by Sonia in memory of her parents, to
Temple Emeth Shalom in Margate, NJ

Sonia and her two daughters, Ellen (on left) and Gloria (on right)
at the United States Holocaust Memorial Museum in
Washington DC November 2003, at the Tribute to Survivors

Sonia with four of her grandchildren, from left to right, Shayna Wetzel, Leah Wetzel, Jeffrey Heaton and Matthew Heaton, after viewing "Broken Silence", a documentary of Sonia's life, shown on November 20, 2003, at the Richard Stockton College of New Jersey.

Family and friends after the viewing of "Broken Silence" on November 20, 2003

Ellen (producer), Sonia, and Christine Farina (filmmaker) at a showing of "Broken Silence" at the Ventnor Movie Theatre in Ventnor, NJ in December 2003

# "MY ENDLESS WAR

## ...AND MY SHATTERED DREAMS"

## THE AUTOBIOGRAPHY OF SONIA KAPLAN

Sonia Kaplan lives in Atlantic City, New Jersey with
her children, grandchildren, and
great-grandchildren close by.

Made in the USA
Middletown, DE
23 March 2019